GW01311836

Into My Fourth Quarter

Going for Overtime

TRISTAN MACDONALD

DEDICATION

This book is dedicated to Alex, my wife of more than 50 years, who has joined me on more adventures than even this book records. She has been known to complain, but if the outcome is satisfactory, she has always agreed it was a worthwhile enterprise. To our two children, Gaere and Lorna, I say thank you, for the love and understanding you have always shown, to a sometimes obsessive father.

Tristan MacDonald

CONTENTS

My First Quarter

My Second Quarter

FOREWORD

After I wrote this autobiography, I realized that my life has been divided into three distinct periods. The first quarter was obviously my early life up to my escape from Canada, from a childhood that I did not enjoy. The second quarter was my life, marriage and the wonderful times spent in England, raising two children and making my way in the world of business, learning all the skills that made it possible to sail into my third quarter. This third quarter has been spent in the United States and opened up a world of opportunity that I never realized was possible. The fourth quarter is what I hope to live in the next 25 years, and I think I am making a good start.

Although these quarters refer to periods of 25 years, making a total of 75 years of life, they fall more easily into the three periods into which I have divided this book.

MY FIRST QUARTER

1 THE BEGINNING

The first part of my story is only hearsay, but it is first-hand information from my mother, Lorna. At about 10 pm on the night of October 3rd, 1936, she felt the oncoming pain of childbirth. My father Keith was not at home (which often proved to be the case) so she went out and caught one of those unique London cabs to take her to Hampstead General Hospital. She did not make it and I was born with the taxi driver's help, somewhere on Hampstead Heath.

My father and mother agreed to a divorce, or separation, when I was perhaps three years of age. Around 1940, my father moved to Barbados (more of that later) and my mother moved back to her native Cornwall. I went with my mother at first to live with her parents in an old, rambling manor house called Chyanhall. This is where my recollection of childhood begins.

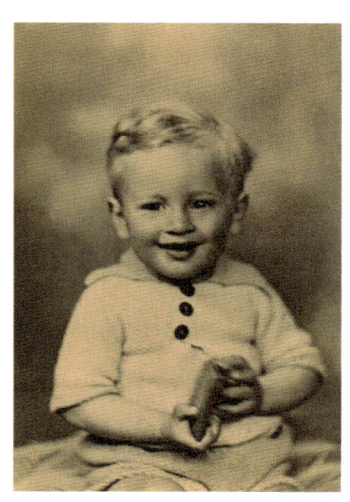

Tristan, age 3

First we had a nanny whose name was Duffy, and she—like most nannies—spoiled us. The "us" refers to my sister Wendy, who is almost exactly two years older than me. The house as, I have said, was large by any standard and had stables, garages and other outbuildings that led down to a garden of perhaps 2 or 3 acres. Some of my first memories are of the people who worked there, in the house and in the gardens. I used to spend hours with the gardener and the kitchen staff, watching them do their work. It was an arduous task every evening with no fewer than 12 guests a night.

Secondly, I was aware of the two elderly people who also lived in the house. They were my grandparents. Although I do not remember much about Lady Ellen, she often sat and read with her lorgnette in the sitting room. Colonel James on the other hand, never went a day, winter or summer, without swimming in the ocean. He swam the day he died, at age 94. I also remember going for drives with him in his Rolls Royce. I felt like an egg in the back seat. He was the first person in Penzance to own a car, and would stop wherever he pleased to visit a shop, even in the middle of the road. After an indeterminate period of living in Chyanhall, we moved to a house out in the country about 6 miles from Penzance. This new place became home, I would guess it was 1941. Sadly, since our departure, Chyanhall has been subdivided into several flats and the outbuildings have been turned into houses. The garden that ran down to a stream has been covered with an assortment of spec-built bungalows.

My second Cornish home had two stories with a large garden. That garden became a showpiece for my mother over the next 30 years. Behind the house was a large fenced-in piece of land that became a vegetable garden and chicken run. Although we were in the early stages of World War II and rationing was in effect, our family was well supplied with food. Perhaps my very first clear memories were of excursions to the cliffs where we walked among the flowers that grew profusely. I particularly remember corn flowers. They were a pale sky blue and I was told they were the color of my eyes. There were many places to discover in the immediate area. The closest neighbors were down a lane opposite the house, it was a small holding and they had a well with a bucket and winding gear on the top. They had three children, two girls and a boy, and we played endlessly near the well, dropping stones down to see how deep it was.

At some time that first summer, the pond which was just down the road had dried up and become mud. My sister and I misjudged and thought it could take our weight, but we went in up to our thighs. On our way home, covered in mud, we met an elderly lady walking towards our house. This woman, never having seen us, did not recognize us and was disgusted at these two urchins, barefoot, following her up the drive. This was our first meeting with our paternal grandmother, but certainly not the last. She created a huge row with Lorna and left after a couple of hours. We had no idea at the time how much this episode would change our lives.

2 FROM WHERE I COME, MY FATHER

I deal with my father first because he was a complex man, and to tell you the truth, I never understood or knew him at all. This was probably more to do with his upbringing than anything else. However, I don't think this is an excuse for his lifetime behavior, or failures as a person and a father.

His parents, my grandfather and grandmother, were products of a typical late Victorian childhood. In my grandmother's case, she was the daughter of a wealthy family who made their money supplying the ships of the Cunard line and others that plied from Southampton, a large port on the Southern coast of England. I know little of my grandfather, except that he was the son of prosperous parents, who left Skye in Scotland around 1850 and settled in Edinburgh. There, he became a provost of the city and the editor of one of Edinburgh's newspapers. At about this time, the family converted to Quakerism and decided to move south into England. Their choice of location was Southampton.

My grandfather worked for Camper and Nicholson, the premier yacht builder in Europe at the time. From their Portsmouth location, they launched virtually every J class and early America's Cup yacht built to compete for that honor. During the time between 1900–1914 and 1920–1930, the whole of the Solent River was full of those huge sailboats, with clouds of masts, rigging and sails. These yachts are unimaginable today, with their paid crews of over 30 men and no expense spared to win the coveted cup. My grandfather, Ian MacDonald, rose in Camper and Nicholson to become the General Manager of the yard, from about 1920 to the early 1930s. In the early 1900s he married Alice Stewart and they had one child, my father, Ian Keith, on the 27th of June 1906. I believe that Alice was probably a good mother but very controlling. He went off to prep school, Fursey Close, one of the several prep schools that also had to tolerate me. He then went on to Winchester Public School, and finally to London University where he studied Electrical Engi-

Keith MacDonald

neering. Meanwhile, his well-meaning mother had reduced him to a stammering, indecisive adult.

Early in 1933, he met Lorna Norman, who was the exact opposite. She was confidant and successful as a concert pianist and soprano (singer) with the music world at her feet. They married on the 10th of March 1934, to the very vocal disapproval of his mother. She proceeded to intervene in the marriage and made life difficult for both of them. Although they were living in London and she was in Southampton, the telephone rang constantly. On one occasion, Lorna being fed up with the constant harassment, pulled the whole phone off the wall and threw it at my father. Into this marital scene my sister Wendy arrived and as I have described, I joined them two years later. I do vaguely remember some happy times spent at a cottage in Dibden with the adjacent farmers, called Longland. I might remember this only because I have been told about it, but I can still taste the fresh milk from the cows. Going back to the thread of his story, by 1938 the marriage was coming unraveled. Lorna decided to go back to Cornwall, taking Wendy and me with her to her parents' home aforementioned. On the 10th of March 1939, Keith filed for divorce in the High Court of Justice, Probate Divorce and Admiralty Division. I have no idea how the admiralty comes into it, but I do know that in the year 1939, only 586 petitions for divorce were filed. With a population of over 50 million people, marriage must have been a happier affair then, than now. More likely, couples just tolerated one another. The divorce was made absolute on the 15th of January 1940. Lorna was named the respondent and a gentleman named Eric Thomas was the co-respondent with the grounds for the divorce being adultery on Lorna's part. So ends, rather sadly, that chapter of my life.

We were in Cornwall loving it, and he was in Barbados, perhaps loving it, too. His work in Barbados was first to develop a public supply of electricity and after that, to develop a telephone system across the island. At this point my father disappeared from my life for several years.

I probably should just mention his father's death in the early 1920s. He was a significant party go-er and one of his tricks was to drink a glass of champagne and then eat the glass. He died of a perforated stomach. No surprise there.

3 FROM WHERE I COME, MY MOTHER

Lorna Norman

Lorna was born on the 18th of June, 1913 to Fredrick and Beatrice Bullen, in Newquay, Cornwall. Her birth certificate shows that Fredrick was a fruiterer, but that tells only part of his story. There were 11 other children, so to keep the family going and fed, he caught rabbits which were plentiful in those days. He was also part of a fishing consortium, and in season collected seagull eggs from the cliffs. All of these things were shipped to London on the train and turned a small profit. He passed the expertise for these enterprises onto his son, my uncle Harold. In due course, Harold passed them to his sons and to me. Regardless of everything Fredrick did, things were very hard in the Bullen home. Lorna and another brother Frank were close in age. They explored and played together on the many beaches around Newquay. One of their favorite things to do was to walk down to Fistral Beach and look in the many rock pools for tiny cowrie shells. After a lifetime of collecting, she had a vase of perhaps a gallon of these tiny shells. Immediately behind the beach and overlooking it, was a huge hotel called the Headland Hotel. It is still there and remains a popular resort hotel that attracted many upper class people to take in the fresh Cornish air.

Colonel R. Donne L. James and his wife Lady Ellen Craig Fitzgerald walked often on the low cliff overlooking Fistral Beach. One day they happened to notice these flaxen haired children crouched down, searching through the sand in the pools for treasures. They descended to the beach to speak with the children and probably found out a lot about them, as well as what they were looking for. Obviously, these two apparently perfect children appealed to the childless couple, who were by then in their late 50s. They lit upon the extraordinary idea of visiting the family and trying to convince Fredrick and Beatrice to allow them to adopt Lorna and Frank. They were at this time around four or five years old. Colonel James and Lady Ellen were of minor aristocratic stock and it is hard to imagine their negotiating this exchange of parenthood in the small attached cottage where they all lived. I have visited this house, but never met Fredrick or Beatrice. For some reason, Lorna never allowed that to happen. I have no idea if any money changed hands at the adoption. The Colonel and Lady Ellen were too proud to give either of the children their name, James. So, Lorna became known as Lorna Norman and Frank retained the name of Bullen. They were taken to live with the James' in many parts of the country where they had manor houses, and in Wales, a castle. My wife Alex and I visited the castle on our honeymoon. It is quite small as castles in Wales go. There was also a town house in London for the London season, the same in Dublin, and a summer place on the island of Jersey.

These two children had been lifted from poverty to extreme wealth in a moment. Neither of them went to school as they were tutored at home and wherever they went. In particular, Lorna was taught the piano and singing and became very accomplished at both. I never met Frank, but I understand he became a successful business man and racing car driver. The family lived a life of society gypsies, spending much time at Chyanhall and Trevaylor, an alternate house a few miles away. The two children were not allowed to visit their parents at any time. The break was supposed to be final. Lorna, by now in her late teens and very beautiful, was noticed as a talent by a couple who were the directors of music for the B.B.C. She broadcast from there and was noticed by the conductor of the London symphony. She performed with that orchestra often in the next few years. I have no idea how Keith met Lorna. I would like to think it was backstage, although I think it more likely it was at a society event.

They married in March 1934. My sister Wendy was born on October 10th of the same year. This brought Lorna's career to a standstill. At this time Keith was working for the London North Eastern Railway as an electrical engineer. The railway was proposing to electrify the railroad from London to Scotland and this was probably Keith's finest hour. The completion of that project was sometime in the late 1960s. On the day the service started, *The Times of London* used a full page to describe the project. Some 30 years after the event, *The Times* also gave Keith credit for its design, but not its execution.

They were living in London, with Lorna filling engagements whenever possible, and Keith staying very busy. During this difficult period, I was born on October 3, 1936. The marriage became very strained, and in 1938 Lorna left with Wendy and me to return to Cornwall. First to

Chyanhall, and then to the two-story house called Chyfor. Lorna continued to live there and work in her garden for many years. Unfortunately, Wendy and I were not to be so lucky in our upbringing.

In 1942 Col. James died at 94, with his wife Lady Ellen following him six days later. They together had a great deal of money and property, however World War II was raging, resulting in heavy taxation on death. The two deaths were taxed separately and the balance was much diminished. At that time, Wendy and I were both wards of the court because there was no agreement of custody subsequent to our parents' divorce. We were beneficiaries under Col. James' will, which made us of much greater interest to my father. He applied to the courts for custody of Wendy and me based on the fact that Lorna was living in sin with a married man. He won his plea and Lorna was instructed to transfer our

Tristan and Wendy

custody to Keith's mother, Alice. Lorna was devastated at having to give up her children, ages nearly six and nearly four, to a woman she despised. Arrangements were made and Bernie Durrant, her now live-in companion, Lorna, Wendy and I drove the 250 miles to Brockenhurst, Hampshire to Alice's home called the Martins (after the little bird of the same name). I will never forget the screams of rage and pain from my mother as she was forced to leave us. It must have seemed that she had lost us forever, but that was the sentence of the court.

We started a new life with Alice (Phelan). She had remarried but her second husband had died. We now completely lost contact with our mother for a number of years. We were not allowed to receive presents from her, or any other form of communication. We were both traumatized, and the game of "you never had a mother" began. Many years later I was to learn that the renewed interest in us by our father was the result of the trust fund set up by Col. James. Accessible by the guardian, it had no provision for audit as to its use.

4 WHERE I HAVE BEEN SENT, JULY 1941

We were now in Brockenhurst with a grand-mother, Alice Phelan (MacDonald), we had seen only once in our lives. She was a woman of about 5 feet 5 inches tall with an unusually severe expression on her face. I am sure she had no wish to become the caregiver of two children ages six and four. Of course, to us, she seemed extremely old, being in her sixties. Our first order of business was to see what our new surroundings could offer in the way of adventure outside of the house. The house was surrounded by a large garden, equally divided

Alice Phelan

front and back, with flowers and shrubs along the front and sides and a vegetable garden behind. There was an adequate tool shed for hide and seek and one other small building and garage with no car, attached to the house. The vegetable garden was very productive and over the next few years we learned a lot about pickling, bottling and preserving. To the side of the house was a large orchard, with several apple, plum, damson, and pear trees dotted about. They were to become our refuge in a time of need, by climbing and hiding in them. At the back of the orchard was a chicken run with perhaps 30 chickens. The need to get all the chickens in their coop at night was demonstrated by regular visits from foxes. They would disturb the chickens frequently and of course we would wake up and have to go out and chase the fox away.

Behind the orchard and the house was a deep ditch and then fields running down to the Beaulieu River, which was strictly "out of bounds" as the child of a near neighbor had drowned in it previously. In front of the house and across the road was the New Forest, a very large and well wooded forest, created by William the Conqueror in 1066 A.D. It was used as a private hunting preserve for the King and his cronies, but it unfortunately became the place of death for William's son, William Rufus II. He was hunting with a group of courtiers and got in the way of an arrow loosed by Sir Walter Tyrrell. I imagine there was a lot of panic and the best thing they could do was load the body of William Rufus onto a grocer's cart and head towards Brockenhurst. The grocer's name was William Purkess. When we moved to the village, the grocery shop was still run by a William Purkess. However, I diverge from my story. This forest was to be our main entertainment and source of adventure for the next six years.

We arrived in July and a school had to be found for both of us. The choice was made, uniforms were purchased, and in September we were taken by Uncle Roddy to our new (and first) school. I was nearly four and Wendy was nearly six years old. A convent had been selected in Boscombe, a nearby town, and we were to board at the school. The school was strictly segregated with boys in one wing and girls in another. The nuns were very strict, but on the whole, I think quite well-meaning. I must explain that we had nothing to do with the Roman Catholic Church, and as such were told constantly that we would be excluded from heaven if we continued in our disbelief. Up to this point religion had not entered our lives. We were later told that Alice and Ian Mac-Donald had both been raised as Quakers. I am sure that they lapsed in their practice, if not in their belief, in that religion. So here we were, denied all of the benefits that a good Catholic religion could give us.

I learned how to be lonely in that first term. I was nearly four and not allowed to see Wendy. I felt very abandoned. By September of 1941, the war and the bombings were in full swing. Trips and long stays in air raid shelters were a regular part of life, day and night. Boscombe was close to several other larger towns and cities, which attracted many raids. One night in early December before breaking up for the Christmas holidays, the impossible happened. The entire boys' school was destroyed, but we were all safe down in the cellars of the Convent Church. Triumphantly, I went back to the "Martins," thinking maybe I would never have to go to school again.

In an incredibly short space of time, I was registered in a new school, in fact the one my father had gone to, Fursey Close. Wendy would continue at the convent and she did for the next six years. I was only to see her in the holidays. Life in an English boys' prep school was tough. No heat, no hot water, one shared bath a week, short pants regardless of the temperature and many other restrictions, including just awful food. I began to thrive in the environment and it was not long before I would look forward to some aspects of this life. I loved Fursey Close and its headmaster, but it was not to be. After only a year, the school was taken over by the army for training purposes, so a search was made for an alternative. We visited several schools in the summer holidays, and the one I liked least was chosen. This was called Savages and its headmaster, called Savage, proved as brutal as his name. He believed in a good beating now and again as the only way to bring boys to heel. My grandmother visited one afternoon, midterm, after hearing bad reports, most likely from me. She heard Mr. Savage shout at one of his dogs, named Lady, "*Shut up* you stupid arse!" That was the end, for he had uttered the two words that were forbidden in our vocabulary. I escaped after one or two terms to be sent for the next few years to what became my favorite school.

Southey Hall was a huge rambling manor house outside a small Surrey village called Little Bookham. The place had everything a boy could want; a swimming pool with more newts in it than boys, a skating pond, playing fields, endless park lands and lots of great teachers. By far the best time in every week was on Sunday afternoons when the Headmaster would read from Kipling, Haggard, Buchan and many other authors. We sat spellbound on the floor, in front of a huge fire, imagining the exploits in our lives to come. I learned to play sports there, not all of which I liked. We played cricket, soccer, rugby, cross country, squash and many more. I also started to run with the beagles, catching hares. My Uncle Peter was the Beagle Master and specifically asked for me to attend. I have seldom been as exhausted as I was that first day, but I sealed my fate by keeping up with the hounds. From that day on I always had to run when there was a meet. During all of this period up to 1945, World War II was raging in Europe and air battles took place overhead. We had few problems at school, but back in Brockenhurst, it was another matter. Across the road from the "Martins," a large anti-aircraft emplacement was built and almost nightly they would be firing away. In the mornings we would go out to collect the shrapnel from the garden and road. We spent a lot of time talking to the gunners on the A.A. site. Only once did we have a German aircraft downed in the immediate area. The pilot bailed out and was captured by the village policeman. The skies after these incendiary raids were red from the burning buildings and could be seen from miles away. Of course, when the war finally ended in Europe, we all went to the celebrations with fireworks and parties long into the night. Food shortages and rationing continued long after war's end, although with the vegetable garden, chickens, orchard and the bargaining power that these gave my grandmother, we seemed to have food, but never quite enough.

After the war finished and it became safe to go across the Atlantic in a liner, my father, who had remarried and moved to Montreal, Canada, decided we should join him there. In the spring of 1947, Wendy, grandmother and I set forth on the Aquitania from Southampton to Halifax. At this time the ships, which had been used to carry troops during the war, were very run down and overcrowded with emigrants like ourselves trying to get out of Europe and into the New World. We joined the mob and listened to the band on the dock playing "Goodbye England and Its Slow Gray Rivers" as we pulled away from the shore.

5 EMIGRATION AND INTEGRATION

As the last bars of music faded and the gap between ship and pier widened, we knew we were headed for adventure. April on the North Atlantic can be quite rough. Once our grandmother had negotiated a new and better cabin for the three of us, we set out to see what the ship had to offer. After our first game, ping pong became an obsession. Rough weather soon laid us all low, but not for long. We soon got back to the dining room but noticed that the crowds had thinned out.

After nine days at sea, we sighted land and were quickly moored up in Halifax harbor. This was the last trip that the Aquitania made before she was taken to the breakers. The trains, which were to take all the people west into Canada, were drawn up at the dockside. It took more than a day to get us onto our train and headed for Montreal, and one and a half days of being shunted around before we reached our destination. Alice, my grandmother, had already decided that she did not like the new world and made her feelings clear to anyone who would listen. The inconvenience of a long distance train journey was not lost on her.

Finally the train pulled into Montreal's station. It was April and I still had on my short pants, totally inadequate for the time of year. We did not have a lot of luggage. After a long wait, Keith showed up on the platform and we were put in the back of his navy blue Buick with all of our belongings. Of course we did not recognize him at all, so it was not an easy meeting. Mother and son were to be together again for an unspecified amount of time, and Alice was planning to return to England as soon as she could. She did not realize it would be within the first week of her arrival.

We drove the 18 miles out of Montreal to Rosemère, a suburb of Montreal at the time, in the dark. Wendy and I did not know what to expect for the next phase of our lives. We had, of course, been told that Keith had remarried and that we had two new half-sisters, Susan age four, and Angela, eight months old. As we pulled into the driveway, we saw through the window (that turned out to be the kitchen) a rather fierce looking woman with her auburn hair tied tightly in a braid on top of her head. Wendy and I took an instant dislike to her and exchanged glances to that effect; hardly a fair assessment from 12- and 10-year-old children!

Of course there was much fuss about our arrival. We were shown our bedrooms and everything at once seemed better than we first imagined. It was a nice, large house with forest behind that lead down to the Ottawa River, invisible except when the river flooded. There was a large garden surrounding the house with a separate garage and several terraces leading down to the flood plain. The village was perhaps a half mile away and very limited in

Tristan, Angela, Marjorie, Susan and Wendy

scope. Of course, the only language spoken there was French. Marjorie, Keith's new wife, tried exceedingly hard to be welcoming to us, although she had her hands full with her own two children.

Keith continued to commute into work after a few days and she was left with these three strangers that she needed to fit into her life which was basically raising two children and looking after the house, cleaning, and cooking. Friction between Marjorie and Alice started almost immediately as they were two very strong-willed women and Marjorie was not about to let anyone get the better of her. After a very short time, Granny Phelan was packed up back to Brockenhurst. I was devastated at the time because she had represented some stability in my life.

We did not stay long in Rosemère, perhaps only a few months, as Keith had a new job in Toronto. So, it was proposed that we would move to Midland, Ontario. Marjorie's parents lived and worked at the shipyard in the town and had a large house in which we would live until a house was found. Keith commuted weekly to Toronto and his new job. Midland was a pleasant town on Georgian Bay, Lake Huron, with quite a lot of industry as a wheat port, but, the largest employer was the shipyard. Herbert (Bertie) Whitmell, Marjorie's father, was the general manager and had done sterling service in the war, building Corvettes and Fairmile class ships. Perhaps the greatest asset to the town was a park surrounding a small lake, called Little Lake, which was about a mile across. As the summer progressed, Wendy and I spent our lives in the water of the lake, first learning to swim, and before school started in the fall, swimming the mile across the lake. It was our first recognition in the press. We had not been able to swim previously because of wartime restrictions.

We had three cousins who lived about a block away. They were a little younger than us but never the less made up a nucleus of friends when we entered school that fall. On returning to Midland many years later, of the two schools I had attended, both had been pulled down. Living with Marjorie's parents did not work out well. Although I was unaware of it at the time, her father was a sexual predator/pedophile and molested Wendy at that time, and later at least two of the cousins. When this was finally exposed, we rented a house closer to Little Lake but were able to continue at the same schools. This episode, as you would expect, had lasting repercussions for Wendy and the cousins, but in common with everything that ever happened in this dysfunctional family, was never discussed.

Bertie and Minnie, Marjorie's parents, owned and ran a really beautiful 50-foot lake cruiser called *Pandora* in and around Georgian Bay. We went on frequent trips up to Honey Harbor and other spots where we would swim or have a meal. To show this man's total disregard for other people, we were leaving the Magnetewan Inn one evening, headed home I believe, when we spotted two canoes with a couple in each in full evening dress. We pointed this out, but he made no effort to slow down and both couples ended up in the water, to be regaled with laughter and no offers of assistance. Midland was a happy place for me, as I made friends there, swam in the summer, and skated in the winter. There were lots of beaches nearby, and I went often to the Saturday matinees. It had to end. My father got tired of the commute, and it was decided to move to Toronto.

6 TORONTO, A NEW LIFE

We left Midland for Toronto in the car with Keith, Marjorie, Wendy and me. A house had been bought in the west end of town. It was very close to High Park, which at that time was a fairly natural block of trees and ponds with a few roads leading through for access to different parts. The park was 20 x 30 blocks in size and was to become my escape from home.

The moving van was to follow the next day, so a rare night was spent in a hotel. For entertainment that evening, we went to the Odeon Cinema downtown where Oliver Twist was playing. I must admit to having been a little frightened at the plot and the position Oliver found himself in so often in the movie. It reminded me of my days in boarding school.

184 Westminster Ave. was a two-story house with really insufficient bedrooms to house the whole MacDonald family. It had a postage-stamp-sized garden on a steep bank in the front. I did not know it at the time, but this meant that getting snow off the sidewalk required a long throw. To one side of the house was an extremely narrow driveway leading to a small garage. Getting the car up the drive without hitting the walls of our house or the next door neighbors was quite difficult. In the back was a larger garden of mostly grass with a flower bed down one side, the whole of it being overlooked by neighbors to the side and behind. It was a typical house built to fit families in an expanding city in the early 1900s.

Wendy and Tristan

The street on both sides had similar structures along the whole of its three block length. The best part of this neighborhood was that all the people living there had kids. I know that Wendy and I both made lots of friends when we were allowed out to play. All playing was done in the street—the garden being too good to use—and if a car turned up, they would have to wait while we cleared the street of whatever game we were playing. It worked well.

I went to public school and into grade six. I think Wendy went straight into high school, which was quite a long way from home. She and I both walked to school, but mine was a much shorter distance.

It was about this time I began to feel that I was not being treated as part of the family, more like someone who could do chores. Wendy and I both began to have restrictions on our free time and where we could spend it. Specific jobs were allotted and we were expected to do them despite our schoolwork. At this point I got my first paper routes, delivering before and after school. I was expected from the start to give 20 percent of my profits to the family fund. This was supposed to represent income tax. School was free, and there were no costs for uniforms involved. I knew nothing of the educational trust that had been set up for Wendy and me. I realize that Marjorie had a big job with four children and the house, but there appeared to be a great inequity in our minds.

The whole house, which at the roof was three stories, needed painting. With no previous experience, we were expected to go out on an extension ladder to paint it. This did lead to one memorable disaster, when a gallon of brown paint spilt over Wendy's head. Marjorie's response was, "A good job she has brown hair." I do not know if there was any thought to the next disaster, but I was told to get 70 years of wallpaper off the main bedroom walls. I did get it off using vinegar and water, but maybe a little too much! The living room ceiling below came down, plaster and all. I often still laugh about that.

Another job was to remove a very large lilac tree in the back garden that was blocking light from the house. I set to work cutting all the top branches off and then started on the root ball. I dug and hacked for hours before coming to a large black root. I went at this with an axe until I was through it in two places. This released the stump, so I rolled it out, refilled the hole and thought, "What a good job!" Shortly afterwards Marjorie realized the telephone was not working and that the entire neighborhood's telephones were out. After much searching for the possible cause, the telephone company found my efforts in the backyard. I had cut through a main cable, 3–4 inches in diameter.

Surprisingly, I did not get into trouble for this incident. By this time Marjorie, who had a fierce temper, was often slapping and hitting both Wendy and me for the slightest infraction, or for a job that was not up to her standards. We could expect to have a slap on the head or face on these occasions.

By this time I had acquired a number of paper routes, both morning and evening. Based on my early rising, I moved from an upstairs bedroom to the cellar. I liked this as it gave me more opportunity to beat the system. Like all good taxpayers, I worked out a method of depleting my profits so I paid out less than the required twenty percent. When Keith discovered this, it was considered an offence that warranted his administering a good whipping, which was carried out by actually using a large whip. Keith was only brought in on two occasions to punish me, otherwise he said nothing in our defense at all and failed to contribute to our lives in any way. We rarely spoke and never hugged or shared our feelings. When I was there, an incident occurred that shows that Keith took an almost sadistic pleasure in cruelty to children. While driving to the cottage, he would mention we were passing an ice cream shop. "There is an ice cream shop," and drive by. When he had a block of Neapolitan ice cream, he would divide it so each child would get either chocolate, vanilla or strawberry instead of the three flavors intended. There is a litany of annoying little behaviors which were very cruel to a child.

Tristan, age 14

It was a barren life but I did have the benefit of some wonderful friends, who shared their families with me. In the summers, the small farmers west of Toronto came into town each morning to hire kids for a day of labor on their farms. Wendy and I were there every day, a wonderful way of having a long day out of the house and earning good money as well. It was on those farms where we learned the value of hard work. Bent double under the sun, picking strawberries, raspberries, thinning beets, etc. On a good day I could earn $3.50! Each day we usually worked for the same farmers because they knew we worked hard, so they picked us out of the crowd. I don't remember ever being sent home without a job. Again, twenty percent was levied on our labor.

Keith and Marjorie then decided to build a summer cottage on Lake Simcoe. The land was leased from the Indian owners and building began. Both Wendy and I took an active part in the building program, as did several neighboring owners. That summer is when I first met Oliver and Gladys Summers. They lived in the cottage next door and took me into their home and hearts. They realized, I'm sure, what a strife ridden family we were and, although they were good friends with Keith and Marjorie, came out on my side a number of times. The last job on the cottage was to paint Solignum on all the eaves and overhangs. Yes, Wendy and I got that job. This stuff was almost impossible to get off of our skin and when it went into our eyes it "stung like hell." I will never forget that torment. We helped dig a well, which was over 20 feet deep by the time we reached the water. After the cottage was completed, I did have a good time there. I would spend part of the summer and odd weekends there walking, swimming, canoeing and boating. In fact, the first time I ever sailed in a dingy was from the next door dock. I think on the whole, there were happy times spent up on the lake. At home in Toronto, things were quite different.

I had moved into high school by now and I cycled there while Wendy still walked. I had lots of friends and my life in school was fun and rewarding, but the cancerous growth of rancor grew worse and worse at home. I had joined the Air Cadets and was going to learn to fly in the

Tristan, age 15

summer of 1952. This would require me to be away from home for the month of July. I decided in the winter of '52 that I had finished with abuse and would escape back to England and my mother, even though I did not know whether she was dead or alive. I wrote a letter to Chyanhall and one of the tenants there passed it on to my mother who, of course, wrote back to the address of a friend. Yes, as you may have guessed, Marjorie opened all mail. We started a clandestine correspondence and planned my return to England for the following summer.

I booked passage on a tramp steamer belonging to a small Greek line sailing from Quebec. The next thing was to get a passport, which was not easy without parental permission. As a substantial businessman, Oliver Summers stood up and answered all of the questions to the satisfaction of the Passport Office. A Reverend McLean also helped in this regard. He was the father of one of my closest friends and knew of my situation. Both knew I intended to run away from home. As the time to leave was drawing near, I had to sell all of my paper routes, but not until the last moment for fear that the ever watchful Marjorie would get wind of my intentions. I was ready, ostensibly to go to the air cadet camp, but actually to escape. The day I was to catch the train for Quebec was particularly tense. I went over to the Rev. and Mrs. McLean's house where I had dinner and then they took me to the station to catch the train. Once on board, the enormity of the secret I had kept for so many months hit me. I had not even told Wendy, for fear of reprisals for her. I have always felt guilt for abandoning Wendy without a word. I was traveling at night and as the train pulled into Montreal, the whole platform was full of police. They boarded the train and started to check all of the passengers. I had watched enough spy movies to think the game was up, but, they passed me with little more than a glance.

The following day, I arrived in Quebec and took a taxi down to the docks. I was traveling very light and had little luggage with me. I was delivered to the dock and had to find the ship, unfortunately I don't remember its name. When I did find it, I was not surprised at the shabby exterior, but I mounted the gang plank and was made welcome by some of the crew. They could not figure out why a 16-year-old boy would be traveling on his own. The passengers on board were all being deported from Canada, mostly for jumping ship. I got on well with them and we drank Beck's beer together. They assured me that I would drown before I got drunk on Beck's. The food was taken at a central mess table. All I can remember is that it was mostly sausage and sauerkraut. The chef was German and he had a small budget to work with. My passage cost me $50 and I am sure all the deported seamen were not paying. The ship was small and well run, by a Greek captain, who I got to know well. He had to eat the sausage and sauerkraut as well. The ship was very slow and took more than two weeks to get to Southampton where, because of the cost of moorage, the ship had to lay off and everything was tendered in by a small boat. The dozen passengers and I were first. We were delivered into a great hall where our passports were checked; my fellow passengers were all arrested and taken to jail. I was left standing with my small suitcase, looking for someone that I did not remember. I did not care. As far as I was concerned, I had escaped a tyranny that I did not understand. I hated both Marjorie and Keith; Marjorie for her constant physical and verbal abuse and Keith for his absence and his quiet ignoring of the problems of our young lives. I do, however, still have a love of Canada and all the good times I had there.

These eight years of my life had made a deep impression on me, and on the way I would react to the people who I was to meet, know, and love in the future.

I had developed a great mistrust of virtually everyone. I reacted viscerally to any physical contact with another person. I had developed a shell of isolation which took some years to crack, and without Alex's help, I might never have managed to do this. This did, and still does, manifest itself in the rather unemotional way I appear to treat life. The emotions are there, but I learned to suppress them. I said earlier in the book that as Wendy and I were dropped off at Mrs. Phelan's house by our mother, I cried for the last time. It is still that way, although I know that I am far more vulnerable now to the normal emotions of the people around me. This was not a passing thing, and affected my whole life.

MY SECOND QUARTER

7 A NEW LIFE, JULY 1953

Eventually I was reunited with my mother and Bernie, my mother's common law husband. The last time I had seen both of them was when I was four years old and I was being delivered to Alice Phelan's house. The 12-year gap had obviously changed me more than it had changed them. Initially I felt I was with two total strangers, but things warmed up and we were telling each other about the intervening years. It was late evening and it was decided not to drive the 250 miles straight back to Cornwall. We started to look for a hotel. Southampton had been destroyed in the war and although rebuilding was underway, hotels were scarce. Eventually we found a pub that had a room and a place for a small bed under the stairs. This accommodation suited Bernie very well, as he liked to have a drink or three. In fact, I was under the stairs long before he and Lorna had finished, or the bar closed. I'm not quite sure which came first.

The following morning we set out early. Having been used to Canadian roads, I couldn't comprehend the narrow twisting road, marked as a main road on the map. By 11:30 am, we were still a long way from Cornwall at the first of a series of pubs where we stopped along the way. It was ostensibly to use the bathroom, but of course the pint of beer that was consumed required a stop for the same reason down the road. This progress continued until closing time at 2:30 pm. By this point, things in the car were best described as happy and I realized then that Bernie was the nicest person you could meet, but he did have a drinking problem. I was too young to join him in each pub, but Lorna did even though she couldn't keep up. I must explain. Bernie was 6 feet 3 inches and very big while my mother was 5 feet 2 inches and very small, so it was hardly a match. Between 2:30 pm and 5 pm when the pubs opened again, we just about completed the journey. However, a stop had to be made at the village pub, The Trevelyan Arms, to show me off to the locals. I had a tremendous welcome from all sorts of people and this was to become my local pub when I was old enough to drink (a bit before, actually). Only one more stop had to be made, at the second pub in the village, The Crown. I never liked it but the same welcome was given again. By this time, I was floating in a non-alcoholic haze. Finally, home to Chyfor, I had a meal and was introduced to my new room. Before finishing the description of our drive home, I must say at no time on this long drink and drive was I ever aware of any impairment in Bernie's judgment.

As I said earlier, I came with a small suitcase and very few clothes. The following morning, it was to Penzance for a complete outfit. All the shopkeepers knew Lorna well, and I was greeted with great enthusiasm. With new clothes and an English accent I never really lost, I was absorbed into the community ccccccto disallow Keith's access and to protect it until I turned twenty-one. It was at this time I discovered that the trust had been milked for the seven years I was in Canada. The answer came back from the court that because I was 16 and had apparently made the choice to be with my mother, I would be allowed to stay in Cornwall.

Penzance was a small market town in the 50s with pony and traps and other horse-drawn vehicles not being an uncommon sight. Our milk at this time did not arrive in bottles. Mr. Trevaskis would make his rounds with a pony cart and the milk, which came unpasteurized from his farm, was sold by the jug-full out of a churn. You had to walk down to the road with your jug, get your milk and return with it to the larder, there being no refrigeration at this time. There were lots of things like this, soon to be gone for good. I was, unfortunately, often comparing life in Canada to life in England which brought a sharp rebuke from Lorna. I made the comparisons but kept them to myself in the future. It happened that this habit was required later in my life when we came to the U.S.A.

I was 16 and quite interested in girls at the time, in fact, I still am. As a cycling club, we used to do rides here, there and everywhere. Our finish was often Newlyn, a small fishing village attached to Penzance. In particular, we would stop at the The Pixie Cabin at the bottom of Paul Hill. I had noticed a girl walking to school and in fact, I would make sure I saw her each day. She had a very special walk. In fact the Beatles later put it in a nutshell when they sang, "something in the way she moves." She went to the Pixie regularly. In fact, there were a number of girls who did. I was completely smitten, but very shy, so it took me a while even to find out her name. When I did, I found that she already had a boyfriend, but I persisted and took out her best friend, Tessa. I figured it would keep me close to her and, you never know, the situation might change. Her name was Alexandra, but she went by Alex. The waiting paid off. She was only twelve when I met her in October of 1953. Her birthday was early the following month. When she had just turned 13, I was 17.

Alex came from Newlyn; in fact she didn't live more than a few hundred yards from the Pixie Cabin. I learned that her mother had died when she was only three years old. She lived with her grandmother, father, uncle and sister Pam. Pam is three and a half years older than Alex and later when their grandmother died, she became Alex's mentor. I remember Pam at that time as being very bossy. Maybe we needed a lot of control! Alex and Pam's father, Alexander, always known as Alec, was a wonderful man who had not remarried. He was a builder, carpenter, painter and undertaker, an odd mix but quite normal in Cornwall. Uncle Frank was a plumber, deeply hating his job, and would show it regularly with outbursts of temper directed at anyone around. I was lucky enough to meet Alex's grandmother before she died. She would notice me down the lane behind her house and would remark, "That boy is there again."

I had decided that I needed to work to make some money. Bernie was willing to employ me and train me in his business, so I started at £5 per week in his wholesale newspaper and magazine business. This was great experience for what came later in my life. This job also allowed me plenty of free time for cycling and the pursuit of other interests.

Most weekends were spent in Newquay with my Uncle Harold, previously mentioned, as one of my mother's brothers. He had been injured by a ship's gun barrel being fired when it was against his head. This resulted in a permanent disability, but he was able to do many things without trouble. He had chosen of be the sexton of a church burial ground, so often I would arrive as a grave needed to be dug. He had two sons about my age and a wife named Olive, who made the best Cornish pasties ever. Summer nights were spent on the beach, fishing with a long line of 150 hooks all baited and ready to catch what was out there. At low tide, someone, usually me, had to swim the line out as far as he could. This would often entail being carried a long way down the beach by the current. I knew where the beach was because there would always be a huge line of driftwood. The idea was to swim across the current back to shore. Quite scary in the dark; however, we never lost anyone.

On weekends when the tide was wrong for fishing, we went rabbit hunting. At first we started on a small scale with only snares, a dog, and a ferret or two. We would catch perhaps 25 to 30 rabbits for a night's work. It was not very productive for a man and three boys. I read of a rabbit clearance society who used nets. The premise was to go quietly at night around the field on three sides with your net, then drag a rope down the fourth side while making plenty of noise. Then the rabbits would bolt for their warrens in the hedges. This worked exceedingly well and our rabbit count went up to between 250 and 500 per night. We sold them for half a crown each, i.e. fifty cents. This soon paid for the net and we approached the farmers to see if they wanted their fields cleared. The answer was always yes. We charged £25 per field. Rabbits were a major problem in Europe at the time. Little did we know that a disease that killed rabbits was being introduced from Australia, called Mixamatosis. It was my first experience in biological warfare. Once introduced, it spread throughout the colony, killing every last rabbit. We were out of business!

In the spring of 1954, I was taken out on the cliffs of Newquay when the seagulls were laying their eggs. It was our jobs as youngsters to collect the eggs from the nests, each containing two apiece. These would be freighted up to London for use in cake baking. The price was a half crown for a dozen. We would often collect 200 dozen at a time. So many years later I was learning about the life my maternal grandfather had lived just to keep his family fed. Sometime after that, I was talking to author Winston Graham about life in North Cornwall many years before. He wove our family's fishing story into one of the novels in the Poldark series. I still have the signed copy with a dedication.

Meanwhile my life back in Penzance continued with a driving license. I was able to deliver newspapers to all the stores. This was done in an ugly green van, which was inevitably rattling with empty whiskey bottles that Bernie had thrown in the back as he was driving. I was now able to take Alex to school, if the train that brought the papers from London was ever on time. Yes, Alex and I had become firm friends by this time. We spent a lot of time together, swimming in the summer, walking and spending time with each other in a couple of secret places we had found. The first of them was known as Carn Rock and was just behind several lines of row houses. There was a great view to be had at this highpoint. This was not, however, to be our favorite place. Newlyn has a quarter-mile long fishing quay with buildings and workshops up against the quay wall. There was one break in these buildings and when we climbed up the wall, we could access a shelf which ran along the entire wall. We would climb up there and sit for hours looking out to sea and across the bay at St. Michaels Mount. The moon would come up over the other side of the bay and the moon path would be several miles long.

Alex was, of course, very young, as was I. Her father and sister kept a very close eye on her, and strict curfew hours were imposed. I always tried hard to abide by them. Her father must have thought I was very dependable, or very boring! These were some of the happiest times of my life; however, they were shortly to change. As I reached seventeen and a half years of age, I became eligible for the draft, so I needed to make some decisions. If I was to wait to be drafted, I would have no choice as to which branch of the service I would go into, let alone what job I would be given when I got there. So, in June of 1954, I signed up for three years in the regular army and five years in the reserve. My choice of service was in the Parachute Regiment, quite glamorous if I could make it. My induction date was set for January 1955. This single decision was to change my life completely and forever. Lorna encouraged me to go for the experience and the opportunity for adventure. I was extremely fit at the time, and very confident that I could endure this rigorous selection process I was about to go through.

8 THE ARMY, TRAINING

In the early fifties all young men, if medically sound, had to sign up for National Service. The specified period was two years and the pay was very low with only 28 shillings a week, i.e. $2.25. I joined as a regular because the pay was somewhat better, about $6.00 to start, with lots of opportunities for increase in the future.

I received a railway warrant, which enabled me to get a free train ride up to Aldershot, about 50 miles from London. Aldershot claimed to be the, "home of the British Army," so you can imagine what kind of town it was. I arrived at the station with my little piece of paper telling me where I should report, as literally millions of young men must have done before me. I thought someone might be there to meet me, but no. After asking anybody who was wearing a red beret directions, I could see they felt nothing but contempt for a boy like me. I was a "grockle," i.e. a new man on the base. I was finally at Airborne Forces Depot, Maida barracks where I was treated with even greater contempt by everyone I met. There were a few other young men dressed similarly to me and looking very unsure of themselves. They were milling about the area, and as I rightly assumed they would be the people I was to train with. Eventually a very fierce sergeant shouted at us to fall in. This was a familiar order for me, as I had served in the Air Cadets while in Canada, while the others just milled around. Finally some order was established and I realized that people there did not speak, they shouted. We were headed into a barrack room which was to become home for the next sixteen weeks.

Our barrack was a two-story building built back in 1857 with a central door that was always open, winter or summer. There was a staircase going up to the second floor immediately as you entered. Both upstairs and downstairs had one giant room on each side. Both rooms were identical and contained 33 beds a piece, housing a training platoon. Every two weeks a new draft, as we were called, came into one of these rooms that had been vacated by the previous group of semi-trained soldiers. What little comfort there was to be found was in the open fireplace in each one of the rooms. In front of each was a large iron box for storing coal. Over the century since they had been built, the bins were two-thirds full of coal dust. This was January 2nd and this part of the country could be, and was, extremely cold. When we had chosen a bed, preferably not next to someone who was too frightening, we had a few moments to put our civvies in the box provided alongside the bed.

Then the shouting began again. We had to leave everything and run to the Company Store about two or three blocks away to get "kitted out." We got boots that appeared to have no reference to the size of our feet, a beret, shirts, and underwear that I was never able to figure out how to wear. They were known as "Drawers Dracula." The trousers were too long; jackets were too small or too big and so on. This all took place under pressure from the fierce looking sergeant that I soon realized was going to play a major part in my life for the next 16 weeks. Eventually all the new recruits, as we were now called, were back in the barrack room. The shout went out to go to the battalion store for bedding, so away we went, on the run again. We had to pick up pre-sorted bundles of mattresses, blankets and pillows, but no sheets. I hope everything had been fumigated. Then we had to run back to the barrack to make up our beds.

This is when I suddenly realized I was well ahead of the crowd; most of the people had never made a bed before. They certainly had not been away from home before. Through the night I heard sounds of sobbing. I had been at a boarding school since I was four, where I had always been expected to make my bed. I had long since forgotten how to cry.

The next morning—yes, we had survived the night with no heating and the temperature below freezing—we were shouted out of bed at 5 am. We were told to fall in and the guys were beginning to understand what this meant. Roll call was taken and, surprisingly, everyone was present. We were told to wash, shave, and be back on parade in 30 minutes. With only five or six basins to wash and shave in, this was not possible. I made a mental note to wake up at 4:30 am. to ensure access to a clean basin. There were no excuses for not being shaved, or anything else for that matter. Some shaved and some unshaven people were back outside in the allotted 30 minutes, with our knife, fork, spoon, and mug in hand, ready to run to the mess hall. A huge line of diners in front of us precluded any possibility of everyone getting breakfast, given that we only had thirty minutes for this function.

Then we were back to the barracks for basic instruction on the stowing of clothes and blankets each day, and how to clean boots until they shone. This was overseen by a nasty little man who we found out was our platoon Corporal. He lived in a little box by the entry to the barracks opposite the washroom. He would emerge from his nest to strike terror into our hearts at any time of the day or night.

After about a week, we had become accustomed to the idea that we had to run everywhere. We were getting our boots to shine, if not to fit. We swapped boots with other people until everyone's sort of fit. Brasses, i.e. cap badges, buttons and anything that could be shined were beginning to make us look more soldierly. Uniforms had similarly been swapped about and pressed, but most of the time we wore khaki pants, shirt, hat and our black boots.

Training had started on day two and consisted of the basic instruction of drill until everyone was going the same way at the same time. This instruction was carried out by our platoon sergeant plus our Corporal and another equally fierce sergeant, who was perhaps still learning to be fierce himself. They had pitiful material to work with and never failed to tell us that. We started running outside the camp; first a mile or so, then longer distances. We were told that we were never to be seen walking anywhere and with this very full schedule of cleaning, inspections, running here or there, drilling and some basic instruction; we had little time for anything else.

There was a Navy Army Airforce Institute, otherwise known as NAAFI, in camp where you could spend some of the money that you had left after the deductions for any barrack room damages. I think the army was funded by those deductions. We had to line up on Thursday afternoons for our pay. It was dispensed with much ceremony by our platoon officer, a 2nd lieutenant, who was about as green as we were. The difference was that he had a "pip" on his shoulder. We had little or no time to spend the money in the NAAFI. Going into town was forbidden as we would be a disgrace to the regiment.

By this time, about a week, I was finding things to be quite easy and felt even more comfortable with being shouted at. I hid myself in a sort of cocoon and I did everything inside it. Running and cleaning equipment was not difficult for me since I had drilled in the Air Cadets. As training increased its pressure on us, we had to survive assault courses, carrying weapons (which we did not yet know how to use), being run over by tanks and fired at. All were great incentives to keep our heads down. After about two weeks, we began to notice the empty beds of people who chose not to continue or were weeded out for other reasons. This did not mean they were out of the army, just out of the Parachute regiment. Before the end of the sixteen weeks, there were fewer than ten men remaining.

There was a particularly brutal test called milling, in which each platoon member had to go in the boxing ring and take on a member of either the platoon ahead of them by two weeks or behind. The platoons were given a colored sash, either red or blue. We were Blue and frightened with the stories that the platoon we were going to fight consisted of all pro-boxers. A major sat on a podium beside the ring and allotted points to the Red or Blue as each bout finished. A single round was five minutes long, an eternity to us if we were being beaten to a pulp. I had some previous boxing experience years before at Savage Prep School when I had to fight Carter of Carters Tested Seeds, Inc. He came out of his corner and I, having no experience of this sort, got my nose broken. That is no excuse for the size of my nose, but it probably helped. Going back to milling and my upcoming bout, I had to think of a strategy that might confound my opponent. I decided the best defense was offense. When the bell rang, I charged out of my corner and using the force of my run, I punched him in the nose. I saw his nose break and spread across his face. He dropped like a log so I walked back to my corner, fully expecting a win for the Blues. It was not to be. The Major, fancying himself as one of the Caesars said, "Jolly unsporting contest, Red wins," as they carried my opponent out unconscious. I never saw him again, which was probably a good thing. This taught me a lot about fighting which would help in the future. Never let your opponent have a first chance, let alone a second.

Training continued in a monstrous procession of runs, assault courses, drills and route marches with all our equipment. We were introduced to what we were going to fight with in the fifth week. Before that, the rifle was not a weapon; it was just something to be kept clean and to drill with. I was assigned a Bren gun, which is a light machine gun weighing 23 lbs, with prefilled magazines containing twenty rounds of .303 caliber ammunition. I liked it even before I fired it later on. The remainder of the platoon was assigned the Enfield rifles that had been left over from the First and Second World Wars. As we were to find out they were obsolete, but were extremely accurate up to seven or eight hundred yards. The first thing after issue was to disassemble the weapons, examine all the parts, and put them back together again. Finally in the sixth week we got to fire our weapons. As we were doing so, a very large cock pheasant walked across the target area. Our platoon officer called "cease fire," which of course we obeyed. He took a rifle from one of us and fired at the pheasant which disappeared in a cloud of feathers. The moral of the story was, 'Do not use a .303 rifle for pheasant shooting.' That is about the only thing I remember about shooting on the range. I had previous experience with rifles in Canada, so I was able to put up a good score on all of the weapons. This resulted in my being awarded 'triple marksman,' the third weapon being the Sten gun, at the Passing Out parade, giving me my first badge on my left sleeve. 'Passing out', or finishing basic training, still seemed a long way off.

I had chosen my bed in the barrack room well. My next door neighbor, David Gollop, was a very pleasant companion. We became fast friends and he volunteered to become number two on the Bren gun, only two were required. Later in our service, we became army champions using this weapon. We served together for all but a few months of our army careers. He was tall and quietly spoken with dark hair and rather sunken eyes. His humor was always waiting for an opportunity to be displayed. This always got him into trouble, as it was made quite clear that this was not supposed to be fun. He was training to become an accountant before he was drafted. To his mother's disgust, he missed that goal by a long way.

By this stage in the training, we were down to about fifteen in the platoon, so they merged us with the platoon ahead of us. This raised our numbers to thirty strong once more. There was only one thing wrong with this idea; we had a lot of catching up to do and only six more weeks to do it in. We were spending more and more time out of camp on exercises, weapons training, firing practice and route marches. We were getting close to twenty miles a day in full marching order with weapons. David and I shared the burden of the Bren gun on these long hikes. I would carry his rifle and swap about as we got tired. With all of this we arrived back at camp, exhausted after a long, hard day, often late in the evening. We still had to be back on parade the following morning, with all our kit cleaned and ready for the rigorous daily inspection. By this time we were inured to all the abuse poured on us. It hardly made a difference. On one occasion, at a drill, the platoon sergeant barked out, "Smith, you're holding that rifle like a Princess would hold a navie's penis." We all had to suppress our smiles, let alone laughter. As far as David and I were concerned, we were classed as educated idiots and treated as such. Whatever and whenever they could cut us down, they took the opportunity both verbally and physically.

I began to realize it was a game and that I could play it, too. It required a certain stoicism, a word I am perfectly sure that the sergeant had never heard. David and I decided to use our limited education to confound and confuse them through our willingness to accept anything they could throw at us. It worked. Collectively, all of our peers knew. We were going to make it through despite our education which our superiors had supposed had made us soft. There was an iron will inside us, bred from years at boarding school and more outdoor activity than most of our fellow sufferers had ever experienced. They then began to pick on other unfortunates and left us alone because they had realized we were survivors. As we approached the end of our sixteen weeks of torture, we were looking forward to our Passing Out parade and a 48 hour pass. We realized that out of all the survivors, there were just twelve ready for the next stage. It was called P. Course and it comprised an even more rigorous physical challenge. With little to no emphasis on weapons, drill, or anything else, it was six weeks long and involved marching, running, and assault courses; 24/7 if necessary. I have forgotten much of this because I was too tired. During all of the 22 weeks in training, Alex and I kept a constant correspondence. Her letters were very important to me and I couldn't wait to go home on leave. There was to be no leave, just a 48 hour pass, which was hardly enough time to catch the necessary trains to Penzance which was nearly 300 miles away. I decided it was worth it and took off on a Friday night. I had to be back in camp by 8 am on

Alex, age 15

Monday. It was worth every penny. I stayed with Lorna, but spent most of my time with Alex. Sunday night soon came and the train left Penzance at 8:45 pm. This train was named the "Passion Express" because there were so many soldiers, sailors and airmen going home from brief reunions with their loved ones. Over the next three years, apart from overseas duty, I would be on that train very often.

There was now only another four more weeks of Parachute training to complete. It was to take place at R.A.F. Abingdon in Berkshire. There was altogether a different atmosphere there; clean, nice modern barrack rooms with every facility. The Royal Air Force was responsible for packing our chutes, training in jumping techniques, getting us to the drop zone and every other aspect of what the airborne forces are about. The first morning, we began training in a vast hangar, learning to roll on impact and everything else we needed to know and practice. After about ten days, we completed our first jump from a balloon at about 800 feet. I was scared. We were split into parties of eight who then simulate jumping out of an aircraft from a static balloon. It was awfully quiet up there, except for our chattering teeth. Everyone jumped, and everyone landed; each group of eight going after the other. On our third jump, we were in an airplane. The airplane was much noisier and our nerves were much more strained. This was our last chance to refuse a jump. After that we were refusing an order. After eight jumps and four weeks, there was a splendid parade and we received our wings with pride. We had become full members of the Parachute Regiment. We were allowed a week's leave and I was going home to see Alex.

9 THE ARMY, ACTION

I returned from Penzance, Alex and Cornwall to a very different life. I was still in Aldershot, but different barracks. I had been assigned to the 3rd Platoon C Company, 1st Battalion, in the Parachute Regt. We were in Albuhera Barracks, which were similar in every detail to our previous ones. David was miraculously posted to the identical platoon. So, we settled in, two companions, for the foreseeable future. During training I had been chosen for officer selection. This process required me to travel down to the middle of another county. We were about twenty or so candidates to be officers. We were each others' competition in the series of tests devised to test and judge our leadership skills.

Officer selection consisted of multiple trials over a ten day period, each with various solutions. Every candidate had an opportunity to solve each problem in a set time, leading seven or eight of our peers. I was lucky enough to be down the line, so my turn usually came after several people had made a complete "cock up" of the task. The point was to learn from others' mistakes. After I completed several interviews on the last day, I was informed that I had been accepted. This was the beginning of a long and frustrating series of interviews with different regiments in the army. The Parachute Regt. had no officers of its own as they were all taken from other units. No regiment would accept me, knowing I would transfer back to the airborne after my acceptance. In the end, I

3rd Platoon, C Company

just forgot about being an officer and decided to spend my time as a soldier, which was a good decision.

I went back to C Company for a routine of maneuvers and exercises. With a bunch of guys of like mind, we had a lot of fun. We went to the pubs when anybody had any money. At this time I brought my bicycle up to Aldershot and started to train for the army cycling team. As a result, I was able to get away with not doing many sports that I didn't like. When I returned from a bike ride, all I had to produce was a postmark from a post office a suitable distance away. I joined the Cyclists Touring Club and this enabled me to spend weekends, when I didn't have leave or was unable to go home, cycling. I would travel out in all directions, a hundred or more miles, and stay overnight with an old couple that hosted CTC members, and return the following day. These were wonderful weekends for me. Unfortunately, David did not share my enthusiasm for cycling. I was accepted onto the army's team, which brought a competitive edge to my sport.

Aldershot was only a short distance from Guildford where one of Alice Phelan's sisters, Janet, lived with her daughter, Sheila. Sheila had joined the Women's Royal Army Corps at the beginning of World War II. Because of her ability and drive, she had risen fast and was the first woman in the British Army to become a General. When I enlisted in 1954, she was a Major General and had her Women's Royal Army Corps headquarters in Aldershot. I had always liked Janet and Sheila as they had been very kind to me during prep school exeats, which were usually spent with them. There was always a spare bed in their house for me. They lived in genteel luxury on a road of exceptional houses just outside Guildford. Sheila's position came with a large chauffeur-driven car, complete with flag showing her rank. All I had was a bicycle, which I could cycle between the barracks and their house. Later, she chose to send her car, or come to pick me up. The car would pull up to the guard house and a runner would be sent for me. I am not sure if this gave me status or was an annoyance to my superiors. Once at the Croft, Ganghill, Guildford, I was treated very well indeed. Their cook would always prepare something special. This happy arrangement went on through the time I was in Aldershot and would often include David as well.

During my last leave, I spent most of my time with Alex. By that time, it was certain that I was in love with her. I hoped she felt the same way. She was now fourteen and very tall for her age, and I thought very beautiful. We had written to each other almost daily during training. This continued whenever possible and we added a call from a phone box in camp every Wednesday night at 7 pm, to a phone box in Newlyn where she lived. There were few phones in private homes at that time. Perhaps we talked about the weather, but I don't think so. Wednesday was chosen as few of my mates had any money left by that day of the week. Payday was on Thursdays.

We jumped regularly, and this was always a good day out. Sometimes if it was a balloon jump, we could do three or four a day. On a particularly windy afternoon, we were all lined up in the plane in Farnborough Airport. One of our guys, named Keith Jones, a Welshman of very small stature, jumped with all of us and was found to be missing when we were on the ground. We waited, but still there was no sign of him. It wasn't until later in the evening he was located on top of one of the hangars! He had been blown there, with no injuries, except to his pride. He was also very much in love, with a really beautiful girl, also from Wales. He was doing a two-year stint in the army and couldn't wait to get married.

He said to me, "Won't it be nice when I'm married and can have sex regularly . . . Once a day and twice on Sundays." I never followed his marriage after he was "demobbed," but it sounded good to me. Shortly after Keith's roof landing, I had a minor accident. A strap with a buckle caught in the slipstream and then whacked me in the temple. There was not a lot of blood, but the whole thing went septic and my head doubled in size. I was in the sick bay for several days, and not allowed to go home on weekends.

In 1955, a nasty terrorist war started in Cyprus, an island in the eastern Mediterranean. The island was not partitioned at that time but Greek people lived in one part of the island and Turkish in the other. The island had been Turkish until the end of the 1st World War. It was taken from the Turks and a mandate was given to Britain to keep the peace between the ethnic groups. This worked well until Greece started to overpopulate their side of the island.

The Greeks were in the majority and they were attempting to take over the whole island. The method they chose was to use terrorism against the Turks, but they chose the wrong enemy. The Turks are a determined, strong, even ruthless people, as the British found out to their cost in World War I. The Greeks were led by a full-time, mainland, Greek general whose name was General Grivas. It became Britain's job to mediate and eventually suppress this smoldering war, which later became a full confrontation. By the time it was decided to send the Airborne to Cyprus, there were significant clashes daily. The three battalions of the regiment were posted in January of 1956. We built a tent city outside the capital city, Nicosia, complete with showers, toilet blocks, dining area, and cooking facilities. We lived in eight-man tents, which were in rows called lines.

We were allocated a tent, and once again, David was in the same tent. There was only one thing wrong with the site chosen; it was on a fairly high plain between two mountain ranges. This made it hot in the summer, up to 130°F, and bitingly cold in winter, often freezing. One other drawback was the winds that blew across the plain. Often the tents and all their contents, not counting their soldiers, were blown with them. This happened twice to our tent and required recovering the tent and all our gear that was often spread for a mile in every direction. This promoted theft, as it was much easier to steal a missing item from someone else, than look for your own. There was a very small civilian population in the neighborhood and I can imagine the locals, both Turks and Greeks, would have clothed themselves from this source.

The airport was about a half mile away and could be relied on for plenty of noise as the conflagration expanded. The reason for our proximity to the airport was so that we could use a hitherto untried method for the delivery of troops to any location where there was trouble. Cyprus is an island about the size of Connecticut and from our central location, using Westland and Sikorsky helicopters, it was possible to deliver hundreds of battle-ready soldiers in a very short time. It would be totally impractical to drop troops by parachute. The island itself, as we were to find out, had every kind of landscape; from deeply forested, to desert, and even mountain ranges over 6000', which were often snow covered, even in summer.

Our packs and weapons were always ready and within half an hour, we could be ready to take off. After a short flight, the helicopters would descend to about twenty feet above the trouble spot. An R.A.F. sergeant would dispatch us and our kit out of the door, and as each heavily laden soldier exited, the helicopter would gain a little altitude. This made for some very heavy landings. It was good that we'd had all that training. Some of us had the bad habit of using the time-saving method of jumping out of the windows, even from the second floor, as a means of getting on parade. I suppose these jumps may have contributed to my multiple hip replacements, and now a knee. This method of troop delivery was much used by the U.S. forces later when they fought in Vietnam. In fact, our company commander at that time was from the 101st Airborne, who was seconded to our unit for study of this method.

Let's return to Cyprus. The northern part of the island was mainly inhabited by Turks. In fact, on a clear day, you could see mainland Turkey from the mountains on the coast. The whole island and most of the mountains are limestone, with the odd exception of a few volcanic mountains in the south. All ages of history are represented, from prehistoric stone huts and tools, to the much more advanced civilizations that came later. Ruins, shards of pottery and tools are everywhere. If you go diving off the coast, which we did, amphorae and shipwrecks abound. So, you can see that we landed in a wonderful place, the only problem being that the people were fighting with each other. The coastline consists either of limestone rock or beautiful sandy beaches for swimming and recreation, but a guard was always posted. It seemed that both ethnic groups had decided that the British were the enemy.

The Greek paramilitary organization that was running the operations went under the acronym of EOKA. I have no idea what those initials stand for, but for the Greeks, it stood for "Cyprus for them." Led by General Grivas, they were a potent shadowy enemy, well armed from mainland Greece, and ready to resort to any means to achieve their goal. We found this out the hard way, on one of our operations, when our company had trapped a number of EOKA fighters, including Grivas. We were in a forest quite high in the mountain ranges and the terrorists, to avoid capture, started a forest fire, with the wind, conveniently for them, in the right direction to envelop us in flames. I was very lucky to survive the fire. My boots were burned off my feet, running over the recently burned area. Five from our company were not so lucky and died in the flames. We did not bag a single terrorist on that operation.

On another occasion, we were doing a routine cordon-and-search operation around a village in the mountains. Our job was searching house to house to find any EOKA fighters. Our company commander, Captain Chiswell, David and I were trying to enter a home with a balcony. The C.O. decided to kick the door in, and putting all of his weight into kicking, the door gave way a little and then sprung back. He went through the balcony rails and landed on his neck 15 feet below. This was a bad situation because it was nearly dark. He was unconscious and obviously seriously injured. David and I got him into his jeep and started to drive him to the nearest hospital. Because it was not quite dark, we were able to pass through our own cordon around the village. The curfew was strictly enforced over the whole island at dark. Anything moving, vehicle or pedestrian would draw fire. We found this out as we drove with all lights out, for many miles through the mountains. We were fired at at least a dozen times. None of us was hit, but the jeep was full of holes. We eventually arrived at the hospital in Nicosia and delivered Captain Chiswell to the emergency department. He had a broken neck, which he survived, but was out of the army. David and I got an oak leaf to be put on our General Service Medal, and were mentioned in dispatches for our exploit. The medal was stolen in a robbery of my house in St. Augustine many years later.

I once had a picture of me up a flagpole, in a village in the mountains. The purpose of climbing the roof, and then up the pole, was to remove an EOKA flag. It was a Greek national flag with the letters EOKA written across it that I had for many years. It was a very foolish escapade, because before I was even up to the top of the pole, bullets were whizzing by. I still continued to the top in a hail of bullets. This had a good ending, because as the terrorists were firing, they gave away their position in the village and four of them were captured. They were taken away to Nicosia Prison for internment.

By this time in the terrorist war, there were over 20,000 soldiers in Cyprus trying to suppress it. The Turks on the island had realized that the British were not their enemy and had stopped shooting at us or trying to blow us up. This afforded safe haven in the Turkish villages and towns. We were able to stop and have one of their incredibly strong coffees and have a chat with the locals. All conversations on these occasions were political, or about how bad the Greeks were. We still were always armed if we were away from camp. The camp was guarded 24/7 and there was a barbed wire entanglement surrounding the whole area, patrolled day and night by whoever was unlucky enough to get guard duty. Staying awake all night was sometimes difficult after a hard day of soldiering. On one occasion, a quick thinking young soldier from our platoon, named Marks, was on guard, became tired, and knelt down with his rifle, holding it to his forehead, went to sleep. He was awakened by the duty officer's approach. He saw a pair of boots before his eyes and he crossed himself like a good Catholic (he was Jewish), and stood up explaining he was praying. The duty officer, Major Potts, who was a devout Catholic, told him to pray standing up and that God listens to all prayers, advising him to stay alert in the future.

Marks was prone to accidents and incidents. On another occasion, as a section was patrolling in the mountains we came to a long scree slope and thought this would be a great place to go down the mountain. Putting our rifles between our legs, like a witch would ride a broomstick, we were off down the mountain at speed, and no effort. Marks was first and what he didn't know was there was a twenty foot cliff at the bottom. He went sailing over and landed hard, but unhurt. His rifle followed him and landed on his head, bending the barrel. This was pretty hard to explain to the armorer when he got back to the camp. His luck held out, as a couple of years before, he had started up a pen-pal relationship with a girl in Los Angeles. He never intimated at any time that there was any-thing more in the correspondence than a passing interest. One after-noon, a large car came to the guard gate with a very glamorous woman and a very beautiful girl of 19 or 20. They asked if they could see Private Marks. We happened to be in camp so he was summoned. The young girl was his pen pal and the mother was Dorothy Lamour. After a couple of days of negotiation, he was bought out of his commitment for the remaining ten months of his service. We never heard from him again, so presumably, all went well.

Shortly after this incident, David and I were given the opportunity to travel to Jordan and stay in Jerusalem for a week. These trips were orga-nized by the same Major Potts who, through his Roman Catholic connec-tions, enabled us to stay in a monastery in the heart of Jerusalem. There were a few rules and the doors of the monastery were locked at 9 pm, rather early if you wanted to have a good time. We missed the doors once, which resulted in our spending a night in a shop doorway. Meals were served at specific times and we had to be there for the benediction. The meals were simple and no other beverage than red wine was served. The monks made this wine in the surrounding countryside. It was very effective and one of the hardest parts of the trip was exiting the dining room, down the lines of brothers still seated. We lived in cells, but were not expected to turn up for prayers with the monks. The trip enabled us to see all of the holy areas of Jerusalem, Nazareth, Bethlehem and the Dead Sea, where we had a float, it being impossible to swim because of the salt. We had a guide for these out-of-town bus trips and his name was George. I can remember that he never mentioned Jesus without first taking off his hat. On one trip, the bus was stopped and without expla-nation, George got out of the vehicle and walked into the desert. He never came back, but his brother did and we carried on our journey. We never figured out how anyone could live in the middle of nowhere, with not a building in sight. George and his brother had an encyclopedic knowledge of everything in the Holy Land and the tours were free, apart from the tipping.

We hated to be in camp for more than a few days at a time, because it was very boring and almost always hot. Only the W.O.G. (Westernized

Orientalized Gentleman) hut offered respite as it was a little oasis of cool where you could buy a Coke or ice cream. It was operated by a Greek Cypriot (familiarly known as Wogs), who charged quite good prices for everything you could imagine. There was always competition for his fried-egg sandwiches. He could only make a certain number of these. He was murdered by his own people for collaborating with the English. I believe he had a wife and family, and the store never reopened.

Our lives changed considerably after about six months when it was realized by the guerrillas that helicopters coming meant trouble for them. So, we switched tactics to section level hikes in the mountains. Each section of six to ten men would be dropped off by truck somewhere in the foothills and it would be the job of the section leader to map read across to a prearranged pickup point, anything from five to ten days away.

As there were about 2,500 active soldiers in the regiment, many groups were moving at any one time. It became impossible for the terrorists to move around, as no one could possibly know where all the sections were. This afforded my section the opportunity to kill four of them one night outside the village. They were trying to get a restock of food, but they didn't make it. Helicopters picked up their dead bodies the next day for recognition purposes. I had been made a Corporal a few weeks before, which gave me the job of section leader. A few important guerrilla leaders could provide you with a trip back to Britain, as their capture could lead to reprisals. This was not the case with our group, who were just ordinary foot soldiers. This new scheme worked really well and incidents dropped dramatically.

Humorous incidents never declined. Preparations were made to move the complete regiment at night for a lightning strike into a mountain area. Everything was going well with 400 vehicles following a Land Rover with a Lieutenant and a Sergeant, with David and myself covering them with our Bren gun. The Lieutenant and Sergeant were supposed to read the map and lead all the vehicles to a predetermined point. David and I had both been on this road before and knew that the road taken dead-ended about two miles further on. We said so, but were ignored. The column following us was about two miles long, Every vehicle entered the dead end road, which was barely wide enough for two to pass. The entire convoy had to back out, taking until noon the next day. All surprise, if there ever was any, was lost, so we went back to camp.

By July of 1956 across the Mediterranean in Egypt, General Nasser was making threatening moves to nationalize the Suez Canal. By August, he had accomplished it and Britain and France, who owned the canal, retaliated by sinking a number of ships in the canal, rendering it useless for navigation. Britain and France decided to go to war to recover the canal. A joint operation was mounted with France and troops of both countries began training for what was to be the largest airborne landing since World War II and proved to be the last major airborne operation ever. Most of the jump training was from Nicosia Airport, just a half mile away. I spoke French, although limited, so I was seconded to a French parachute unit. My new friends were vastly more experienced than me, most having survived Dien Bien Phu in Vietnam only a year or so before. They were friendly and good company. I learned a lot, and perhaps even a little more French.

10 BACK IN CYPRUS AND HOME FOR CHRISTMAS

The worst part of my arrival back in the same camp was my allocation to a different tent with alternate companions. I was to find out very soon how serious it was, as the leader of this little band was called Reg Melody. He was 6 feet and as strong as an ox. Like me, he was a Corporal and led this group of misfits into all kinds of trouble. They would get horribly drunk most nights, and come back to the tent to continue drinking and making noise. This particular night, I was already in bed, very much tucked in, as it was cold. They had made their feelings about me very clear and tonight they were going to do something about it. After about half hour, one of them, Rick Smith, got up and in a drunken stupor came to my bed with a knife in his hand and sat on me so I couldn't move. He asked the question, "Shall I kill him now Reg, or later?" After a little thought, Reg answered, "Later." As Rick Smith stumbled back to the group, I took off out of the tent as fast as I could. It was about 10:30 pm and I had to find a berth for myself. The next morning, I asked for a transfer and it was granted. I moved back in with David and life started to get back to normal.

It was now the middle of November, and there was a strong rumor going around in the Oasis that we would be going back to Britain for Christmas. I should describe the Oasis, because it was really the source of all "gen" (part rumor and part fact); the terrible trouble is, you don't know which to believe. Going back to the Oasis, it was a building about 30 feet long and 10 feet wide, which contained 14 khazis (toilets) on one side and 14 on the other. This would accommodate 28 soldiers at a time. You can't imagine the conversations that went on in there. Periodically, the whole apparatus had to be moved to a new site after a large hole was dug by the unfortunates who happened to be on "jankers" (extra duty, which was always hard). The old hole was covered with wood and then earthed over. You might not know it was there unless you walked over it. One of my friends, Nelson by name, was backing up a 1-ton truck and went over one of the holes. It swallowed about two-thirds of the vehicle, but fortunately, the engine was okay. He was told that he must get it out and then clean it. This took several days. Nelson came in for a lot of ribbing on that one.

Operations against terrorists were resumed, still using helicopters, but more often trucks. I must explain that the roads, often not much more than tracks, were extremely narrow and the side of the road would often give way from the weight of a 3-ton truck and its contents. Far more people were killed going over the side of a mountain road than from any other cause.

We were on a long patrol over the mountains in an early evening in November, when it was time to stop. We happened on an old stone chapel, long since abandoned, but the structure was still sound. The roof was still on, and inside was much warmer than outside. We were 15 in the patrol and I was the leader. The altar was still intact and the windows were all in place. It was decided that we should make this our home for the night. During the evening, five of our group decided to urinate on the altar. I remonstrated violently against their behavior and desecrations, to no avail. The following morning, a signal came over the radio for us to rendezvous at a road 6 or 7 miles away. The distance was soon covered and after a short wait, a truck drove up. The sergeant got out with his clipboard and read out seven names from our group, which included all the names of the desecrators from the night before. They were told to get in the truck with their equipment, as they had been granted leave. This usually meant time in a very modest hotel on the beach, taken over for this purpose. They pulled away and the road was extremely narrow. They went maybe 2 miles and one of the culverts on a corner gave way. The truck went over the side and rolled down the side of the mountain for several hundred yards. There were 15 on board; although some were badly hurt ten survived, five died. Yes, all five desecrators were killed. I have never been strongly committed to any religion; in fact, my dog tags stated I was an agnostic. This accident did not totally change my opinion, but it did however, make me reconsider my disbelief. As the saying goes: "There are no agnostics in a foxhole under fire." I didn't change my dog tags.

As our time in Cyprus was winding down, the Oasis "gen" was correct. The brigade was to start moving on the 20th of December by plane back to Aldershot. This was a big enterprise with over 3500 soldiers and their equipment. At that time in the British Army, each soldier had one daypack and one duffel bag in which to fit everything he owned. Many of our unit threw away their kits and substituted anything from cigarettes to guns. While I was in Egypt, I had disarmed a couple of Egyptian officers and they both had 9mm Luger pistols. One was a competition model from 1917 and the other a standard Luger. I had also liberated a

.262 Czechoslovakian light machine gun, complete with about 1000 rounds of ammunition. The question was how to get them all back into Britain without detection. Britain is very anti-weapons in the public sector. I found a spare duffel bag and loaded it with all of these weapons, then packed around them with gear. There was a large pile of company stuff and I casually put my extra pack with this, hoping to intercept it at the other end of the journey. This worked, for when I finally arrived back in Aldershot, there was my pack unopened, just laying there.

We flew from Nicosia to Malta in a York, a very old World War II bomber with no seats and about 25 soldiers lying around in whatever space they could find. It was very cold as the plane was open to the elements and it was early winter. In fact, it was the 22nd of December already, and most of us thought it unlikely we would make it back for Christmas. These thoughts were amplified when the York approached Malta, and the landing gear wouldn't come down. We were warned of the impending crash and told to lie down and hold on. We could see nothing of the outside, because there are no windows on a York. Everyone, of course, was nervous of the outcome. The crash came and we held on as the aircraft skidded along the runway for what seemed a very long time. Finally, we came to a stop and everybody on board was alright. The firemen, who were evidently following our landing, poured foam over everything and we didn't catch fire. The pilot came and said, "Sorry about that chaps. Is everyone alright?" We answered in chorus, "Yes sir, well done."

That was late afternoon on the 22nd of December. After checking with the tower, the pilot came to this disconsolate group of soldiers and said, "I am going to hitch a flight back to Blighty (Britain) and come back and pick you up." We all thought, not in a month of Sundays would that happen. We messed around at the airport all of the 23rd, losing more hope all the time. The 24th dawned a blue sky day and every plane that came into view, was scrutinized. Sure enough, about 10 am, a plane, complete with our pilot, landed. It didn't take long to get ourselves and gear on board, and after refueling, we were off. This plane, a Hasting, could travel at twice the speed of the York, and before long we were at St. Mawgan Airport in Cornwall. This was not more than 35 miles from Penzance and as it was Christmas, I thought it would be easy to hitch a ride in uniform. It didn't prove to be easy, but a few people did stop and I finally made it home for Christmas, late that night.

We were not to go back to Cyprus. The political situation sputtered on and finally the Greeks took over the government. It was a pyrrhic victory for the Greeks as the Turkish Army invaded the island shortly after the withdrawal of British forces. They rolled the Greeks back into the southern part of the country and declared the northern part Turkish. The capital Nicosia was divided by a wall, a bit like the Berlin Wall, and they continue to this day to snipe at each other on the border. There are no crossing places to allow people from both ethnicities to visit relatives on the other side. The southern Greek portion has become very successful as a holiday destination, drawing tens of thousands from all over Europe for holidays and second homes. The northern Turkish side spends its time sleeping in the sun under lemon trees.

Alex and I visited the northern part a few years ago, hired an ancient Renault car and toured all of the mountainous regions that I had patrolled lots of years before. We visited the old ruins of abbeys and castles that the Crusaders had built 800 plus years before. We stayed in the small but beautiful harbor town of Kyrenia in the Dome Hotel, which was out of bounds for anyone who not was an officer in those "other days." Cyprus made a big impact on me, for in that year, I grew up and became responsible for myself and for others. I saw, and meted out death, a sobering experience in itself.

My love of that Island will never leave me. If you *walk* in any country, you let the feelings soak slowly into you and understand the country and some of the people you meet. Conservatively, David and I, with our troop of friends walked over 5000 miles in the year we were there. It's hard to forget that. We left 123 men behind, some were friends and some were not, but all of them were young and deserved a longer life.

The harbor of Kyrenia in Northern Cyprus

11 SUEZ, NOVEMBER 6, 1956

As the day set for the attack approached, we were involved in much more training for this operation. Our concerns for the terrorist war in Cyprus became irrelevant. I was spending this time in the French camp, just a few miles away. I was not sure with which unit I would jump. On November 1, 1956, I was recalled to 1st Para., and preparations became urgent; packing weapons containers, drawing parachutes from stores, and of course, live ammunition for all our weapons. There was not enough time for all participants to get the right immunizations, so it was decided to inoculate the whole regiment with every relevant shot necessary. This brought with it great discomfort. This process was completed by November 3rd, so we were shipped over to the airport, sleeping out, and generally not knowing what to do with ourselves, or what was going on.

Reveille on the morning of November 6th was at 2 am. The time was irrelevant as nobody was sleeping anyway. We were trucked out to our airplanes, a real mixed bag, mostly remains from transport planes from World War II. All equipment was loaded with each jumper, who was responsible for his chutes, weapon containers, helmet, and premade sandwiches for breakfast. This amounted to 150–175 lbs per man, depending on which weapon he was carrying. It was found that the easiest way to load all this was to wear it, and shuffle aboard as best one could. In order to avoid the inevitable confusion on landing, wherever possible, one Platoon was in one aircraft. Each Platoon of any one Company was in the next airplane and so on. The thought behind this was that Companies and Platoons could rally that much quicker on the Dropping Zone (DZ). This, like on every other massed parachute drop did not happen, in fact you could be almost a mile away from the first man out of the plane. There followed a very long wait on the runway, while all planes were loaded and brought to readiness for takeoff. By about 4 am, this was achieved, and we trundled down the runway and were airborne.

One would think that an element of surprise was part of any airborne operation. This was not to be the case, as a massive leaflet drop had been made for several days in advance of our arrival. This was supposed to reduce the number of civilian casualties. We were given the time of 5:45 am as an exit time and that jump height was to be 100 feet. No one had ever made a descent from that low before. The jumper had to get out of the plane, let his parachute develop and unclip his weapons container that hung about 15 feet below him from a rope attached to his harness. Then, make sure that the rope wasn't between his legs to avoid possible castration. It was not possible to land properly in this time, in fact nearly everyone landed in a heap. There was the added distraction of heavy fire being directed from the ground at all the jumpers. As all of us had at least five injections, no one could raise their hands any higher than their shoulders. This made the control of our chutes difficult, and use of our weapons more so.

As we landed and got our weapons out of their containers, we realized we had landed where the map provided said, at Port Said airport. There were a few casualties, people who had been hit by fire, broken ankles and other bones; but, on the whole it was a very successful drop. The enemy, who should have been defending the airport, were to be seen scattering in every direction. Mostly not in the direction of the town, Port Said, as this would lead them into further fighting.

The town and docks at Port Said were to be the scene of an invasion of ships of every kind that would be carrying further troops and equipment and should be arriving at 10 that morning. We were quickly sorted out in our Platoons and Companies. This was made easier by only desultory fire from what was left of the enemy.

We marched in battle formation down the road to Port Said. The Royal Air Force and the French Air Force had already destroyed all of the aircraft on the ground, so there was no need to worry about resistance from above. It was not until we were perhaps a mile from the city that there was any incoming fire. At that stage, we dug in and returned fire, waiting for the entire front to assemble and roll on into the city. This didn't happen until the following morning, and during that night we saw many Egyptian soldiers running around in what appeared to be pajamas. Possibly, this was a way not to be identified as soldiers. As day broke, we proceeded into the city and to the banks of the canal, where the ships of Britain and France were still unloading. We dug in and waited for the tanks to clear an arc of fire for us. This was carried out by a tank for each row of houses or buildings and without reference to whether any of them were occupied or not. The tank would gain some speed and momentum and just crash straight through the houses, until stopped by something solid, and then they would start again. Rows of buildings were demolished in this way. As the destruction continued, the enemy, or just people, appeared out of the buildings and were taken prisoner or shot if they offered the least resistance or were armed. I didn't feel very good about this at the time and still don't. We spent a troubled and noisy night in the city. In front of us were mounds of rubble and the remains of the Egyptian Army firing at our position, near the banks of the canal and docks.

The following morning we were told that there had been a negotiated cease fire, insisted on by the American government. I have always thought, then and since, that we surrendered our right to property belonging to Britain and France and this was the beginning of all of the nationalization carried out in the area since. It would be a few years before Egypt was able to reopen the canal and clear all of the sunken ships. When they did, despite the belief they wouldn't be able to operate it successfully, everything went smoothly upon its reopening. Basically our job was over and after a couple of days sitting around in our foxholes we were loaded on to the Empire Parkston. This was a troop ship in the Second World War and probably a long time before. It was beyond uncomfortable, and I spent the days and nights on the deck. It was extremely cold, but better than being down below.

Up to the time of the Suez operation, I had resisted the temptation of smoking. Even in Cyprus where we were issued a 20-pack a day, I gave mine away. In Suez, everybody was smoking. This now included me and it would be almost 25 years before I would kick the habit for good.

We arrived back in Cyprus after a few days and disembarked from the Empire Parkston in Famagusta. A long truck ride brought us back to our original camp and tent lines. I believe that everyone was very depressed about the outcome, and our feelings were very negative about American foreign policy. This was true also of the Hungarian uprising, which started on the 5th of November, 1956. The American government dropped tens of thousands of leaflets in Budapest and other cities, telling them of the support they would get from the U.S.A. We all know the outcome of those promises, never meant and never kept.

12 ONE YEAR TO GO

All I remember of that wonderful Christmas leave was the question from everyone: "When are you going back?" The last thing I wanted to do at that time was to go back; however, early in the new year, I jumped on the "Passion Express" and headed back to Aldershot. I was traveling with my full kit as I had gone straight home from St. Morgan. This was always a struggle on and off trains as I had to change twice, once at Reading and again in Farnborough. I also had my bike with me, which didn't make it any easier. As I came to the barracks, I checked in at the Guard House, and went straight to the room we had been in before we left for Cyprus, about a year before. David had saved the next bed for me and everything looked good.

I picked up the spare duffel with the weapons in it, and then had to think of somewhere to hide them. I decided the safest place would be the armory. The Sergeant in charge, if not a friend, certainly understood. I left them there until I next went to Aunt Janet and Sheila's. Eventually, I got them all to Cornwall. "Why would you want all those weapons?" you might ask. The answer was quite simple. David and I had become very left in our thinking and, in fact, we were looking forward to a revolution when we would be in charge of something. This all seems very impractical now after 50 years of capitalism, which has changed my life; however, I didn't sell those weapons for a long time, just in case. David did go on and become a card-carrying member of the Communist Party and a union leader.

One thing I had decided was that with only one year to go before demobilizations (demob), I wanted to get in as much experience as I possibly could. I had always been interested in climbing, either on cliffs or on mountains. My weight-to-strength ratio was just right, so I became involved with the Brigade climbing team. This took us up to Wales and Scotland, and eventually to other parts of Europe. The mountains were not particularly high, but they had good rock faces for technical climbing. There were several world class climbers in the group, so I learnt a lot.

Another thing I had been pursuing for the previous two years was education. I had left Canada and high school at 16 with a few G.C.E. O-levels and when I joined up, education and study for A-levels were available. Sgt. Winters, a huge man with a superhuman amount of patience had been taking us through the classes necessary for these exams. Towards the end of this last year, I passed two A-levels.

Concurrent with all these activities I was still cycling and winning races for the Army, especially long distance events. I was selected to go on a heavy drop course, which took place near Swindon in Wiltshire. It proved very interesting as heavy drops were the only way that equipment could be made available to the troops on the ground. We started with a kind of pallet, with D rings all around it, and webbing straps with quick release buckles on them. The idea was to tie down a Jeep, a Land Rover, a small tank or any number of things and then strap on the appropriate number of parachutes. Every strap had to go in the right place and they were endlessly checked and rechecked. It took an average ten man team about two days to complete the work. Then they were loaded on to a Beverley, a vast cargo plane, and pushed out of the back when we were over the drop zone. We all kept our fingers crossed that everything would work okay. We dropped five items in our week there with no incident. I never used the skills I learnt in that week throughout the rest of my service.

During the spring of this last year, David and I were detailed to practice and prepare for the army shooting competition held at Bisley in Surrey. Bisley is to shooting as the Super Bowl is to football. We were still Bren gunners and turned up for the three-day trial. It consisted of several tests, in which our score on the target and the spread with which we accomplished the number of shots allotted, was computed to give us a final score. Each day was different, so sometimes we were shooting at static targets and other times targets would appear. Typically, the test would start at 1200 yards and we would run forward 100 yards at a time to shoot whatever appeared. As time was of the essence, fitness played a major part. Both David and I were extremely fit after a year of active service, so we were ready. I had worked out how to let off one round at a time instead of the intended burst of fire from a Bren gun. This made for extreme accuracy as during a burst the gun recoils and goes off the target. I was never sure if firing one round at a time was legal in the competition and I never asked the question. At the end of the trials, the scores were added up, and David's and mine were far ahead of the competition. I do believe the judges were suspicious of our having cheated. If those targets had been enemies, they would have been dead. We brought back a large trophy, which I understand was displayed in the Officers' mess.

During this summer, my mother, Lorna, had left Bernie Durrant and the only way she could do this was to find another mate. She found an ex-merchant seaman named Bill Wallis, who was as big as Bernie physically, if not mentally. He was a tall, well-built man with a lot of laughter attached to him. I had never met him although he spent lots of time in the local pub, as did Bernie. It never came to fisticuffs, but Bill had to oust Bernie after a 17-year relationship. Not easy because both men could get violent when intoxicated. The first thing I heard about this was a letter from home, saying she was going to get married in a couple of weeks and could I come. I had no leave pending, so I had to apply for compassionate leave. This entailed going on Battalion Commanders orders and getting very dressed up in my best uniform. On arrival outside the CO's office, eight of us had to line up and be approved as suitably dressed for the Colonel lurking behind the door. This inspection was carried out by the Regimental Sergeant Major, probably the most powerful man in the Battalion. He was a lifetime soldier having served in World War II and had lots of time to hone his wit. He came down the line, first inspecting for dress, then reviewing the reason for our being there. He got to me, was satisfied with my dress, and said, "What's this? You want leave to go to your mother's wedding?" There was a pause and I said, "Yes, sir." He replied, "I always knew you were a bastard, MacDonald." Of course there were sniggers down the line, and I tried to keep an entirely straight face. Eventually I was marched in and the leave was granted. Another chance for me to see Alex!

We were having a busy time with exercises, one of which was a huge NATO exercise in Denmark. This consisted of a large drop over the southern part of Denmark, Sjaelland. More than 1000 parachuted into an area of beautiful farmland. Unfortunately the plane missed the DZ and over 20 people were electrocuted after landing on the wires suspended from pylons. I was lucky not to be one of them. It was a poor start to an exercise that was to last five days. Other NATO countries were supplying the men who were to be the enemy and there were referees to tell us if we were dead or wounded. I landed well and moved forward to a beautiful farm in Fakse Ladeplads.

The name of the family was Pedersen, with a husband, wife, and a very good looking daughter named Inge. It was their kindness and generosity that made the next five days so pleasant. The weather was perfect and the nights were cool. David and I had almost constant visitation in the spacious trench we had dug. The only requirement for moving was the old trench had to be filled in, so as not to inconvenience the farmers. We moved a couple of times, but always on the same farm. Mr. Pedersen was a farmer in a very big way, with thousands of pigs, some cattle, and a lot of arable land for growing barley for the local Fakse Brewery. He only had one thing missing and that was a son. He tried his hardest to persuade me to come back after army service, marry his daughter and make a home on his farm. It did sound like a very attractive offer, and I certainly found out a lot about the Pedersens. He had lived in New York for 20 years, amongst other things driving a cab. He and his wife spoke perfect English, as did Inge. The food brought to our trench three times a day was outstanding and several times a night they would bring coffee. During all this time, we never once saw the enemy, or had to move more than a few hundred yards. When the whole thing was over, with so many Thank You's and promises to come back and see them, we felt really sorry to leave. We flew back to Britain in the same aircraft we had jumped from.

Shortly after our return, I was to turn 21. I was very excited as I was to receive the inheritance, what every young man wants and rarely gets, from my grandfather Richard Donne Lee James. I most wanted a sports car. At the time, the Austin Healey was the answer for every young driver, who wanted to make an impression and drive fast. In those days you could order, more or less, what you wanted in your car. My choice was the AH3000 in white with black side panels. I rode my bicycle over to the nearest dealer in Guildford, parked outside the showroom and went inside to see what they could do for me. The reaction was not as I had expected, as they were very doubtful about taking the order from someone as young and scruffy as me. I nearly got on my bike and rode away. I thought better of it and went back in to see a manager or someone in authority. It happened to be a Mr. Jackson who owned the dealership, and he said he would order it providing I would pay for it in full beforehand. Being as green as I was, I agreed to these terms and shelled out £1200 pounds ($1800). It seems a bad way to spend my inheritance, but I thought I deserved it as I still had some money left. I had to wait six long weeks for that car and when it came, I drove out of that dealership, skidding in every direction. In the rear view mirror was Mr. Jackson, with his hands over his eyes in horror. I hadn't driven a car with quite the power of this one before. I got back to the barracks and parked in the Officers' lot, there being no need for parking for the men, as no one had a car of any sort. This car was to stay with me for several years. In fact, Alex and I went on our honeymoon in it.

More about Alex. She and I had kept up a steady correspondence and spoke most Wednesdays on the phone, using the same phone box arrangement as before. I was certainly faithful to the idea of getting together when I got out of the army. I would travel home on the weekends as often as I could, particularly when I had my car. I only caught Alex out once, with a young German. I even remember his name. He was called Werner Schuring. We made up and she promised not to go out with him again. Her father, being one of my stronger supporters agreed and told her so. In fact, even at age 16, Alex was totally her own person, and if she had decided to do so, Werner would have had another date.

About this time, a flu epidemic spread throughout England, and of course, in a fairly crowded environment, the Army was hit hard. The barrack room emptied in a hurry and in some cases, unfortunately, the individuals did not return from the hospital. David contracted it and I seriously thought I would lose him, but he eventually pulled through.

Shortly after the flu outbreak, we were told to prepare for an exercise on Dartmoor, a bleak cold, and windy spot in the west of England. We were to take up a position on the top of Yes Tor, the highest spot on Dartmoor. It is a rocky promontory, maybe 3 miles from Okehampton, where we were to stay and wait for the attack of another platoon. The only problem was we really had no food and the weather was icy. We killed one of the sheep that roamed around on the moor, but we didn't have a lot of experience at that and getting the skin off was very difficult. Eventually we had a large amount of mutton, but nothing to eat with it. I came up with the idea of walking down to Okehampton and buying a sack of potatoes and a bottle of Brandy to cheer us up. I was still ranked a Substantive Corporal but was an acting Sergeant. We had a Platoon officer with us as well who thought it was a good idea. David and I collected as much money as we could and headed for town around 8:30 pm. We easily passed through the fake enemy, entered the town and found a vegetable shop. We were able to rouse the owner and the potatoes were ours. Now to get the bottle of brandy we selected the nearest pub and went to the off license window. We decided that after the walk down and the trying trip back with a 56 lb bag of spuds on our backs, we deserved a pint of beer.

No sooner had the obliging landlord given us our beer than the Company Sergeant Major walked into the pub and spotted us. He was a very fierce fellow with a handlebar moustache to match. He was on us before we could even take a sip, he asked, "What are you doing down here?" We explained our mission to no avail. We were told, "Put that beer down and get back up there." We were disappointed about the beer, but more worried about his parting words, "You will hear more about this tomorrow."

Off we went with the spuds and brandy and made it to the top. Once again, we passed through the enemy lines without being detected. I told Lieutenant Madrell what had happened and he made nothing of it. Little did I know that he would later deny all knowledge of the expedition and also said, "I didn't know about it and would not have agreed to it." The next day dawned and before long the Company Commander, a Major Garten, and the Company Sergeant Major arrived and called me over. They informed me that I would receive a court martial, and the charge was deserting my post in the face of hazardous duty. It sounded pretty scary. I thought maybe a firing squad would do the job. Meanwhile, I was put on open arrest until we got back to barracks. No, it didn't go away, and I was arraigned a few days later by a board of Generals. They had heard from a series of officers and non-commissioned officers, including Lt. Madrell, that I was a trouble maker and should have the most severe punishment possible. Fortunately, being a Substantive Corporal, allowed me to be reduced in rank, so I was a Private once more. It was a lot better than being shot by a firing squad. David was charged with nothing, as he was just a follower.

The downside of this demotion was immediately apparent when I was posted to E Company, now just as a Private. I met with the Sergeant Major of this company who welcomed me with these words, "You stay out of my way MacDonald and I'll stay out of yours." As it happened, I had about six weeks of service left and I was given a job that suited me fine. It was as a Brigade Runner and entailed my being on my bicycle all day, taking message dispatches all over Aldershot. I was happy and I realized that my army service was finished. I was only asked to do one more thing, sign on for another year, get my stripes back, and participate in the Joint Services Himalayan Expedition. The expedition of about 60 men from all services was to attempt K2 and several other mountains. I thought about it a bit and decided I would probably lose Alex if I disappeared into Nepal for a year. Nevertheless, it was a distinct honor to be considered, let alone picked. I have often thought about that year and that decision since. All that remained for me now was to go on demobilization leave of two weeks, come back to barracks for a night, and leave as a civilian. I did visit with Lt. Madrell for a few minutes and told him if I ever met him in civilian life, I would kill him. I think he believed me.

13 CIVILIAN LIFE AND GETTING STARTED

I drove away for what was going to be the penultimate trip, and I have never felt as relieved or free, before or since. I decided to go a different route home, and on the Winchester bypass a car came up behind me as he went to pass. He clipped my rear fender and there was very little damage so he gave me £100 to fix it. However, it was a mood changer and I was still a long way from home.

I arrived in Penzance in the early evening and made my way straight to Alex's house to find she had gone out with friends, so I waited. I talked with her father for several hours until she returned. I think he told her off for not being home, as he was talking with the experience of having been a soldier himself in World War II. We were both very excited at the promise of two weeks leave, and at the end, Alex's father gave his permission for both of us to travel to Aldershot for the final demob process. We drove up, arriving at

Tristan, age 21

the barracks in the very late afternoon. The provost sergeant, who was a good friend, saw us and offered us a cell each in the guardhouse for the night, which we took willingly. The following morning I was processed and we headed back to Penzance. I was a free man, with only five years on the reserve left.

At this time, Bernie offered me my previous job back at a better salary. I increased my knowledge of the wholesale newspaper, magazine and book business and started to think about what I was going to do in the longer term. About this time, I met three people who were thinking of leasing a small store space on the seafront at St. Ives, a nearby tourist town. They were interested in me as a partner as they had no money and I did—the only reason for their choice. The landlord was an old man by the name of Pop Short, a lecherous character who I had met a few times before. He decided that he didn't want to lease the shop to the others, but preferred me. This was to be my start in England. There was a hell of a row from the others, but I prevailed. Before the summer season of 1958, I opened Britain's first all paperback bookshop. It took quite a lot of work to persuade the then few publishers to supply my shop with paperbacks. Having spent time in Bernie's wholesale paperback book business helped a lot, and I soon was able to get wholesale rates on my entire inventory. Concurrent with the opening of the shop, David got out of the army and needed a job, as he didn't wish to go back into accounting. He jumped at the chance of running a bookstore because he was an avid reader.

In that same spring of 1958, I found a small semi-detached cottage in the country on a large estate called Trevethoe, which used to be the butler's house. As I no longer found it comfortable living with Lorna and Bill Wallis, I suggested I buy this house to give them more space. The cost of the half-acre lot and house with kitchen, dining room, living rooms, two bedrooms and one bathroom was £1450 ($2100). The monthly mortgage payment was just over £19 (under $30) which seemed a lot at the time. This suited David fine as he was able to move in. I now had a roommate and a manager for the new shop. We lived pretty simply; our food mainly consisted of pigeon stew. We shot the pigeons out of the bathroom window, plucked and cleaned them and threw them in the pot. We would add vegetables as necessary, and with a little bread, we had everything we needed.

Alex and I were still very much together and spent a lot of time painting and renovating the house. The only paint color I remember was the color of the raftered ceilings, which was Narvik Blue, a sort of glacial blue. The garden, which must, at sometime, have supplied the butler and his wife with most of their vegetables, had gone to seed. We didn't have the time or the inclination to start on this, but we did build a pre-cast concrete garage for the Austin Healey, which was probably my first real experience of building. It didn't prove easy, as from the start, the poured floor was by no means level. As we came round, bolting each precast section to the next, we reached our first corner section and had to rise maybe 2 inches from the start. Every section put in place was worse, until we had to block up each piece to get the bolts through. It was always a drafty garage, with gaps of 5/6 inch in some places under the bottom of the wall. The roof was much easier being made out of wood, which is more tolerant of fools. It looked good in the end, or we thought so.

I was still working in Penzance in the wholesale book department, which I had taken over from Bernie, who was glad to get rid of it. David was working full time in St. Ives and would phone daily for the books he needed to have resupplied. I would bring home a box full and David would pack them into a backpack and walk with them the 4 miles to the shop. This made resupply easy, as the traffic in the town during tourist season was total gridlock.

By now, the house had become really livable and we had furnished it with what we could find. Alex had left the Grammar School by this time and was working for the Social Security Service. I missed picking her up at school in the Austin Healey, as it made quite an impression on her school friends. I drove up the school driveway until I was asked not to by the school's headmistress. The Social Security building was a rather dreary building on a back street. It was closer to home, so Alex more often than not walked to and fro. She fitted in well, but I believe she was appalled by the indolence of some of the recipients of the "dole," as it was called.

In that same year, 1958, I learned that Bernie was in a lot of trouble with the IRS. In fact, so much so, that he might go to prison for evasion of taxes. I knew little or nothing of his business affairs. All I did know was that we would meet at the train station every morning at 7 am to pick up the papers, a huge load of parcels. They were transported to the little distribution center about a block away and counted out into bundles for various shops in the town. After that was completed, the newsagents in all the surrounding villages had their parcels made up and taken down to the bus station, which was a block away. The parcels would then be delivered to these country shops by various buses. Meanwhile, I went around town in a van delivering all the parcels for each newsagent. When I returned from this mission, Bernie would take the car, and drive off. We never knew explicitly where, but it was always a pub. This was before 9 am. The pubs were officially closed, which I believe didn't make much difference to him. Working and looking after his various businesses took him less than two hours a day, so he was spending money faster than he earned it. This, I suppose led him to cheat on income tax.

He had previously bought a small newsagents shop on Alverton St. in Penzance from Charlie White, who wanted to retire. He spruced it up a bit, put a manager in, and the business was doing quite well. In order to get a hold of some cash and pay off the Income Tax debt, he offered to sell me the freehold property, the business and the stock. From memory, I think he wanted £25,000 for the whole lot, plus the cost of the inventory, a lot of money at that time. He wanted £15,000 in cash and £10,000 under the table to follow when he was clear of his IRS problems. I signed a promissory note for the £10,000 and thought no more about it. I was now owner of one shop and freehold with no debt other than the pending £10,000. I had taken over a shop that was being run by a manager, aged perhaps 45, and a staff of five women. I continued meanwhile to work in the wholesale business. The other shop in St. Ives was leasehold, with David running it efficiently and profitably. I should say that my new Penzance shop was known as Whites after the former owner. This business was to go a long way and figures so large in Alex's and my life together, that it is hard to imagine what other direction our lives might have taken.

The store had a frontage on the main street of Penzance of about 70 feet. The shop when I bought it was perhaps 25 feet deep. Behind the store was vacant land leading to a series of stable buildings belonging to a large hotel next door. At this time I was unable to comprehend anything beyond what I had bought, which was the store building and the vacant land.

This comfortable situation continued with Alex and me working at our separate jobs, but seeing each other every day. Our favorite pastime was the movies. We had four cinemas in Penzance and Newlyn: the Ritz and Savoy, both quite nice facilities; and the Regal and the Gaiety being of second class. We knew the managers of all of them and they knew us. Another favorite pastime was to sit on the Newlyn Pier seawall. We had discovered a break in the buildings lining the quarter-mile quay and with a little effort we could climb up on the wall behind. We could then walk along this wall behind the buildings for almost the length of the quay. It was the ultimate private place and I don't think we were ever disturbed. We would talk of our plans for the future, because I think both of us knew we would eventually get married. We watched many moon rises over the Mounts Bay from our hideout.

In late spring of 1958, I was guilty of the sneakiest trick I ever played on Alex. I felt that I needed to go back to Denmark and check out my feelings for Inge Petersen and her family. Charles Hansen, the Danish born landlord of the local pub, and I drove to Harwich and my car was hoisted by crane onto a ferry that took us to the Hook of Holland. From there we drove non-stop to Copenhagen, about 1000 miles. After dropping Charles, I drove back to Fakse where I was greeted like the long-lost son they so wanted me to be. I have to say my visit went well, but confirmed my feelings that Alex was for me. Inge and I had a super time touring in Denmark and into Norway, but there were no illusions that this would continue, so we parted and that was the end of that chapter. On my return to Penzance, I went to Alex's house. She was pretty upset as someone had told her the reason for my trip. I thought this might be the end of our love affair, but fortunately, she forgave me the next day. I agree it was sneaky, but had I not gone, I might never have known absolutely that Alex was the one. Alex was 17 and I was 21 at the time, still very young.

On my return, things started to go wrong, or maybe they started to go right. My manager in the Penzance store went for a drive with his wife on his day off and died of a heart attack at the side of the road. He had two young children and his wife was devastated. I had no experience of retailing at all, but I had to take over where he left off. The first of many problems, were the staff of young women who worked there. They had all been employed there for some time and every one of them was older than me. All of them knew more than I did, which was not a good way to take over management of anything. I learned fast, but they did anything they could to make me feel small, useless and lacking in confidence. I knew that the only way to gain ascendency was to fire the lot but I couldn't do that, as they knew all the secrets of the business. So, I just worked and thought a lot about how to improve the shop by changing its direction.

One whole wall was a vast glass cabinet full of dreary looking gifts of all kinds. I threw all of them out to the horror of the staff. The cabinet went next, to be replaced by the first modern shop fixture in the town. This was to merchandise paperback books, which I knew sold because they were doing so well in St. Ives. This was the time when greeting cards were being taken out of shoeboxes, as a customer requested a type of card, so I set up special displays—units that we have all become very familiar with. I contacted Hallmark cards and became the first shop in Cornwall to sell their cards. To make the space for these displays, I had the serving counter cut by 75%, and displayed the papers and magazines in much less space. The old cash register fitted onto the counter amongst the newspapers.

The staff started to look for other jobs, thinking that all the changes would lead to the closure of the shop. I was left with only two of the most entrenched women, but the books started to sell, and guess what, so did the cards! Bernie's remarks were along the same line saying, "You're ruining that business." I guess he was worried about the £10,000, still unpaid. As Christmas approached, I thought we might find a decline in sales because the gifts were gone. The seasonal cards easily made up for this as our first Christmas showed an increase in sales and profits. I didn't think I was the greatest retailer of all time at this stage, but I knew I was on the right track. I was still operating the wholesale book business, taking advantage of the extra percentage of profit that this brought in. I moved the operation to a new location with more space.

Alex, John and Pam

The most exciting thing to happen that Christmas, however, was not my early success in retailing, but my being able to convince Alex's father to allow us to get engaged. There were provisions of course, marriage couldn't take place until after Alex was 21 and she had just had her 18th birthday. This gave us three years to wait!! Whatever, you take what you can get, and work out the details later. Now into 1959, events directly related to us, made changes we hadn't even thought about. In March, Pam, Alex's sister, was married to John Davis in the Methodist Chapel in Newlyn. Alex was the bridesmaid in a really beautiful short white dress. We both felt very strongly that this should have been us getting married. I know we talked about it on the seawall afterwards. Lorna, my mother, who had watched us grow up together, was, I think, concerned that our hormones would overrule our common sense. After a discussion, Alex and I convinced her that she could intervene on our behalf to convince Alex's father to change his mind and let us marry sooner rather than later. Lorna knew Alec quite well; he had always admired her from afar when she was a child. The meeting took place and my mother convinced him of the advantages of an earlier marriage, reminding him that we would have a house to live in, and it seemed a promising future with the shops. He unwillingly agreed and the date was set for May 16, 1959.

14 MARRIAGE: A DIFFERENT LIFE, CHILDREN

The conversation between my mother and Alex's father took place at the end of March. We had only a few weeks to prepare for our wedding. We both decided that it would be small and held in Madron Parish Church, followed by a small reception at the Union Hotel in Penzance. Half past nine was the proposed time. This would enable me to work on the newspapers before the ceremony. I ordered a taxi to pick me up at 8:30 am from White's. No taxi arrived, so David and I started to run the 3 miles, mostly uphill, to the church. Meanwhile, Alex and her father were circling the village awaiting our arrival. Her father made the classic statement to a young bride: "You've made your bed, now you must lie on it." Actually, Alex and I couldn't wait to get into that bed. David and I finally turned up, making the 3 miles in less than half an hour. We were a little warm to say the least, as it was a gorgeous day.

The Reverend Ram, who was the vicar of Madron, conducted the ceremony in a Church of England service. David was my best man. There were just 13 family members at the service. Alex wore her beautiful bridesmaid's dress from Pam's wedding. She carried a bouquet of white lilies, which after the ceremony were placed on her grandmother's grave. All we had left to do that day was to drive 230 miles to Bristol to the Royal Hotel, which we had chosen for our first legal night together. After starting the drive, we realized we had forgotten our border collie, Jedda. We had left her in the shop during the service. We quickly returned, picked up one excited dog, and were off on honeymoon.

Tristan and David arriving at the church

I think it was probably my idea to go to Wales as I had a great interest in castles and, in fact, I still do. Wales is full of castles, some in ruins and some quite nicely restored. I am not sure how many we visited, but it was a lot. I don't think Alex shared my interest at the same level. We had great weather, great hotels, at some of which we had to prove we were married before they would give us a room. The Welsh are a very devout bunch and didn't want any sinning. We must have looked very young at 22 and 18 years of age.

We came back to our cottage at Trevetho, where David continued to live. He was an excellent companion in our daily life. He had begun to go out with a French girl, Genevieve, who had been looking after Lorna

May 16, 1959

during her convalescence from a hip replacement. About ten days after our return, we were invited to a beach party. Alex said she didn't want to go and I wish I had said the same. David and I set off, arriving at the party site where there was a huge amount of apple cider available to drink. I had no experience drinking that particular beverage, and it had a pretty serious effect on me rather quickly. To get to the party, we had to park in front of some houses that were bordering on a rail line, and then descend by a steep path to the beach below. This was easily done when sober, but in reverse it was a feat. I remember climbing up the cliff path, going through the wires on the side of the rail lines, falling and rolling down the grass cutting to the rails below. I pressed my forehead against a rail, which was some relief for the oncoming headache. I wished a train might come along and cure it. I finally climbed up the grass on the other side and through the wire, eventually finding my parked Healey. I engaged gear and cruised around in the subdivision trying to find my way out to the road. Then it was across the main road and onto the same dirt road that David walked every day going to St. Ives. I did eventually get home, but I only made it half way up the stairs before I passed out. When Alex met David upstairs the following morning she asked where I was and David's reply was, "I found him on the stairs and I didn't think you would appreciate him like that." "So what did you do with him?" Alex asked. "I put him on the sofa downstairs," was David's reply. It was the only time in my life I was unfit for work and Alex had to take the car and go in for me. It was a Sunday so it was only half a day, but it took more than a day for me to recover from that one.

David and I had done some serious drinking in the army, and had some monumental hangovers. He reminded me of the time when we had each drunk 23 brandy sours and missed the truck home from Nicosia. We had to go cross country back to the camp, falling into a dry riverbed and some wet ones along the way. We looked like hell when we arrived back at camp, but we were still on parade in body, if not in mind, the following morning. After that escapade, it was my intention not to let Alex down like that again and I did reform some.

Very soon after our marriage, Alex began to feel sick in the mornings and of course we all knew the reason for this. It was confirmed and we began to look forward to the birth of a boy or girl. It was not possible in those days to detect the sex of the unborn. The cottage we lived in was up a driveway about 1/2 mile long, past the Manor house and through the home farm. Alex had a tough time, as her pregnancy progressed, making the long walk down to the bus, which stopped at the gates, especially if she had shopping bags. The owner of the manor house would often pick us up, but we couldn't count on it. I would leave the house before 7 am and usually not return until 6 pm, so Alex was often rather lonely. We decided that a second car was needed, so for £25 ($40) a Ford Consul was purchased. It was "tummy ache green," had a protruding visor over the windshield, and was really ugly! It ran well, so Alex could come into town as she felt the need.

Gaere's christening

The nine months passed quickly for me. Needless to say it passed much more slowly for Alex. On the evening of March 14, 1960, Ian Gaere Lee MacDonald was born. At the time, the thought of a father being present at the birth of his child was unthinkable, so I had been out at the movies with friends. When the phone call came to say it was a boy, and mother and child were well, I was overcome with emotion. I found it impossible even to dial a correct number to let others know. Alex had the baby at my mother's house using a midwife from the local village of Goldsithney.

I drove from Penzance to Chyfor, probably way too fast to see Alex and Gaere, who we had not named as yet. I didn't want to leave them, but I had to return to Trevetho to take care of our dog Jedda. Alex spent a few days at Chyfor resting and then decided to come home. Trevetho was very much our home; before we were married, and after. We were always happy there in the country and around the really huge estate surrounding us. There was a large lake, crumbling ornamental gardens, a walled garden with greenhouses to grow early vegetables, and a huge

Fishing with Alex

paddock large enough to land an airplane. In fact, the new owner did just that. In each direction of the compass, a road went out to intersect a public road and at each junction there was a gate house and a lodge, no longer inhabited. We walked over the grounds in every direction, whenever we had the time.

It was a grand place to live, but our days there were to come to an end for several reasons. The farmer didn't like Jedda or Lottie, our new Saluki that we had purchased. They would escape and chase his sheep. I don't believe they ever killed one but he was convinced they would. David had married Genevieve and needed to move on to a more orderly and structured life. Alex and I will never forget the day he left and waved goodbye as he walked away from the house, and us, with his backpack and nothing else. We were only to see him once more, but by then I had sunk into a life that he deemed a completely unacceptable capitalist life. The third and last reason was that Alex was increasingly feeling cut off in the country with a baby and two dogs. So, we decided to buy 22 Kings Road in Penzance, a two-story masonry house with three beds, 1 and 1/2 baths, a large living room and dining room with a good sized kitchen. The garden area was nearly all in the back of the house, which was perfect for our dogs to run in. Also, to place the five beehives we had installed at Trevetho.

We had taken up bee keeping as a result of a walk with our friends Liz and Mike past one of the gatehouses on the estate. Each time we passed we could hear a loud buzzing noise. The house had long since been abandoned, so Mike and I entered through the front door, went upstairs and looked into the attic. The rafters were covered solidly with honeycomb in every direction. This was a project for the following weekend to collect the honey and comb. We visited a bee keeping store in Truro; the owners were free with advice, and we purchased the necessary equipment for the adventure. We each bought a hat and a veil, plus smoke to calm the bees. We ventured forth, loaded with pans, washtubs, and anything else that would hold honey, along with a ladder, and departed upstairs. All was prepared so we put on our head nets and started to put smoke up in the roof. The roar of those bees was deafening. Not dissuaded, we started to scrape honey and comb from the rafters. At a little

over 350 lbs we stopped, wondering what we would do with it all. This problem was solved by our local grocery store (long before supermarkets), which bought and bottled all we didn't save for ourselves.

This led to the idea of having our own hives and selling the honey. We started with two hives and soon added three more. The process of moving five hives plus bees the 8 or so miles into town was another matter. We obtained the services of Sid Courteney and a truck. After closing the entry and exit to the hives in the evening when

Anna

most of the bees were inside, we loaded them into the truck. Sid drove very carefully to our new location. This was a very urban area and we did have some trouble. Whenever anyone in town was stung, he or she suggested it was our bees. If there was a swarm anywhere, it had to be our bees, which was not true as we serviced our hives regularly, making sure

Lottie

there was never more than one queen in the hive. Our bee keeping came to an end a few years later, with a cold winter that killed all 50,000 of them.

Shortly after moving into Kings Road, we realized that it was an unsuitable home for Jedda. She was a rambunctious collie, who needed freedom to run and bark when she felt like it. We had a very nice customer called Martin and he said he would love to have her on his farm, so Jedda went out of our lives. To replace her, we bought another Saluki called Anastasia (Anna for short) from a woman who bred them. She joined Lottie on the bed that I had made in our kitchen. We took them on the beach and cliffs where they ran free and very fast. We had a love affair with Salukis and bought another one a few years later, plus the ones we bred. In fact, we only had one litter of four.

Gaere was getting big by that time and Alex was pregnant with Lorna. It was becoming increasingly difficult to reach into the back seat of the Healey and pull out his carry cot. Then, one day, the bottom of the cot fell out, leaving Gaere in the car. It was very sad to come down to a very pedestrian Austin A55 Cambridge. We kept it a long time and it

Young Gaere

proved to be a good work horse for the business and family. Lorna Alexandra was born on the 15th of September, 1961. This time Alex went up to Redruth to a birthing facility, which had been created out of an ancient Silicosis Hospital. It was, in its time, a very busy place, because all the surrounding area was filled with hard rock mining. Silicosis is a result of getting dust in one's lungs, which causes breathing problems and often death. Alex didn't like the hospital or the matron and neither did I. It was 20 miles from home, and when I called up to find out what was happening, I was told that Alex was still in labor. Lorna was born the following morning, a healthy 8 lbs 15 ounces. During the very restricted visiting hours, I went to see Alex, who was so fed up she said she was going home. The matron made a remark, "You people use this facility like a hotel." We signed the documents and left. I should have mentioned earlier that Gaere was baptized in church by Canon Buckley. This was the same church and the same vicar who had christened me 20 odd years before. Lorna was christened at Madron Church where Alex and I were married. We felt that we needed to stop having more children; it seemed to be too easy. So, Alex became a very early user of the birth control pill.

Now we had two children, two dogs, five hives of bees and two relatively successful businesses. David's place in St. Ives was filled by a man who became and still is a longterm friend, Peter Noall. He lived in St. Ives and was only a short distance from the shop. I still worked in the Penzance shop and supplied Peter with the books as necessary. Alex, of course, was at home looking after our two lovely children. Gaere, from an early age was very spirited and got into all sorts of trouble. When he was three, he came downstairs on Christmas Eve and turned up the oven to 500°F, which was supposed to be cooking the turkey slowly all night. We had a smoke filled house in the morning and for good measure he found some blue paint and painted the kitchen floor. This made for a slightly different Christmas morning than we had planned. Lorna, on the other hand, was a happy baby, seldom cried, and was always content. After Lorna was first born, a lady came into our lives who literally changed everything. Her name was Kitty Ellis, and she became known fondly as Elly to the children. Initially, she volunteered to help Alex around the house three days a week, but on the very first Friday, she suggested that she take Lorna home to give Alex a break. Lorna and Gaere grew to love Elly as much as we did. She became the Grandmother that Lorna Sr. could never be and Alex's mother, Hilda, who had died when she was just 2 and 1/2 years old didn't have the chance to be.

Shortly after Lorna was born, we decided to do a road trip through France and Italy with our two friends, Mike and Liz. We had two of Alex's friends living in the house to take care of the children and Elly looking in regularly. After staying in Rome for several days, we went on to the boot of Italy, where we caught a ferry to Greece. We traveled in Greece very thoroughly visiting all the ancient sites. I had my diving bottles on the roof of the car and they were not your standard issue scuba gear. It was a set of three bottles on a frame, which looked suspiciously like a bomb, so we were stopped at every border crossing, and had to explain what they were. We only had one mishap, pulling into a Shell station to a Super Shell pump. We filled up with the specified grade and only went a few miles down the road before the car stopped. A hay truck came along and asked what the problem was. We said we didn't know. He promptly siphoned some fuel and smelled, then tasted it. He said, "You have diesel in there." We of course said that we had just filled up with Super Shell. He insisted we turn the car round and attach it to his loaded hay wagon with about 15 feet of rope. He drove off at breakneck speed. We were unable to see a thing around the truck with hay coming off like a snowstorm. He stopped at the gas station and the attendant confirmed there was diesel in the Super pump and then said, "They never asked."

We proceeded being towed at high speed into Olympia, a forgotten village with lots of history, including, being the origin of the Olympic Games. The main street had one quite modern hotel, operated by an extremely lecherous Greek. The street was perhaps 1/4 of a mile long, with the usual cafes and bars, all frequented by men smoking and talking politics. There was a grocery store and in the window there were some wheels of cheese, with a cat sleeping at the side. In the middle of one of these cheeses was a mouse standing up on its back legs eating a large morsel of cheese. The grocery store didn't seem to be doing any business, in common with the other stores.

Our car was dropped at the only garage in town and it was obvious from appearances that this might take a long time. We were told that we would need a new carburetor and some other parts. These could only be obtained from Athens, a considerable distance away and over the mountains. There was no regular delivery, as the Austin A55 Cambridge was not a common car in Greece. We settled in for the long haul with the lecher, who was becoming more of a nuisance every day. He encouraged the girls to sunbathe on the roof of the hotel and suggested they might want to take the tops off their bikinis. The next thing we watched was the lecher coming up to join them. Eventually after seeing everything that Olympia had to offer (at least twice), the car was ready and we set out again for Athens. The rest of the trip was exciting, as all four of us had never been to some of the European countries we went through on our way home. Our trip was a month long, and we were still friends with Mike and Liz at the end. The only sore point was that since I was doing most of the driving, each time I parked the car, they would get into the hotel first and be sure to take the best room—every time.

15 DIVING AND ROUND TABLE

In the period between the births of Gaere and Lorna, in the summers of 1960 and 1961, there was a new business starting from Penzance Harbor; scuba diving for sea urchins, along with catching lobsters, crabs and crawfish. The urchins were plentiful in water from 30 to 100 feet, and the shellfish, mostly 100 feet plus. I had done some diving off Cyprus, so I was attracted to the idea of making some extra money. I went into the business of collecting sea urchins. I had joined with Malcolm Brounker in partnership, which was to last several years. The basis of this was that I supply the boat and all other expenses we split. He supplied the cleaning site for the shells and all the equipment necessary. The process required sacks to collect them. The sack was kept at negative buoyancy by putting a little air from your mouthpiece into a gallon jug attached to the sack. We then swam them up to the boat, which was anchored above. The person in the boat was responsible for cutting around the mouth of the urchin, shaking out the insides, and then re-sacking them. I had bought a 17-foot boat with a small cabin up front. We had a series of outboard motors that frequently let us down.

The cleaning site was a very small backyard attached to Malcom's house. We each had our own diving suits and bottles; the compressed air was a shared expense. This arrangement went well, and we were soon processing 1000 urchins a week. After the initial cutting and shaking out of the insides, the sacks of urchins were taken to the cleaning site. They were immersed in a solution of caustic soda and water, in old bathtubs that had originally been used in houses without bathrooms. They were galvanized and would hold 150–200 urchins each. This process took somewhere between a quarter to half an hour, depending on the temperature. We then took a wire brush and scrubbed the outside of the shell, taking off all the spines, being sure that the insides were completely clean. The shells would then be immersed in bleach and water to disinfect them and bring out their color. Then ready, they would be placed on racks to dry for a day or so. So, what did we do with the finished product? Tourists just loved them as souvenirs of their holidays in Cornwall. Some of them were made into lampshades, and other decorations. We had my two shops to sell them in, plus a few others which we contracted to supply.

The much easier, but also more risky side of diving was to go for shellfish. It was always deeper water, and usually in more exposed places. With our fairly small boat, we had to be careful of the weather. The coast of Cornwall where we were operating is extremely rocky with strong tides up to 20 feet and weather that can quickly make the ocean very rough. These forages for shellfish were fun and financially rewarding. It was not unusual to catch up to 50 crawfish per trip, which sold in the market at £7 pound. Each crawfish weighed 5–7 pounds, which easily balanced out the extra danger involved in getting them. This diving arrangement went on very well, and we extended the season to include fall and spring. We did try a few winter dives. They were found to be impractical because the water temperature at 47°F was just too cold. Malcolm and I did not see each other socially, so it was entirely a business relationship. After a couple of years, Malcolm became careless, and one particular dive stands out. We were about 3 miles up the coast from the village of Mousehole and it was fairly rough. Malcolm was in the boat following my bubbles from below. He lost them altogether, and after searching around a while, he decided to head for home. I surfaced, looked around, and saw the boat disappearing in the distance. I had two choices, the first was to try landing on the shore a few hundred yards away, but this was impractical as the waves were crashing on the rocks, making any attempt at landing very difficult. The second choice was to drop my weight belt and start to swimming for Mousehole Harbor, about 3 miles away. I had a flowing tide to help me along and after a long swim, I reached the harbor. I was in a full wet suit, flippers, and mask so later I am sure people wondered what I was doing walking in the village. I went to the bus stop, and Mr. Harvey, a friend who drove the bus took me aboard. He took the bus off its route to drop me at Malcolm's house whose response was, "I thought you would show up." I remonstrated with him to no avail.

On another dive, I was down a little over 100 feet with Malcolm in the boat, when my air supply locked completely. I realized I had a long way to go up to the surface, and fast. The little oxygen I had in my lungs as I swam up expanded. Seeing the silvery sheen of the surface above, I kept going. As I reached the top, the boat was right there and I was just able to grab the rail. If it hadn't been there, I am sure I would have drowned.

It was getting too dangerous as we pushed ourselves further and further into harm's way. Malcolm and I agreed to part. He was getting fed up with doing most of the cleaning work anyway. Meanwhile, I was still working the shop. Most of our diving started around 5 am., which made for a very long day, with the shop closing at 6 pm. Malcolm continued diving with his girlfriend, piloting the boat that he had bought. One day he didn't come up and was found later at the bottom, having suffered a heart attack, induced by nitrogen narcosis (bubbles of nitrogen in the blood). He left a wife and son of whom I was Godfather.

I found a new friend who was interested in diving with me. John Bunnell was an ex-army captain, about my height, with a very serious moustache. He had to shave this off because it made his mask leak. He was at one time in his service, aide de campe to the Duke of Edinburgh. He spoke very Oxford English, had a sharp wit and a wife called Patience. They had three children, Bernadette, Benjamin and Bartholomew, known as the three Bs. They all lived in a huge old house in Hayle, a nearby town. It had adequate space for the processing of urchins, so we began diving together, and our relationship lasted at least three years. I eventually gave it up for health and for other work commitments.

One night Alex and I were lying in bed together, talking about our lives, and the lack of friends and social life. It was obvious what the problem was—we were chronologically ahead of most of our friends, who were still not married and without children. What could we do? None of our friends had houses, so we hosted most parties.

During this time, we had both put on quite a lot of weight, so we decided we had a great deal to straighten out in our lives. The following morning, we stopped putting sugar and milk in our tea and coffee. That was the beginning of a new lifestyle of eating, which changed both of our lives.

The next decision was to join Round Table, a club for young men who met every other Monday at a hotel, where dinner was served, followed by a meeting. The evening was usually over by 10:30 pm. There were about 35 young men in the club, all under 40 years old, who, between them represented most of the trades and professions in the town. Penzance Round Table was one of many across the country and indeed the world. This was a good pool of like minded young men and their wives who we soon knew socially. In fact, we made lifelong friends of Round Tablers from many locations. John Bunnell was a member, and as I said before, my partner in diving. The wives of the members had the option of joining Ladies' Circle, who met once a month. The object of both clubs was fellowship, community service and charity work, similar in style to the Rotary Club. Over the years that followed, I became Chairman of our Club and Area Vice Chairman. I put a lot into the organization and received a great deal in return.

After giving up milk and sugar and joining a club that would solve our social problems, there had to be more actions that we could take to reduce weight and get fit. At this time, Alex and I decided that we would look for an au pair to live in the house with us and help look after the children. We contacted an agency and soon had a suggestion of a German girl named Heidi Weinstock, from Neuss am Rhine. We wrote to her and invited her to join us for a year, outlining a very small financial reward, but the benefits of living with us and learning the language. She replied she would love to come, and enclosed a picture of herself. That was quite enough to get Alex started on a strict diet for the several months before Heidi arrived. It worked for me, too. Heidi was very glamorous, with blonde hair and a great figure. Heidi was also the same age as Alex, which was 21 in the summer of 1962.

We went up to Bristol to see our friends, Ken and Bobby Budd and while I was there I was measured for a new suit. As tailors do, they mark in the inside jacket pocket the physical shape or description of the recipient. I didn't know this, but when I came home, proudly showing Ken and Bobby my new suit, Ken immediately looked in the inside pocket. There were the words, "Short/Port," short referring to my height and port, referred to my figure being portly. I had only a few months, but diving was good exercise and I tried hard, like Alex, to eat less. We were successful and by the time of her arrival, we both were in great shape.

Heidi got along in our family very well and she loved the two Salukis. She would parade around the town with them on leashes and was a real head turner. She fit into our everyday life with never a complaint about anything and if there were jobs to do around the house, Alex and Heidi would do them together. Of course it wasn't long before she had boyfriends on the scene, so she would go out on the nights we were at home. This worked well but towards the end of her stay with us, she would want to go to the same parties as us! Then we had to get Elly in to babysit. She loved living in Penzance with us, so she added another three months or so to her stay. She went back to Germany, but soon returned to Penzance for a stay of several months on her own.

After Heidi, we had another au pair, this time from Sweden, whose name was Marianne Larsen. She was a tall quiet girl, and lived comfortably with us for the full year. After she left, we visited her and her family in Sweden, where we were introduced to all the wonders of Swedish cuisine. I think her mother was very grateful that her daughter had found a good home. At the end of her year, she spoke such excellent English;

you would hardly know she had come from another country. She went on to work for Volvo Penta Outboard Motors and lived in London.

The third and last of the au pairs was perhaps the liveliest of them all. Ulla Bohlin also came from Sweden; she was of medium height, with fair hair, a dynamite body and personality to match. She was a hit on her arrival and stayed that way. At the end of her year, she stayed with us for several more months, to pursue the serious love affairs that filled her life.

Marianne and Lorna

We lost touch with all three of our au pairs and often wonder what happened to them. John Davis, Alex's brother in law, heard that Heidi was to get married, but her husband committed suicide the day before the wedding. John kept in touch with Heidi for some time after she left Penzance. We visited Heidi's home in Germany some time later, and her mother was charming and welcoming. Her father, however, only appeared once during our visit. He clicked his heels and muttered his thanks to us for looking after his daughter, turned and left the room, not to be seen again.

16 THE MIDDLE YEARS

In addition to the really good help from our live-in au pair girls, Elly was always there to babysit for a night or a week if necessary. She would take both of them home with her and Lorna even had her own bedroom. Gaere started kindergarten and from an early age, showed an aptitude for disruptive behavior. We persevered with his education at St. Erbyns, a local private school, until he was eight. By this time, he had proved too difficult for most of the teachers, so after much heart-searching, we decided in tandem with two friends that had a son of the same age, to send them both to boarding school in Sussex. The school, named Cottesmore, was 275 miles away and situated in a large mansion, built in the 1890s by an entrepreneur in the Ostrich feather business. The building was surrounded by considerable grounds and playing fields. All in all it was a first class place. We felt very substandard in our Austin Cambridge car. Other parents dropped their children in everything from Aston Martins to a helicopter. Meanwhile, Lorna began school at St. Clares, which was private and just a couple of hundred yards away. St. Clares was also in a large mansion, in fact, our house on Kings Road was built on land originally belonging to that estate. She settled into school life very easily and stayed at St. Clares almost to the end of high school.

Alex and Gaere

When the children were still very young, I had the opportunity to join 245 Round Tablers from all over Europe and their wives on a sponsored trip to South Africa. The sponsors were the South African Round Table, with a great deal of help from the government, who wanted to introduce and represent their country under apartheid. Apartheid means separateness in Afrikaans and I don't think they convinced many of the participants that this extreme system of segregation was acceptable. We saw and felt this regime everywhere we traveled. On the whole, the black people were treated kindly, but sternly, and "kept in their place."

All participants had to go to Frankfurt where we boarded a chartered 707 that flew us to Johannesburg. On arrival, we were divided into busloads, and this was the way we traveled for most of the next month. The buses took us to a reception at The Cricket Club of Johannesburg where we were met by the President of the Republic and a number of his ministers. A sumptuous lunch was served, with lots of wine to accompany it, and then the speeches of welcome were made, explaining their strange behavior towards 90 percent of the population. I was appointed to respond to his speech for the group. We were then taken to the houses of our first hosts. My hosts, Ian and Elma Hunter were to become good friends, remaining in our lives to this day.

One morning we were up at 5 am to take a trip down "Western Deep Levels," a gold mine on the Rand, about 30 miles away. We descended into the mine in an elevator going down 1 and 1/2 miles, then a 1/2 mile out to the face where they were extracting the ore. The temperature in the mine was a blistering 140°F. After finishing our underground tour, we had a much needed shower then another big lunch. I sat next to a very nice gentleman named Harry Oppenheimer. He was to diamonds what Warren Buffet is to American business. After leaving Ian and Elma, we boarded the bus for Mafeking and then on to Kimberley, where we were taken into the diamond sorting rooms where visitors are not normally allowed.

From there, Gerald, a friend that I had made on our bus tour, and I flew to Cape Town and Paarl, where as in every case, we stayed with Round Tablers in their homes. In Cape Town, the hosts had heard I was a diver, so I went out with the local club for a dive from shore on an old wrecked ship. The dive went well until we were coming back in. I was caught by a large wave and my snorkel, mask and flippers were ripped off. I was still perhaps 200 yards from shore, not able to see without a mask, and found it difficult to swim with no flippers. The shore consisted of extremely sharp rocks, but I came in on the next wave and held onto a piece of rock as the backwash tried to drag me back out to sea. Covered in scratches, cuts and abrasions, I was taken to hospital for cleanup.

The trip went on to Graf Reinet, where Gerald and I stayed on a farm with over 20,000 sheep. Then we went to Oudtshoorn where the animal of choice was ostrich. We were able to ride one and had some races. We also enjoyed ostrich steaks. The ostriches are still grown for feathers and hides. In the 1890s this was really big business. We each came home with an egg, the insides of which had been blown out. We made our way north in our bus, stopping at several small towns, where people were just as hospitable. At the end of the trip, we went to Kruger Park, a game reserve of immense size. Here we saw nearly all of the animals of Africa. From Kruger we went back to Johannesburg to Ian and Elma's house. We were all very sorry to leave after a month of incredible experiences.

On arrival in Penzance by train, Alex came to meet me with Gaere and Lorna, and they ran up the platform past me. I think I was very tanned and they didn't recognize me after my having been away for a month. So ended a perfect trip, apart from Alex not being there. I had been told it was Round Tablers only and no wives, which didn't prove to be true. I broke that news to Alex much later, when we were in Denmark and met with two friends from the trip, Hans and Schmouni Warrer. Luckily, Alex believed me when I told her the trip was represented to me as only Round Tablers.

It was during this period that I went with our next door neighbor, Alan, to the London Boat Show. I had always wanted to try sailing and Alan had a small cabin cruising boat of the Silhouette Class. I had been out with him a few times and enjoyed it. While viewing the incredible selection of sailboats available, I spotted one which was afloat in the large pool in the exhibition hall. It was called an Eventide. It was 27 feet long and had twin bilge keels that enabled it to stand upright on the mud or sand in the harbor. Penzance harbor was a mixture of both. Eventides were built of steel in Holland, and one could be delivered to Dover before the next season. It came with a normal sloop rig, main and jib, plus a storm foresail. The mainsail could be roller reefed in bad weather. I bought it, and then went home to Alex to tell her of my purchase. The news wasn't greeted with much enthusiasm, and it was pointed out to me that we hadn't yet bought a dining room table. I had not thought that a table was more important than a sailboat, but one was purchased within the next few days. In the spring, before the delivery of *Pipers Moon*, I went off to the Hamble River to learn how to sail. From the moment I got on that sailboat, I knew that it was to become a passion for me. In that week, I learned a lot but knew that there would be a lifetime of learning ahead.

The name *Pipers Moon* was selected from many choices. Our Hallmark Card representative, Andy Ramsay, was dating, and threatening to marry Ann Sheppard. Her father owned a couple of racehorses, one of which

Pipers Moon

was named Pipers Moons. We liked the name and the horse, so we named the boat accordingly.

The date arrived for the delivery of the boat, so we piled a crew of four, plus a driver to come back with the car, into the Austin, including lots of gear needed for its maiden voyage. On arrival at Dover Harbor, my disappointment was complete, because instead of the gleaming example I had seen at the boat show, there was a dirty, scruffy, totally filthy vessel. They had moored it by a coal dock and the dust was inside and out. The sails were just stowed on deck, not bagged and covered. We went on board and started to clean up. I had the necessary charts for the passage of 350 miles (direct) and a young mariner named Ken who was to navigate. He became famous later as the navigator who put the Royal Navy's *Ark Royal* aircraft carrier on the rocks in Plymouth Harbor, for which he was court martialed, and dismissed from the service.

We got started towards dark on the first day of arrival and there was a fresh breeze coming out of the west, the direction we wished to go. Being purists of sail, we sailed away from the dock and into the crowded harbor with several ferries per hour from France to avoid. We shot out of the harbor into a very choppy sea and a fresh wind. We pointed the bow into the wind as high as she would sail, with a reefed main and full foresail. The compass showed us going almost due south towards France. The night passed slowly and coldly, as we completed the 21 miles to France before putting about and leading on the other tack, this time towards England. These are dangerous waters, with lots of tide running, and shipping as dense as any place in the world, so a lookout was kept day and night. On the second tack back to England, it didn't look good, as our estimated arrival destination was Dover Harbor, which of course was our original departure point. Sure enough, after covering the same 21 miles, by mid morning, there was Dover Harbor and we reached land roughly 100 yards upwind of the entrance!

We decided that perhaps a little engine power might be needed to make it up to windward and against the tide, which seemed always to be against us. The engine, a single cylinder Norwegian diesel, was started by revolving a very heavy flywheel using a metal cranking rod. When one had the wheel going at sufficient speed, it was necessary to move a compression lever so that the engine might start. There was one thing wrong with this design, the starting handle was too short and the companion way stairs stopped it turning. We had no tools, just a knife that I carried. With the aid of this we were able to cut off the bottom steps. Sure enough, the diesel started and we could make a much better heading upwind.

On this tack we made the eastern entrance to Cherbourg Harbor and were soon resting alongside one of the many quays. It was decided to spend the night in Cherbourg, get a meal, buy some groceries, and perhaps get a night's sleep. We phoned home to notify them of our lack of progress and a new estimated time of arrival in Penzance. The response was not good, as we were supposed to be home the next day. It looked as if it would be three or four days, and "What are you doing in France anyway?" was the question asked. We couldn't find an answer to that.

The following morning, we put to sea at 6 am, leaving by the western entrance of the harbor. With the tide following in the correct direction for the next 6 hours, we made really good time under sail alone, as the wind had moderated considerably. Before first light on day three, we spotted the lights of Plymouth, a scant 85 miles away from Penzance. Encouraged by this, we decided not to enter Plymouth, but to make a tack south again, thereby missing the Lizard, a very large headland that creates a significant tidal race. This tack paid off and we made a good distance westwards against a persistent headwind. One more giant tack and we were in Mounts Bay and entering Penzance Harbor, feeling quite pleased with ourselves.

At 27 feet, *Pipers Moon* made quite a splash in the harbor of mostly small boats, particularly with the man on the next mooring, Albert Willoughby. He was an irascible character in his seventies who had served on tall ships as a sail hand. His work was as a sail maker and ships chandler, and there was nothing he didn't know about sailing or boats. I knew him from visiting his ship for all sorts of reasons. All customers were greeted in the same gruff manner, "What do you want?" He became a very dear friend, and I always visited him on my return to Penzance after we had moved away. He made many sails for us, including most of the sails for our main trip to the U.S.A. He even forgave me when I attempted, and failed, to sail on to my mooring. I collected his boat on the way, pulling up his mooring chain.

We used *Pipers Moon* that summer for short sailing trips mostly in Mounts Bay. Towards the end of the summer, we sailed to the Isles of Scilly, which are about 35 miles from Penzance off Lands End. This was the first of many trips in this boat, with no assistance with the navigation.

Sailing on **Pipers Moon**

The following summer we made the first of several trips across the channel to France. As we gained confidence in our abilities to sail and navigate, we went further afield. We had some tense moments off the coast of France. On one occasion, we had made a faster passage than expected, bringing up the coast and the entrance to L'Abervrach Harbor before daylight. Good sense told us to stand off and wait for the light of day but we decided to go into the harbor. When we reached the point where rocks were sticking out of the water in every direction, we turned and headed down the coast towards another port. Our companions on these early sailing trips were David and Jill Eddy. They became the very closest friends we had and continued to sail with us for many years.

On another of these early trips in *Pipers Moon*, it was decided by the committee of four that we would head to the Channel Islands. These are a number of islands off the coast of France, the most well-known being Jersey and Guernsey. They, of course, at one time belonged to France, and French is spoken as well as English on all of the islands. The tides here are as high as any in the world; 40 feet is normal, so navigation and timing is of the essence. You can, and we did find, ourselves sailing really quickly with the boat going backwards along the coast. We visited Alderney, Guernsey and, lastly, Sark. This island is unique in that it is still run on the lines of a feudal demesne, with its own rule and government. There are probably no more than 600 people living on the island. The navigational hazards of arriving in Sark Harbor are considerable, if not timed correctly: number one, there is no water in the Harbor much of the time; number two, if you don't spot the entrance, you will be swept past as it is impossible to go back even under power. We made it and had several wonderful days of walking and sightseeing. On leaving the harbor for the trip back to England, Alex and Jill had prepared a stew in our pressure cooker. As we came out of the harbor, it was so rough, that the pressure weight on the cooker fell off. It was impossible to go below to turn it off, as the stew was being extruded through the pressure hole in the top of the pan. It went everywhere and there was no dinner for the night passage home, but lots of clean-up!

17 EXPANSION

We were still living on Kings Road in the early 1960s and we had divided one bedroom into two for Gaere and Lorna, the third bedroom was for our au pair. I was still diving and the shop in St. Ives, now called White's Bookshop, was doing well and was well managed by Peter Noall. White's in Penzance was also successful, but I thought I would use some of the vacant land behind for an expansion of floor space. After consultation with an architect, we decided to build on about 2,000 square feet. This allowed us to increase the space for greeting cards and to introduce several new lines.

This proved so successful that the following year we built further extensions of another 2,000 square feet. Then Alex's father, who did the renovations, reminded me that each time we made one of these extensions, we had to remove the back wall which, of course, was wasteful. I went to my banker and asked to borrow the money necessary to purchase the stables belonging to the hotel behind. The hotel was owned by an old gentleman named George Redfearn. He was an accountant of the old school, in fact, the principal of the firm of accountants I used. After much bluster, he agreed to sell and we arrived at a price.

The next step was to figure out if we could incorporate any of the hotel buildings into an expansion. We found that the building to the rear of the shop was worthless, but the two-story one to the side was sound. This would be a very large expansion indeed. Plans were drawn to build back another 3,000 square feet to the back and to remove the wall into the old stable at the side. There was only one problem. The adjoining property on the other side had a large wall that towered over the proposed extension. The question was: Could we undermine the wall sufficiently to dig footings, etc? The answer was made clear shortly after starting when the entire wall fell onto our lot, into a huge concrete pour, which we had just completed. We took a week with jackhammers to remove it and start over. In due course, the construction was completed and we had 8,500 square feet. All of this was on the ground floor, with a new stockroom on the second floor, in the stable which we had saved.

Obviously, this large expansion required many new lines to fill the space. We made an area for pens, typewriters, hard- and soft-covered books, many different household items, and we began supplying commercial stationary. The following year, we opened a record department, beginning with Peter Sarstedt. He was #1 on the charts at the time, with the record, "Where Do You Go To My Lovely." The opening was a huge success and the business instantly thrived. At this time, Alex joined me full-time at work. Previously she had helped whenever she could.

With our move into hardcover books, and our wholesale book business, we started to attract libraries to buy their books from us. This was soon followed by the local schools, which would buy hundreds of copies of the same book. This led to a huge expansion of our gross income and of course profit. In 1963, at the time of the second expansion, I decided to give up diving, which was a decision I didn't regret.

The business, now known as Whites of Alverton, continued to improve with a new modern shopfront built in 1965. In the late '60s, Alex and I talked of building a penthouse flat on top of the existing store, but we had no idea how this could be accomplished. After consultations with an architect and an engineer, a plan for a 2000-square-foot flat was drawn. As the roof of the store was flat, we decided to build over it, and not on it. Steel joists were hauled in by crane and placed on prepared steed stanchions. This operation closed the street while the 70-foot steel joists were swung off a truck and into place. Alex's father then built the house on top of these foundations. Alex and I were totally involved in the construction and design of this beautiful apartment. Many trips to London were taken to various design centers. On completion, it was a showpiece and we moved from Kings Road to the center of town.

All of this had occurred in ten years of marriage. We did not realize at the time that we only had about ten more years remaining in Whites of Alverton. Alex and I worked really well together. She could go through a door next to the office into our home whenever she liked. As Lorna was growing up, when she came home from school, she liked to collect Alex on the way up to the flat.

This chapter is about expansion. We were now ready to make the final move, to make even more expansion possible. We found a really beautiful conversion of a barn on a hill overlooking Mount's Bay and Penzance. It was only partially complete, as the developer had gone out of business. We bought it, and when we had the time, we renovated it sufficiently to move in.

This took only a few months. Meanwhile, we made plans to further extend Whites of Alverton into the space we were vacating. The entire back of the flat became a record and music department, with the office

Gaere and Lorna

Alex on the cliffs

behind. A new staircase was built to get from the ground floor to the record store. The space made by moving music upstairs was taken by a new line of artists materials, which was managed by Peter Noall, with Alex in command. During this period of expansion, we closed and sold the lease of the St. Ives bookshop, bringing Peter in as an assistant manager. He was still responsible to me, and to a salaried partner, John Phillpots, who had joined the organization a couple of years prior. The four of us got on famously, and our best times together were at a coffee break in the mornings and at a tea break in the afternoon, when we discussed everything.

There was only one setback to the expansion. Bernie Durrant called in his note for £10,000. It was very inconvenient timing, and we had to scurry around to find the money, but with help from my mother, Lorna, we paid it off. Not thinking at the time, and wrongly assuming that Bernie would destroy his copy (remember the note was under the table to avoid the tax man), we then thought that debt settled.

We now owned a store that was the largest in the west of England for most of the retail lines we carried. We had great management and the opportunity to travel was open to us. We took that opportunity as often as possible.

Gaere and Lorna rowing

18 TRAVEL, 1961–1979

I really don't know how we did all we did, and still had time to travel, but these years were full of exciting trips. Some were on the boat of the moment, and some wherever we felt like going. I have already described my solitary trip to South Africa with the Round Table. This club was the reason for some more trips in this period. I won't mention visits to other Tables in England as they were commonplace, but always fun. The trips to other countries were much better. I believe the first one was to Chartres in France. This was to celebrate the formation of a new club. It was held in the ballroom of the city hall and featured a mayor who had not been told what to wear. All the guests were in dinner jackets, the ladies in ball gowns, and there was the mayor of Chartres in a woolen sweater making speeches. Both Alex and I were not feeling well, but we managed to eat the 26-course meal. This was presented French style, so each vegetable or item was served as a course and it took a very long time. The couple of days spent in Chartres, for the men, were spent in meetings, at which, one Englishman in particular kept falling off his chair. He was either drunk or bored. The ladies, Alex being one of them, had an exhaustive tour of Chartres Cathedral. This medieval masterpiece is as cold as a morgue in the summertime and this was winter! The entire tour was in French and lasted some hours. This resulted in Alex being so cold, we had to give her a brandy or two to revive her. We went on this trip with Derek Charldwood and Gerald Waldron, who were both fairly new friends at the time. Derek was the driver, and up until that point, we had no idea how frightened one could be in a car.

Our next Round Table trip was to Denmark, where we were to go to Aalborg for a World R.T. Conference. As the word conference implies, there were quite a few meetings. The main agenda was to have a good time, and this we did despite the miserly currency restrictions in place in England at the time. The government would only allow a total of £75 to be taken out of the U.K. between the two of us. This wasn't even enough for the gas. We drove to Harwich, took a ferry to Esberg in Denmark, and then went on to Aalborg. We were accompanied by Gerald, and were traveling in our E-Type Jaguar, which we had recently bought. The E-Type certainly turned heads everywhere we went, but looks can be deceiving. We really could not afford to eat, so we picnicked whenever possible. At the closing dinner, our friends Hans and Shmouni, who I had met in South Africa, asked us to stay with them in Aarhus. We were all certain that they had said, "Come and stay with us in our house," so we accepted and turned up at the suggested time. After a very long dinner and some more time had passed, Hans said, "Where are you staying tonight?" Alex looked at me and said, "Where are we staying Tris?" I responded with the truth, "I thought we were staying here." At this Hans and Shmouni got up and went upstairs, presumably to see if that was possible. On their return, Hans said, "You are not able to stay here, but I have a room for you in town." We were escorted to the hotel, by an apologetic Hans. It was then 3 am, and we were taken up in the elevator by a bad tempered night porter. When all three of us got into the room, we could suppress our laughter no longer. The only problem we foresaw was paying for the room. The following morning, we found, to our relief, Hans had paid for the room. We pooled all our money, put some aside to get from the English ferry terminal to a bank and saved enough to buy a gin and tonic each on the ship. The rest we spent on a huge flower arrangement with an apology to Hans and Shmouni. Unfortunately, our friendship did not survive this occasion.

In the fall of 1963, there was a major earthquake in Skopje, then Yugoslavia. Round Table Penzance decided in tandem with other tables in the area to send help in the form of trailers, blankets, food and other useful articles. The trailers were to be left there as accommodation for the many thousands of homeless. A campground in the area donated a trailer. A farmer loaned a Land Rover to tow it and all the articles were donations.

We set out with a convoy of 21 trailers for the nearly 2000 mile trip to Skopje, with all trailers completely loaded. The cross channel ferry tickets had been donated by the ferry company. Unfortunately, the Land Rover did not perform well, as we hadn't made it to the boat before the clutch burned out. We pulled into a dealer, and a new clutch was fitted free just in time for us to catch the ferry. The long drive was taken in two-hour watches, day and night, so we made quite good time; however, traveling in a convoy takes patience.

Arriving in Skopje, none of us had ever seen the results of an earthquake before—neither the devastation nor the plight of the people. I have photographs of some hollow-eyed and frightened survivors, who were very grateful for the help they were receiving. The magnitude of the damage was evident everywhere, with hardly a building left standing. One wall of the Railway Station remained and on it was a clock reading ten past four, the time of the quake a few nights before. We didn't stay long in Skopje. It was too depressing.

There were six of us from Penzance in the Land Rover. On the way back, we stayed in Belgrade for two nights and toured the city. It was very dark and dreary with an overwhelming feeling of grey people, looking worn down. In 1963, the communist regime of General Tito was still in power, the people were very poor, and there was nothing in the shops for people to buy, even if they had money. We left Yugoslavia, pleased to leave such a repressive regime, but not knowing of the bloodbath that would follow its collapse.

In the time between these two trips, Alex and I went to Switzerland, Italy and returned through Germany to see Heidi and her parents, as previously described. We did a similar trip to Sweden to see Marianne and Ulla and their parents. Both were more than hospitable and we saw a lot of Sweden. We drove in all cases, putting our car on a ferry.

The next Round Table trip was for the formation of Round Table Malta. Andy and Ann Ramsay were the sponsors and originators of this extension, as it is called. We had been friends with them since we were married. In fact, we were friends of theirs when they were married. They invited us to come on their honeymoon with them, so after their wedding, we met them at the airport and flew to the Canary Islands. It took Ann's father a long time to figure out how I had taken pictures of their wedding and then continued into the honeymoon. We had an outstanding time and played some great tricks, at the hotel's expense, on the other guests.

We had the good luck to meet Harry Worth, who was a top comedian at the time, in a bar in Palma. We invited him to join us for drinks in our hotel. He turned up with his wife and it did a lot for our image at the hotel, as autographs were requested. He spent the remaining evenings of our vacation with us, saying, "You are all much more fun than the lot in my hotel."

Back to Malta. It is a rocky group of islands in the southern Mediterranean. The town and harbor of Valetta, a walled city from the days of the Knights of St. John, is truly magnificent. Above the town, and set in its own grounds, was the Hotel Grand Vidalla. It was luxury in the extreme and the center of activities over the next few days. We had friends on the island and decided to have a visit with them. They lived in an old farm house in the countryside. We were to return to Malta a few years later with Andy and Ann, who by this time had bought a house on the coast for summer use. We stayed in Valetta this time, and toured the island, which is steeped in history, both ancient and modern.

Our trips to London were frequent and we were always able to stay at first with Derek Charldwood and then Gerald Waldron. They both lived in apartments close to London. We would take the underground into town most days, then go to the galleries, museums and shops. From the latter, we would often stagger back with so many bags and parcels, we could hardly walk. We had a lot of fun and it was relatively inexpensive.

We also visited London, Manchester and other cities to show our Salukis. We went to Cruft's Dog Show in London several times, and although we never won Best in Show or Best in Breed, we always came home with ribbons for 2nd or 3rd place.

Lastly, we made frequent trips to Bristol where we stayed with Ken and Bobby Budd. I had met Ken on a Parker Pen sales course in London, and made friends with him. Then a few months later, I met him again in Dover on a Parker Pen repair course, which cemented the friendship. Ken was unmarried at the time, but was shortly to marry Bobby, so I invited him to spend a few days of their honeymoon with us. This was accepted and they are still two of our best friends. Basically being in the same business and of the same age and interests resulted in some wonderful visits both ways. One of our favorite pastimes was to visit fine restaurants in the area. The all time favorite was the Bell House in Sutton Benger, a country village with a population not exceeding 25 people. So, obviously, they didn't rely on the locals for their business. People came from all of the surrounding countryside, Dukes and their Duchesses, Lords and their Ladies, Counts and their Countesses, and we four. The owner was Jack Stratton, with his wife and Barnaby the dog. Behind the bar, Jack kept a copy of Debretts Peerage and another volume that dealt with lesser folk. Needless to say, we were in neither. This created an early interest from Jack as to who we were. On each visit, he would do a little more fishing, suggesting that we might be doctors or veterinarians. He was sure we were important people in our communities; otherwise we couldn't pay the exorbitant prices asked on his menu. On one occasion, we ordered strawberries in February. They cost over £1 each! We continued to frequent the Bell House for some years but Jack never did find out that we were just shopkeepers.

Since the halcyon days of our youth, we never return to England without visiting Ken and Bobby. On three occasions in the 1980s, we rented bare boats in the Mediterranean with them, and once in the Virgin Islands, and had lots of adventures.

19 SAILING

Meanwhile, our travels on our sailboat, *Pipers Moon,* continued until 1970. After many trips across the channel to France and also the Isles of Scilly, we decided to buy a bigger and more capable boat. Our last trip to the Scilly Islands was in company with Gaere and Lorna, a family boating trip with many good memories.

Our travels and trips on *Pipers Moon* can never be complete, without mentioning a chance meeting with a man, who became a friend and mentor to Alex and me. His name is Leo Kramp, by birth a Belgian, but he had lived in France for most of his life. I was sailing alone one early morning before work, and I saw a boat of about the same size making for Penzance Harbor. Often, when any two boats are going in the same direction, a competition ensues. There was a very light wind, but *Pipers Moon* was the first boat at the harbor entrance. Leo called over a friendly recognition of my victory and went on into the harbor. When I finished work for that day, Alex, Gaere, Lorna and I went down to the harbor to say hello. We were greeted with Gallic enthusiasm and went aboard to meet Leo and his crew of two. The next time we saw them was to invite them for dinner and a shower, the latter facility not being a part of *Brabo*'s equipment.

Leo became a family friend, and he loved our two children as his own. After that, he would call into Penzance most years and we would get together. He lived in a small village in the center of France, in a house that was originally built in the 1400s. We became regular visitors to this house when we started to keep our boat in the Mediterranean.

The best story is one of Leo's Atlantic crossings. He came as always into Penzance and stated that he wanted about five or six chickens. The reason for this request was that he would like to have fresh eggs in the mornings on his trip. He had constructed on the foredeck of *Brabo*, a chicken coop that would hold up to six chickens. We knew several farmers who had chickens and asked them to make sure they were laying eggs. Within a day or two, the chickens were delivered and installed in their coop. We waved goodbye to Leo and heard no more from him until a call some 12 months later, saying he was in Penzance Harbor, and could we come to pick up the chickens. He had crossed to the Caribbean, up to the U.S.A., and then left from Charleston, South Carolina, to

Penzance. During his entire trip, he had not enjoyed one egg from the chickens. He didn't like the idea of eating the chickens themselves either. John White, the farmer, picked them up; they started to lay eggs immediately. I guess chickens don't like small boats on big oceans!

Before we move on to our next boat, our last and perhaps our most ambitious trip was to the north coast of France. We were sailing to Roscoff, a fairly good sized port, which is famous for its onions and its artichokes. It now has a ferry service to it and is a very busy port. The purpose of this voyage was twofold, we were having our usual early summer cruise with David and Jill Eddy, and secondly we were to go to a Round Table Formation in central France. Destination Blois, we set out for L'Abervrach aboard *Piper's Moon* at 6 pm, and were off the coast of France in record time at 2 am. We changed course to almost due east and sailed quickly along the coast to pick up the approach buoy to Morlaix by 8 am. We found a spot with 17 feet of water and dropped anchor to wait for the tide and to get some sleep. We went on to Morlaix at 4 pm, and got through the lock gates by 6 pm.

The river leading into Morlaix is particularly beautiful. After two days of sightseeing, we sailed to Roscoff in very rough seas. A French Navy ship waited for us to negotiate the entrance, which was made rougher by a vicious outgoing tide. Ten minutes after tying up to the north wall of the harbor, we went aground. We intended to leave the boat there and, after hiring a car, we went off to Blois. On arrival, we were greeted by very enthusiastic French Round Tablers, who allocated us to various member homes for the three nights we were to stay. There was so much to see, with the Chateau de Blois being the center point of the city. The Biltmore mansion in Asheville, North Carolina, is a scaled down version of this chateau.

To me, the high point of this trip was the picnic arranged on the grounds of the de Maintenon chateau. This most beautiful, small, chateau was given by Louis XIV to his wife, the Madame de Maintenon. It is still owned by her family. The picnic on what was a bright, sunny day had an almost dreamlike quality to it. The only sounds we heard were of people having a wonderful time and the buzzing of bees in the wildflowers we were sitting on. I remember very little about the celebrations, only having been surrounded by beautiful women, Alex and Jill being two of them.

Our return to Roscoff by car was straight forward, apart from driving up a one way street in the wrong direction during rush hour in Guinguamps. Unfortunately, we were followed by a number of French cars, creating the largest traffic jam the town had ever seen. We were severely reprimanded in French by an irate policeman. This had no effect on us because we didn't have any idea as to what he was saying. On our arrival in Roscoff, we ordered from the duty-free stores. The log tells me that we took aboard six bottles of whiskey, five of Dubonnet, one Cinzano, two of Cognac, one Crème de Menthe and a case of liter bottles of Vin Ordinaire. This was 1969 and the bill came to £16.18 ($25.00). You can see why we were headed towards alcoholism! The trip back from Roscoff to Morlaix was uneventful. We wanted to be in Morlaix by June 6, the 25th anniversary of D-Day. There were to be parades and celebrations.

On the eve of the D-Day celebrations, a British Minesweeper moored up behind us, which we thought nothing about at the time. We all went into town and had a great meal and plenty of wine and went to bed. We were all sleeping soundly, when we were awoken by loud knocking on the hatchway. Looking out I saw two very properly dressed Royal Navy officers who said, "We see you are a British yacht and the Captain wishes to invite you aboard for a drink." I took a look at my watch and saw that it was 11 pm. Having paid income tax for some years, I quickly started thinking we were going to get something in return for those taxes. We all donned track suits, or similar attire, and made our way up the gangway of H.M.S. Monkton. We were welcomed aboard by the Captain, and the steward offered us the first of many drinks. The assembled guests were people from Morlaix, who were active in the resistance and several British wartime agents, whose job it had been to navigate from the English coast to Morlaix at night. Having accomplished this in the daylight twice, we realized these were special people.

At 4:30 am, hardly able to stand, I announced to the crew that it was time to go. David begrudgingly agreed and we managed to walk the 50 feet or so back to our bunks. June 6 was spent recuperating from this overindulgence. Alex and Jill had hair appointments and kept them. David and I went to the parade, listened to lots of band music, which sounded too loud to our aching heads, so we went back to the boat. The next morning we sailed away before we were invited back to the H.M.S. Monkton for another session. This time we set course for Falmouth Roads and picked up our mooring buoy at dusk of the following day. What a trip to Blois! What a voyage to Morlaix!

The new boat we chose was a Warrior Class sloop and was pre-owned. The boat was called *Valore* by the previous owner, but we decided to call it *Intsholo*. Intsholo means sweet music in XHOSA (pronounced "Caw-sa"). It refers to the wondrous sound of a yacht carving

Intsholo

through water on a pleasant day. This boat was in every way the worst boat we ever owned. It was wet in the sea; its plumbing, a new experience for us, came to pieces in a frost. I labored for hours replacing it. The electrics were a disaster also. Several trips to boatyards were required to repair all of the items. Our first trip in *Intsholo* was down the west coast of France, through Ushant and to Douarnenez, Audiere, Belle Isle, Isle de Ré, Isle de Oleron, and eventually up into a canal leading to Marrennes.

This trip was the first of many long voyages with the children. They particularly enjoyed the Isle de Ré with the whole harbor and town being walled. It was the island where French prisoners being transported to French Guiana (Devil's Island) were held until a convoy could be made. The little town with the harbor has a moat around it with only one bridge in and out and was like a fairy tale. In the evenings, the sounds of music would drift over the harbor as musicians played on balconies. There was also a beautiful church in the center of town and while walking by one evening and hearing music, we were drawn inside. There was a chamber music group playing in the nave of the church. The sound, echoing around in the near-dark building, was enchanting.

We spent some time on Isle de Ré, and one of the high spots, was the Bouglione Circus coming to town. We had John and Pam, Alex's sister and her husband, with us and John generously offered to take all of us. It was a small circus, but they thought they were big, and every performer had several roles to play. We had a wonderful time, I'm sure Gaere and Lorna still remember the cry, "Which is the greatest circus in the world?" The answer as loud as the small crowd could make, "Bouglione."

We all left the Isle de Ré sadly with a very difficult task ahead. The channel into Marrennes was narrow and shallow. Luckily, the entire mussel fleet was coming in from all the mud flats at the time of our arrival, so we hooked onto the end of the parade for the entire distance to the canal leading to Marrennes. It was a straight shot from there and we locked into a basin of perfect tranquility, apart from the very earnest fishermen lining the banks. Upon inquiry, they informed us they were fishing for sardines. Gaere was immediately on the bank with his rod to find this wasn't normal fishing with bait. You needed a four-hooked grapnel and when you thought you were in a school of sardines, you jerked your rod and snagged one. The French men and women were very good at this and they gave Gaere one of their special hooks. He was off. He spent several days trying and finally he caught one, to the applause of the whole basin. We did have a sardine dinner eventually, as Gaere became more proficient. He was 10 in 1970.

The trip home was uneventful apart from a couple of breakdowns, which was an inherent problem with this boat. Each problem was fixed underway. We had a new harbor for *Intsholo* and after much bartering, we obtained a mooring in Mylor, where there was permanent deep water. This yacht had a single keel and would not easily go aground on each tide. The only drawback was that the Mylor mooring was a good hour's drive from Penzance.

As we were becoming more proficient at navigation, our thoughts were roaming further afield. The idea of keeping the boat in the South of France appealed to Alex, with the prospect of warmer sailing than previously experienced. Plans were made, charts were bought, and a crew was assembled for the 2500 mile journey across the Bay of Biscay down the Portuguese coast and into the Mediterranean at Gibraltar. It was still another 800 miles from there to St Mandrier in the Rade de Toulon where we planned to keep *Intsholo*.

The crew consisted of Roy, Barrie, Phillipe, Mac, and myself. I was to be totally responsible for navigation and the running of the boat; i.e. decisions and sail changing. We set the date for departure for 10 am, May 8, 1972. The weather was beyond bad on that day, so we watched the weather in frustration, until the 13th, when I decided we would leave at dawn. We left at 4:30 am, a little early, with very rough seas, which made it too rough to boil water or cook all day and night. The following morning saw winds of Force 7, with a very long swell. Some of the crew were gradually recovering from "mal de mer." We were still sailing very fast as we brought up the first light on the northwest coast of Spain. As we drew closer to Cap Finisterre, large mountains could be seen to the port and mountainous seas to starboard. I decided not to go into Vigo, the first port on the west coast of Spain, as the wind was favorable. By the 18th of May, we could see the entrance to the Tagus River and Lisbon a little way up river. We made for one of the many docks cut out of the riverbank and tied up alongside a particularly unpleasant Englishman. We were going to enjoy Lisbon despite his mean attitude.

An excellent tram service ran all along the river and into the center of the city. We all hopped on and enjoyed the ride. With the afternoon to

Going south

shop and find the best restaurant, we came across the Cervejariad and took full advantage of their food and wine. In fact, we had five 6-pound crawfish between us, and so many bottles of Portuguese wine we lost count. We were in bed by 2:15 am, which made for a late start on the 20th heading for Portimao on the south coast of Portugal. With great difficulty we found the entrance to a small river leading to the town and harbor, which was very basic. We anchored there and were taken ashore by a local entrepreneur with a boat called *Rent*. We dined and drank until *Rent* wanted to go to bed, then we continued aboard until 3 am. Needless to say, another late start ensued. After refueling and getting more water, we sailed to Cadiz the following morning, tied up at the Club Nautico, and had a great dinner ashore. It only cost us £2 a head and we drank copious amounts of wine. I managed to get everyone to bed by 10 pm, ready for an early start at 6 am for Tangier.

As a levanter was blowing hard the following day, we were pleased to find a harbor halfway up the straits of Gibraltar. We were lying alongside a fishing boat with a massive catch of 20 tuna fish weighing in at over

1000 pounds each, plus a number of swordfish. They gave us a 10-pound lump of tuna, which made several delicious dinners.

The next morning, we set sail at 7 am for Gibraltar. With a very strong wind and tide against us, it took seven hours to complete the few miles to the harbor.

We entered the Mediterranean the next day, and after a brief stop in Marbella, we headed past Malaga to Cartagena and then Almeria. We

Delivery to the Mediterranean

stopped overnight there to visit the incredible Moorish castle above the town. The next day we set sail for the Balearic Isles stopping at Ibiza and Majorca, where, in both places, we found beautiful clear water anchorages. We dropped two of our crew in

Majorca, as sadly they had to return to work. We became three, and the watch system became a bit more strenuous. The weather remained idyllic for a couple of days until we reached the Gulf of Lyon when all hell hit

us, experiencing our first mistral wind. With watches of one and a half hours on, three off, we were pleased to go below at watches' end. We sailed hard like this until we reached Toulon and our new home the port of St Mandrier. Leo had arranged a membership for us in the

Raising the French flag

Touring Club de France, whose facility it was. The harbor was all we could hope for and after a couple of days, we flew home from Marseille.

Intsholo now waited for us to rejoin her for a new adventure in the middle sea.

That summer we drove down to St Mandrier in mid-June and picked up *Intsholo* in perfect condition, due to the *guardianage* of M. Mancha. He was to look after our boats for some years in the future.

We had Gaere and Lorna with us, and we were to sail along the French coast to the Italian border. All of this was new territory for us and we were to travel the fabled French Riviera.

After leaving St Mandrier, we had beautiful anchorages in the Porquerrolle Islands, not one of which had a marina at the time. You could drop anchor in a bay of clear water, swim, snorkel or just lounge about. As we progressed eastward along the coast, things were more organized and the marina charged a lot of money for the privilege of docking against the quay, in such fabled places as San Tropez, San Raphael, Juan le Pins, Nice, Cannes, or even Monte Carlo, where we were charged only 10 Francs for ten days with water and electricity included. These were the days before the crowds came.

We could sit on the after-deck of our boat and watch the glitterati and the "beautiful people" pass at the end of our gangplank. I am not sure how Gaere and Lorna enjoyed this, the first of many holidays spent on these most civilized cruising grounds. Before we made the decision to move to the other areas, they no longer wanted to join us for the summer. They wanted to spend the time at home with their friends. There was always a bed and a home waiting with Elly.

Monte Carlo

20 ACCOMMODATION

At some time while I was serving in the army, I was posted on Battalion Orders to appear in front of the commanding officer. No reason is ever given, but you had better be there and be prepared for anything. When I was marched, I could see a letter in front of Colonel Jackson. He looked up and started a tirade of abuse about my being an ungrateful son and with my education I should know better than not to have written to my mother for several years. I really didn't know what he was talking about, as I saw my mother regularly whenever I went back to Penzance. At these interviews you are not allowed to speak, or reply unless a question is asked. He then thrust the letter across his desk and said, "I want a reply to this letter on my desk by tomorrow morning."

I was marched out clutching the letter. On reading it I found that Marjorie, my stepmother, had found out through the War Office, that I was enlisted in the 1st Battalion of the Parachute Regiment. She then wrote to the CO and told him that she hadn't heard from me for three years. I was then forced to reply to this letter and suffer the censorship of my superior. This was the first unwilling contact that I made with my, as far as I was concerned, EX-parents. In due course, I received a gushing letter in return, as if nothing whatsoever had transpired a few years before. This correspondence continued in a desultory way for a year or so, until I received a letter saying that Keith and Marjorie were planning a visit to England and would like to see me. Throughout this exchange of letters, there never was any direct communication from Keith, my father.

The date was set and flight times were given to me. Alex's father agreed to let her go with me to London to meet them. We drove up in the Austin Healey, and foolishly decided to sleep in the car, because the flight was early in the morning. Sleeping in a sports car is not recommended, for any reason. We met them and then drove on to Oxford, where they planned to stay at the Mitre Hotel. We all arrived by lunch time and went to the hotel restaurant for lunch. When the first course was served, the waiter tipped an entire bowl of tomato soup down Alex's back. This helped considerably to loosen things up between us all. I think they felt very sorry for Alex's plight. After a couple of days in Oxford, we returned to Penzance and a loose truce was declared.

Keith and Marjorie made two or three other trips to England in the 1960s, and at least on two of those came down to Cornwall to see us. The first time, they stayed in the Queens Hotel on the seafront in Penzance. This hotel was not to Marjorie's liking, so on the following expedition, they rented a house a couple of blocks from Whites of Alverton. I later found out that this was an exploratory trip to see if they would like to retire in Cornwall. They didn't like it very much. The cottage they had rented was large and ancient, and it was cold and draughty. They returned to Connecticut.

In 1968, we made our first trip to North America, and finally stayed with my sister Wendy and husband in Toronto. We then drove down to Connecticut to visit with Keith and Marjorie. They had moved from Toronto for work reasons a few years earlier. Gaere and Lorna came with us and to help us with the children, we brought Sally Farrer, who was a young senior student at the school Lorna attended. It was Sally's first trip to the U.S., and she was very enthusiastic, as were we.

We stayed with my half-sister Susan and her husband David at their large and beautiful Victorian house in Westport. The entire subdivision of huge houses was built on the farmland of the house. The accommodations were superb, but the eating arrangements were very sketchy. We were lucky to get a meal, as these would be taken randomly by different people at different times, often only consisting of a sandwich. It is no wonder David ate most of his meals down at the local hamburger joint. During one of the few evening meals served at home, David's beeper went off and he was required to don fireman gear and race off to a fire somewhere in the community.

We really didn't get to see much on this trip as we always seemed to be waiting for something to happen. It seldom did. Gaere and Lorna had a great time in the swimming pool and with the neighborhood kids. It was arranged that we would visit again, without the children, and go on a car trip with Keith and Marjorie.

We returned to visit a couple of times and each trip was set out like a military operation, with each function planned down to the minute detail. There was seldom anything random or fun. The first trip was to Washington, D.C., and the battlefields of the Civil War, which was exhaustive but must have been quite a trial for Alex, who didn't necessarily share our enthusiasm for history. We did a fall leaf tour in New England and a trip to upstate New York, which was made humorous by Marjorie's indecision as to what motel we would stay at each night. She had always been very "sniffy" about the suitability of any establishment that might be required to render hospitality to her. On this occasion as lunchtime passed into tea time, with no suitable place being found, we finally stopped at your average country restaurant. Marjorie made no bones about informing the hardworking owners that she didn't know how anybody could live like this. Despite her alienating tone, we were still served a delicious meal. Whenever she traveled in America, she feigned this very "plum" Oxford English accent; however, if we were to meet English people, she would become an American immediately.

Despite all these shortcomings, I'm sure on both sides, we managed to stay civil and have a good time. At no time in this period was there any mention of what led to the separation in the first place. The most I ever heard were a few oblique references to my failed career as a lawyer, because I chose another path!

21 SAILING II

By the end of the summer of 1972, we had all we could take of *Intsholo*. After numerous breakdowns, all of which were handled with ease, I had become a qualified diesel mechanic. In the winter of 1972, I decided to travel to Peterborough, the home of Perkins Diesel. The company offered two-week courses on each engine they built for marine use, and at the end of the course, we could completely disassemble and reassemble your engine of choice. Mine was the 4-cylinder 4-236. Its application in this boat was not brilliant and resulted in every problem that a diesel engine shouldn't have.

The *Intsholo*'s troubles were not only related to the engine; the ports leaked, and so on. We decided to sell her and find a replacement boat. This was achieved at the London Boat show in January of 1973. We traveled up to London with David and Jill Eddy, with whom we sailed regularly. Once before, my eye had been caught by the boats of Michel Dufour, as he was a very practiced marine architect and was a fast rising star in building sailboats. His boat works were on the west coast of France in La Rochelle. We had sailed into this port several times before; if we were to buy one of his boats, we would do so again.

The deal was made for a 41-foot ketch-rigged yacht of the Sortilege class, which drew about 6 feet 3 inches, and could be completed in the early summer of 1973. This was a center cockpit boat. It had a large cabin astern with rather difficult access through a passageway so low that you had to crouch to make it through. The engine access, another Perkins 4-236 was to the side of this passage. The only alternative entrance to this stateroom was from a secondary small cockpit in the extreme stern and down a couple of steps. The very adequate double bed was on the starboard side. The separate shower and head was to port. Forward and down the companion way, the galley was to the right down a step. To the left was an excellent navigation station with a shelf behind just large enough to accommodate a cardboard wine container. Forward on the starboard side was a great dinette, with a long couch opposite. Ahead of that were two single berths, a toilet and shower leading into sail storage. The whole boat was light and airy, because of the very numerous Goiot hatches. These did not leak, as the previous hatches had.

We called our new acquisition the *Intsholo II* and registered her in Jersey Channel Islands, for tax purposes. She proved to be a very fast and seaworthy vessel and any impromptu race was inevitably won. We took delivery in May/June with David and Jill aboard, and we sailed along the west coast of France, calling at a lot of the ports we had previously visited, and some new ones. After this shakedown cruise and a little work carried out by the builders, we headed for home in the car. It was our intention to come down again with the children and Pam and John for a cruise in the La Rochelle area. This was a huge success; we met lots of new people and made new friends. This western part of France, which once belonged to England, contains so many interesting fortifications that tell the story of a very troubled history. Whole towns and villages are fortified, and there is always a person behind the massive stone walls who can tell you this history.

At the end of our summer cruise, we took the boat back to Mylor and our mooring, with the intention of taking the boat to the Mediterranean the following spring. During the winter months, preparations were made for this, our second voyage, around Spain and Portugal.

Concurrent with all the sailing we were doing in our own boats, an acquaintance named Lou Doble, a chicken farmer and processor, bought a quite famous racing boat, called *Vashti*. She was 39 feet long, named after the Queen of Persia who did not obey her King, as she had a mind of her own then, and in the form of the boat named after her. Lou's boat was as wet as a submarine. In fact, she went through waves, not over them. I was asked to join the crew as a navigator, on the numerous races Lou entered. They were almost always across the channel to France, or occasionally Ireland. There was never a race that I went on, when adequate food was available. You had to scrounge around in the bilge for a forgotten can. These were usually unlabeled, as there was always water in the bilge, and the label had soaked off. No amount of cajoling would convince Lou that food was an important part of winning a race!

After numerous trips and several wins, a race across the channel to Douarnenez was scheduled. As we crossed the starting line outside the Royal Cornwall Yacht Club, the wind, even in this sheltered area, was blowing at over 30 miles per hour. When we hit the open ocean, it was 40+ mph. I looked at Lou and said, "Do we really want to do this?" His reply, "Sure, it will probably go down this evening." It didn't, and as we entered the narrow channel between the Island of Ushant, and the mainland of France, we were underwater more often than not. There were over 30 starters and we hadn't seen one of them. It transpired that we were on our own. We were all permanently wet and cold, and still he insisted on continuing. I made a vow at this point, that if I survived this adventure, I would give up racing and stick to cruising. We did eventually get home, and when I rang our doorbell, Alex came to the door. Her words were, "What happened to you?" I was standing there with not a dry piece of clothing and a kit bag containing more sea water than clothes. I never raced again!

The following spring, with *Intsholo II* now moved to Penzance for final fitting out and storing, and with the same crew as the trip with *Intsholo*, we stood by for several days as a massive gale blew through. We finally left with the wind still blowing hard, at 4:30 am, April 20, 1974. It didn't take long for the violent motion of the boat to have some people looking a bit green. The wind did not go down, but blew harder as we entered the Bay of Biscay. A large ferry boat bound from England to Spain, hove to and protected us from the worst of the breaking seas. We virtually had no sail up at all, but were still doing 6 knots over the ground. After about ten hours of this, the wind started to moderate, and the ferry radioed to say she was leaving. This left us with huge seas and swell, and a boat rolling around with sails and boom banging and flapping, despite the rope preventer we had rigged.

All good and bad things come to an end, and we were grateful to reach the Tagus River and Lisbon, where we stayed and rested for a couple of days. The remaining part of the trip was uneventful, and we made the usual stops when absolutely necessary. I had learned from the last trip, that if you let the crew ashore, it was often not possible to motivate them again until late in the day. So we sailed and motored up the southern coast of Spain and into the Gulf de Lyon in comparatively calm seas. Nothing occurred of note until we were only a few miles short of Toulon (St. Mandrier). We were stopped almost dead by the thickest fog we had ever seen. It was so dense, we had to feel our way through at under half a knot. Fog rarely occurs in the Mediterranean at any time of the year. We eventually rounded the point of the enormous bay that is Toulon Harbor, and then into the ancient harbor of St. Mandrier. We took up our mooring, cleaned up and prepared for the flight home from Marseille.

Only one thing about the flight home is worth mentioning. I had bought the tickets for all of the crew for the return flight to London. When we all checked in, I was not among those of the crew who were upgraded to first class, although I had paid for the tickets. While we were in coach, eating sandwiches, my crew was being served champagne and pheasant in first class. There is no justice! We returned from London by

MacDonald family, 1974?

train, and I looked forward to the summer on board *Intsholo II* and the cruise we had planned for Corsica, Elba and several ports along the Tuscan coast.

The whole family arrived by car on the 24th of July and prepared for the upcoming cruise. The weather was good and no storms were forecast, so we headed east towards Italy, stopping each night for a stay in marinas and harbors. We crossed the border at Menton with the weather remaining superb, but hot. During the day, we frequently stopped the boat and jumped over the side for a cool off in the amazingly clear azure water. It was many hundreds of feet deep here, but it seemed as if you could see the bottom.

We were now dealing with Italian yachtsman, a lot less proficient than their French neighbors. It was always a hassle coming into any harbor, but in Italy it was made worse. Even after you were safely moored, with an anchor dropped from the bow, you had then to motor in stern first to the quay, put your stern lines on to the bollards or rings, and pass the port and starboard lines back to the boat. This enabled you to leave the mooring without having to go ashore. You merely had to take in the anchor on the bow. In most Italian harbors, this didn't work, as invariably some late-comer had dropped his anchor over your chain.

The worst case of this was in Porto Venere, a small harbor with lines and chains mixed up like knitting. I always carried my diving equipment and this time I needed it with a vengeance. After perhaps half an hour we were free to go, leaving a still-tangled mess on the harbor floor.

We were headed for Porto Fino, a very scenic town. The harbor was crowded, and we had to sail in as the engine had stopped a few hundred

Porto Fino

yards out. We dropped our anchor under sail and managed to pass our stern lines to an English boat named *Carmalou*, then winched ourselves into a tiny space, all that was available. The next requirement was water, all of which had to be shipped by tanker, so they had a suitably named official, *Supratendcia de Aquadotti*, dressed in a very special uniform, who dispersed small tokens, that, if you were lucky, you could put into a slot and a small amount of water was delivered. One problem, I only had a million lire bill and he had insufficient change. The impasse was solved by the same Englishman who took our ropes; his name was Philip Wand. He and his wife Betty had tokens to spare, and lent us some. These two were to become very good friends over the next few years.

This harbor, which is the subject of tens of thousands of pictures, both painted and photographed, was truly a Mediterranean gem, provided you came by yacht. The town and the land were so overcrowded with traffic and tour buses, one could hardly move. So we stayed aboard *Intsholo II* and were adopted by Philip and Betty on *Carmalou*. The engine, of course, started right up when I tried again, and this was to become an ongoing problem, until I found a piece of wadding in the fuel tank, which when stirred up blocked the fuel delivery pipe.

From here we planned to go on to Elba and did so in company with *Carmalou*. The same water restrictions applied there and I still had not been able to split my million lire bill. So we were staked again by Philip whose knowledge of boating was restricted to motoring between ports in his 37-foot Princess Motorboat. Betty was an extremely nervous passenger, and was constantly terrified by Philip's promise to sail regardless of weather. He would say to Betty, "I don't like the look of it, Betty," but he would go on regardless of her terror. The next move was onto Corsica, and once more *Carmalou* accompanied us. I don't think Philip had a

In Corsica watching the weather

chart aboard, he navigated using an Exxon road map. As we rounded the northern end of the island, we were both hit by a strong mistral from the northwest. Philip ran due south into St. Florent and we headed for L'Isle Rousse, which we could just make with sails sheeted in. We didn't realize this was to be our home for the next ten days, due to bad weather. We made our escape at night and ran under motor with a big swell into Golfe Juan, arriving at 7 am, just as the wind started again.

From a sailing point of view, the next five years were spent in the Mediterranean, using St. Mandrier as a base at first and then moving to the west a few miles to the Isles Des Embiez. We had met a great Belgian family on their boat *Escapada*, which was about the same length as *Intsholo II*. Renaud and Yola, with their two daughters and a son, of much the same age as Gaere and Lorna, became family friends, and so we moved to Embiez and sailed with them quite often. Later Renaud was to accompany us on our Atlantic crossing. Their son Sven was a very keen

Windsurfing

windsurfer, a sport I had taken up a few years before. We carried two windsurfers tied to the stanchions, on the after deck, and he and I had many competitions going around the island. Alex, Gaere and Lorna all became proficient windsurfers, and would spend hours out cruising whenever we moored.

There are a few events in these sailing years that stand out in particular. Our discovery of the Isles des Frioles off Marseille being particularly memorable. The island had in the past been designated as an area of quarantine for the port of Marseille. During the period of 1650 to the early 1900s, many buildings, including hospitals, barracks and churches, had been built for the people who were waiting for clearance into the

port or for those who would die there. The island was supplied from Marseille, and the enormous anchorage, where the quarantined ships used to lie, were open to yachts, but they seldom came. We would lay at anchor in complete isolation, surrounded by the ruins of these extraordinarily ornate buildings. When we went ashore, there was always somewhere to explore and when we were aboard, swimming, snorkeling, or windsurfing were always options. If we needed stores, the city of Marseille was just 4 miles away. I don't think any place caught all of our imaginations like this harbor.

Just along the coast was a remarkable series of fjord-like bays cut out of the high limestone cliffs of the coastline. The Calanques, as they were known, were exploited for their limestone, which was quarried in the 1800s for use in building locally and abroad. The most important use was for the construction of the docks, quays and buildings of the Suez Canal, so in the course of the 1800s, millions of tons of this stone was quarried, cut, dressed, then loaded onto ships, which could come right

In the Calanques

into the Calanques because of the deep water. The whole scene now is of serenity with pines coming down to the edge of the crystal clear water, and no sign of the industry that had existed a century before, apart from the steel rings in the sides of the cliffs, which the ships previously had used for mooring. Now these rings are perfect for the yachts that use this sanctuary.

No description of these sailing years would be complete without mention of a storm in which we were included, probably in 1977. We had left the Isles des Embiez headed east towards the French Riviera, and put into one of the last bays that had not been marina-ized on the Isle de Porquerolles. This particular bay is perhaps 500 yards long and at its mouth about the same. It gets narrower as you go up and of course shallower, with a sandy beach at the top. As we pulled into the bay, there were many yachts at anchor and the weather was idyllic. We went ashore for a walk on the cliffs overlooking the bay, and noticed that we were anchored perhaps one-third of the way into the bay, with many boats almost on the beach. There was no wind and all the boats were riding to anchors facing the south. I said to Alex, Gaere and Lorna that there was something funny about the light, but thought no more about it. We rowed back to the boat, went aboard, made dinner and went to bed. I have no idea what time things changed, but it was very sudden. As I came on deck and looked around, it was pitch dark and blowing perhaps 40 miles an hour from the north. All the yachts, many rafted up, were all facing south. The entire anchorage changed direction with dis-

Pensive Lorna

astrous results as boats pulled anchors and were swept down on one another, heading for the beach. The wind stayed in the north, blowing at over 60 mph, with an accompanying deluge of rain. By this time, lightning was light-

ing up the whole bay, and there were several strikes a minute. The bay looked like a battle scene.

Immediately I thought of Trafalgar, and the headland and battleground I had visited and studied. The question was, how do we get out of this situation? I thought the best move was to get our anchor up, under power of course. Gaere and I went up to

Catching pinner clams

Alex

the foredeck and with the use of power, windlass and the engine's help the anchor started to come in. The anchor was gotten on deck and stowed, but boats were flying around under bare poles, in every direction. Rain was coming down as though we were under a waterfall. The wind was so strong that boats were sailing at 6 or 7 knots under the windage of their masts and hulls. We managed to avoid most other yachts and thought we had a clear opening to the sea. Wrong! Out of the darkness there appeared a 50-foot sailboat with the owner maniacally shouting, "Nouveau bateau," new boat. We struck him a glancing blow on his

Tristan with a beard

starboard side, ripping off the first five or six of his stanchions and lifelines. Then he disappeared into the dark from whence he came. During all this time, we had a parade of dress and undress, ranging from completely naked to baby doll nighties. The emergency was far from over, as we chose to motor to another harbor about 7 or 8 miles away. Visibility was still almost nil, so I laid off a compass course for the mouth of the harbor and started out. By this time it was obvious that it was much more than a normal storm. The water was full of debris; trees, the occasional dead animal and much more. On arrival at the port, I decided against entering, as we had never been there before. We let out the anchor and made sure it was well dug in, and then tried to get some sleep.

I should also mention a couple of missed accidents, which could have been serious. They occurred in these years. The first was Lorna, who being asked to disconnect the electricity from the shore to the boat, was holding the live end of the 240-volt lead. She was thrown around first on the dock and then fortunately struck the mooring ropes, on her way into the harbor. This separated her from the lead, and of course we pulled her out, very stunned and burned. She was taken to the local hospital, where she was put under surveillance for a while, then released, as she could speak little French and they could speak no English. This episode had a very sobering effect on all of us and we were much more careful in the future.

The other event that stands out, was caused by Gaere, who, wishing to help, got his fingers caught in the anchor windlass. He had gone forward in a fairly strong wind, to bring the anchor in, in preparation for sailing. The windlass was electrically powered, and had two settings; one pulled in only when you had your finger on the start button, the other would continue to pull the anchor up until you pressed the stop button. Gaere chose the continuous mode and then helping the chain as it rolled over the gypsy, his fingers got caught between the chain and the gypsy. He was unable to turn it off because he couldn't reach it, so he screamed and I ran forward and turned the winch off. I expected to find his fingers on the deck, but after pulling the chain to get some slack on it, his fingers emerged a bit bent but all still attached. We immediately iced them down, and by the following morning, he said he was okay. I think he was just being very brave!

Of course, in these same years there were other instances of storms and rough trips, but nothing ever came up to match the drama of that night. For some weeks after, we met boats that were damaged, and could tell us their story. There were also several boats left high and dry on the beach.

In the autumn of 1978, we left *Intsholo II* out of the water in the boatyard of Monsieur Montagne, not knowing what the near future would bring to us as a family.

Lorna and Gaere

22 PENZANCE, 1974–1979

We were living in the penthouse built over the shop at 29 Alverton St. It was Sunday morning and we were out gardening in our container garden. We heard a little disturbance in the road below and looking over the fence we saw a van and two or three cyclists heading west on the main road. The van had a poster announcing that this was a sponsored cycle ride from Newquay to Land's End, a distance of maybe 45 miles. Newquay Round Table was doing the ride.

On considering the project, I thought to myself that perhaps I could do something like that and raise a lot of money for Guide Dogs for the Blind, the charity of the moment at the Penzance Round Table. The plan I formulated was a sponsored ride from London's Marble Arch to Land's End, a distance of 303 miles. I was then 38, quite fit, but not for riding a bike that far in under 24 hours. I made the stipulation of under 24 hours, to create more interest and possibly to raise more money.

It was January, and I wanted to do it before the summer, and the sailing I would want to do that year. I started training immediately, at first perhaps 25 miles, and I built on that weekly. I would leave the shop early in the morning, with John and Peter managing in my absence. There were no cycling clothes available at that time, so if the weather was fair it was shorts, if not, a track suit. I would carry a rain poncho and a spare tire and, as the distance became greater, a sandwich. The lanes of West Cornwall became very familiar as I worked out set routes of so many miles, with a hill combination that would test and strengthen my muscles. Talking about muscles, my friend Ian Smart, an osteopath by profession, volunteered a massage as often as I needed it. He didn't realize it would be nearly every day, as I suffered badly from cramps. The University of Bristol got involved from a diet point of view; they monitored my training progress, which was to last three months. Alex, who was a tremendous support to me through the training period, had a pretty dull life, as I started to go farther and farther each day. I stopped all drinking. I was the dullest husband imaginable!

As the time set for the ride approached, I was sure that I needed to put one long distance ride behind me. I chose to go to Bristol where our very good friends Ken and Bobby Bud had a house, and I knew they would give me a big welcome. The distance was just under 200 miles and I set out early in the morning. I estimated about 10 hours for the trip. In fact, I took a little less, spurred on by rain which fell continuously for the last 75 miles. I was, of course, soaked and dirty from the mud that the tires sprayed on me. Bobby offered to wash and dry all my clothes for the next day's ride back. Meanwhile I borrowed a suit from Ken, and we went off to a meeting of his local Round Table. On the following morning, I got up early to start my return ride, and to my horror all my clothes had shrunk so much I couldn't even get into them. I had to borrow more of Ken's things, which fit much better than the dwarf track suit, which had to be thrown away. The return trip was long and lonely, and it started to rain, so I abandoned it at Exeter and went home the rest of the way by train.

The date set for the 303-mile ride was March 15, 1975, and a friend, Brian Leathley, donated a van and his time to the project. We were accompanied by Ian Smart, David Eddy, and George Ostens. George brought his bike as well so we could ride in company if that helped. It didn't work because he couldn't keep up the speed. The van crew's job was to keep me supplied with the food and water as needed. We all arrived in London, and were greeted by Philip and Betty Wand, who lived only two blocks from Marble Arch, the starting place. We had dinner and went to bed early to be woken by Betty at 3:30 am. By 4:20 am, I was ready for the departure, and the van led me west out of London and on to the Great West Road. I had set 22 and 1/2 hours for the ride, but, early on I realized that I was easily going to beat that time. As the towns were ticked off, and I passed into a new county every now and again, I realized I felt good and was going to make it.

The weather was perfect—no wind, no rain, and no sun, just cool March weather. I ate an astonishing amount of food on the short stops I made, never actually getting off the bicycle. At other times a bar would be handed to me, or a cup of coffee or tea, which was brewed in the van. By mile 265, I was beginning to tire and got bad tempered, especially when I found that my crew had eaten my favorite food. I blasted off verbally and physically, almost destroying my chances of success. My increased speed brought on by frustration, caused more fatigue, and as I came into Penzance with just 10 miles to go, I felt whacked. There on his bicycle was my old cycling buddy Geoff Littler. He was ready to ride with me those last 10 hilly miles. He cajoled and encouraged me until I entered the parking lot of the Land's End hotel at 10 pm. I know I wouldn't have made it without him. Just 17 hours, 57 minutes, and 14 seconds from Marble Arch to Land's End, 303 miles at an average speed of just under 17 mph. There was a large crowd at Land's End to welcome me, and of course Alex, Gaere, and Lorna were there along with my mother. After champagne and a great welcome, I found that I had to keep walking so that I didn't stiffen up too much. I was still walking at 4 am.

The effort raised just under £2500, which bought and trained four guide dogs. As a memento of the ride, the Association for Guide Dogs for the Blind presented me with a statue of a dog with a suitable inscription. It is on my desk in front of me now.

One not-so-positive thing happened at about this time. Bernie Durrant, my mother's former common-law husband, died. He left a widow from a former marriage, and a new common-law wife with one child. I had no idea how this would affect me as I went to see him in the hospital. At that time he knew he was dying of sclerosis of the liver. He assured me that the wholesale newspaper and magazine business would pass to me. He couldn't will it, as it was a concession controlled by the supplying companies. I really thought no more about it, until he died a few days later. We went to the funeral and the will was read, and, as expected, all his goods and chattels passed to his common-law wife. She made an appeal to the newspaper proprietors to let her run the wholesale business, which she did, but lost it in less than a year.

This however was not the serious issue. The promissory note for £10,000 turned up in his papers. As you will remember I had paid this off some years before, and had torn my copy up, but he had not. I still had the canceled check, but no other proof of payment. As the court pointed out, that £10,000 check could have been for anything. After much bickering, I had no choice but to pay it again. It was an expensive but good lesson, particularly as I had been doing Bernie a favor in the first place.

During this same period, I went to see a movie with Alex, and in it was featured a raid on the amazing Greek Monasteries, using hang gliders to access the precipitous cliff-top buildings. I was so taken with the concept of hang gliding, I went down to the sail loft where my friend, Albert Willoughby worked, and asked him what he knew about it. To my surprise he knew someone in the area who was not only flying, but was trying to recruit people to the sport. I called Roger Full the same day and by the weekend we were in to demonstrations. By the following weekend I had bought one of his older kites, and was very tentatively practicing running down a small slope, flying a few feet and landing, until I reached the bottom. Pack it all up, take it to the top, and start again. I became possessed, and started to skip windsurfing in favor of hang gliding. Almost as soon as I got started, my windsurfing buddy Ian Hicks wanted to join in. So we both got new kites and started into the sport. At first it was literally just flying off the original hill, until we were able to get enough height to clear the road and land in the field beyond.

The first time we both went to the cliffs over Sennen Beach, to fly from the top down on to the beach, I have to say I was somewhat nervous of throwing myself to the wind's mercy. I landed successfully on the beach below and began one of the hundreds of ascents back up to the top to try again. Ian had problems as he was so light, he wasn't able to penetrate into the wind coming up the cliff. The solution to this problem was for him to wear a diver's weight belt. We practiced at Sennen and other cliff sites, until we were both able to fly along the cliff back and forth until we chose to land on more or less the exact spot from which we had taken off. It was at Sennen that Roger got into trouble, experienced as he was. The wind was a little too strong and he was blown back until he struck the power cables running along the top of the cliffs. This produced a lot of sparks and the termination of power to all the villagers in the cove, one of whom was so irate, she shouted at him, "Get down from there, I'm trying to cook my Sunday dinner." He was having great difficulty as his kite was arcing across the wires, and he was at least 20 feet up in the air. We eventually got him down and power was restored the next day. A letter of apology was sent to the utility company who never charged for the damage.

My only brush with death participating in this sport took place on the cliff of Carbis Bay. A branch rail line, already mentioned earlier in the book, runs along the cliff under the launch site. It was the last flight of the day, and the wind was dying as I prepared to launch. The moment I took off, I knew trouble was coming. The lack of wind meant no lift and the beach was perhaps 500 feet below. I went into a series of controlled (uncontrolled) stalls, each one taking me closer to the cliff and certain disaster. I saw the rail line and the cutting it was in, immediately below me. I decided to head into the cutting and crash onto the rail line. I didn't make the rail line, as the wings of my kite were straddling the narrow cutting. I was left dangling from my harness about 15 feet above the line, and there was a train due shortly. Roger with great presence of mind got down to the line in the direction the train was coming, and flagged him down. It took better than half an hour to get me and the glider off the line. A letter of apology was sent to British Rail.

It wasn't long before Gaere wanted and did get involved in the sport. We flew together often. One of the most beautiful sights we witnessed was at an international rally held in North Devon, where it was possible to see over 200 gliders in the air at one time. All the beautiful colors of the wings looked like a balloon festival.

In the spring of 1975, we were thinking of moving out of the Penthouse, and into a house again. The reasons were twofold: first, the children were getting bigger; second, we could enlarge the shop into the apartment space. We had seen a development of several barns and buildings on a farm about 4 miles east of Penzance. It was being developed by an acquaintance of ours, Lucy Anderson. She had run out of money, and was anxious to sell the biggest of the three as it was. The house was quite large and there was an attached cottage beside it.

The cottage was not included in the sale. The building that had been completed was quite well done and suited our requirements, apart from the kitchen, which she agreed to remove. A price was settled upon and work started with Alex's father doing most of it. As always when there was any building to be done, I wasn't very far away. Alec, as he was called, and I got on very well. At the same time I had a new workman who started to install terrazzo flooring downstairs and in the patio area. He was also a tiler, and he agreed to show me how to do both finishes. I have been tiling ever since. The new house took a long time to complete, and after speaking with the farmer who still owned the attached cottage, he agreed to sell it for £10,000. This put a whole new spin on the work. We decided to remove all of the second floor, and build a new mezzanine floor over half of the cottage. This floor made a bedroom, reached by a spiral staircase to a landing the full width of the cottage. The small bathroom and kitchen were at the back of the house. To gain access from the main house, we excavated over 4 feet of wall and made an arch with a door in it, then descended several steps to the ground floor of the cottage. I cedar planked the entire ceiling of the cottage, which was over 20 feet high. The final effect was a fantastic feeling of space and solitude, because all the walls of this building were 3–5 feet thick and there was a huge walk-in stone fireplace on one end of the ground floor room. Outside we merged the two gardens and built a stone wall around the perimeter, making for a very protected outdoor space. The wall was later jokingly to be known as the Great Wall of Tregellast, the latter being the name of the house.

In the last part of 1975, we moved in to our newly renovated house, it really was beautiful inside and out. The views included all the way to Penzance and St. Michaels Mount to the Lizard Head 20 or so miles away. In the foreground was a patchwork of small fields, some with crops and others with animals. When we moved in, there were no other residents in the other two houses that were being renovated and it stayed that way for a while. Then our friends Tony and Jean Redman moved in. I worked hard in the garden and made a very productive vegetable patch, which was helped along by endless barrow loads of manure from the farm next door. We both loved this house, and felt it was unlikely we would move for a long time.

This was not to be the case however. In the winter of 1978, I received a call from a Mr. Tagliavini who was the CEO of a national chain of newsagents. He said he would like to meet with me to discuss the possibility of his company's buying our business. I was dumbstruck but agreed to the meeting. Less than a week later and before my meeting with Mr. Tagliavini, I received another phone call, with a proposal of a meeting with another national company. Obviously word had got out, and I knew those two companies were in strong competition with each other.

The first meeting went well, and a general discussion took place as to how they would operate the numerous sides of our business if a purchase was agreed upon. In particular the treatment of our staff, some of whom had worked for many years for us. As for the two managers, Peter and John, John's being a salaried partner presented a problem. Mr. Tagliavini agreed that both could if they wished stay on at the same salaries, and I would have to work out some compensation for John's losing his status as a partner.

Then came the million dollar question. "How much do you want for the business and the real estate?" I replied that, "I hadn't thought of selling, but would be open to an offer." At this time, I mentioned I was meeting with his competitor in a few days to discuss the same subject. His face went gray and he became quite flustered, and asked for a few days to consider his offer. This was fine with me, because I hadn't given selling a thought, nor did I have any plans for the future.

His competitor turned up on schedule and we had a very similar conversation. He in turn went back to his head office to consider his offer and terms.

A little bidding war took place by telephone and eventually with a few caveats I agreed to the offer made by Mr. Tagliavini on behalf of N.S.S. newsagents. The caveats were that we could continue to run the business through Christmas, and they would take over on February 1, 1979, after a sale, which was his stipulation to get the inventory as low as possible. Bad idea, as the store was empty after a bumper Christmas season, with no restocking afterward. The remaining inventory was subject to valuation by a professional. The deal was set, deposits were paid, and the lawyers started to work. I realized that quite a lot of our business enterprises were beyond the scope of his business model. This proved to be the case, and the store suffered badly after the takeover.

The next decision was how and what we were going to do in the future. In the mid 1970s Alex and I had invested in a small bistro in the nearby city of Truro. We had two young friends who had been in advertising in London, and had this proposition to buy an existing restaurant called The Bear Essentials. It was somewhat on a backstreet, but had enjoyed fair business. They took over the business, with our being silent partners. This worked quite well, but their taste for fine wines and food would often get in the way of the profit motive. By 1979, Gaere was also working in the business, and became very interested in the cooking side. Still profit was elusive and the most we could expect was a good meal now and again. Philip Grainey and Richard Bate as they were called, both became good cooks, but bad businessmen. They would both play a large part in our future, but we didn't know what that future would be.

23 WHAT TO DO AND HOW TO DO IT

Before the closing of the purchase of Whites of Alverton, we as a family had to decide in what direction our lives would go. I asked Gaere, Lorna, and Alex to consider if there were somewhere they would like to spend the rest of their lives.

Lorna was in college in London, and was definitely prospering, with invitations to Wimbledon and Ascot coming from the very West End crowd she was moving in. She was having a ball. Gaere was spending time at Camborne Technical College, studying Graphic Arts, and probably many other things that we didn't ask about.

Alex and I were now alone in the house, which was built for a big family. I had officially retired from Round Table, but was made an honorary member. We had lots of friends in the area, and a great social life. Somehow I felt that this was a special opportunity not presented to many people in their lifetime, especially not at 42 and 38. We were both working in the business full time, as we were dedicated to having a really profitable last year. When Lorna came home from London in the summer of 1978 and Gaere was off at college in Camborne, I called a family meeting at home. We had a great dinner, and sat as we had throughout their lives, talking into the night.

To move to France was a suggestion, but was dropped because of language difficulties. Several other places were mentioned, but turned down for some reason or another. I waited until last and unfolded my plan. At first I suggested a move to the United States, and that didn't draw much enthusiasm. Then I suggested that we all sail there. I think GOBSTRUCK would be the best description of the reaction. How, when, and where to were questions quickly asked.

I had been wondering for some time if it would be possible, and I had contacted my father, who was living in Connecticut and was an American citizen, to enquire if we could obtain a visa to come to live in the U.S.A. He made enquiries at the State Department and found that my relationship to an American citizen would give me and my family a 5th preference to immigrate to America. The only provision was that I was still alive at the time of immigration. I knew by this time that we could legally enter the U.S. if we wished.

The next item for discussion was what boat we would use. *Intsholo II* had proved to be very seaworthy, and had weathered several storms. Yet we all agreed that a larger boat would be more comfortable, and probably more stable. I knew that the builder of *Intsholo II* also built a 47-foot ketch with a very deep draft of 7 feet 3 inches. It was called a Croisiere Totale or total cruiser. It seemed to be a perfect match for what we all decided we wanted to do. I ordered one for spring of 1979 with delivery in La Rochelle.

Then we needed to sell our house, cars and furniture. We decided to sell some furniture with the house, and the remainder was crated up and put in a container to ship to Connecticut, which was to be our ultimate destination. The house sold within a week, which was not what we had wanted, but very good friends of ours, Peter and Marjorie Bate, offered us their house in the interim, as they were going to Bahrain for a year to teach English.

Their house was not more than a few fields away, and we settled into this very cozy cottage with Bridget, our only Saluki left, and a white cat named Enoch. We had made arrangements with a lady who loved Bridget to have her when we left. Enoch was to go with us as the ship's cat. Unfortunately Enoch didn't make it to the boat. She was staying with our friends Betty and Bill Thompson on their farm. She went missing and was found later drowned in a water butt, a sad end to a lovely white cat.

The movers came and did an outstanding job of packing, and we quite sadly left our lovely home. One car, a Lancia Monte Carlo, which had been hit by a car while stopped at an accident scene with Alex in it, was still in the garage getting fixed. The other car, a VW Passat was to become the workhorse of the family as we intended making several trips to La Rochelle to prepare the boat for the voyage.

Meanwhile, preparations were being made to close on Whites of Alverton, wills were prepared, insurances were improved or altered. Most importantly, we had a large number of forms to fill out with regard to immigration. We submitted them to the U.S. Embassy, and in due course an appointment was made for us to be interviewed, and to get medically examined. The questions asked were often very personal, and rude. One question of note, has your mother ever practiced prostitution? Has any member of your family ever suffered from venereal disease? On and on with questions.

I wanted to ask a question while I was in London visiting the embassy. What is the law with regard to importing, as an immigrant, a large collection of wine? I was directed to the office of the U.S. Customs, in the same building. On putting the question to the officer, I was told that it would be impossible to import approximately 10,000 bottles into the U.S.A., end of story! On arrival in the U.S. some 18 months later, I was told that as it was a collection I would have been allowed to bring them. This was too late, as I had already arranged for Christie's to auction the entire collection, 20 years of wine buying gone without trace. That was the only sad part of our intended emigration to the U.S.

The new boat *Intsholo III* was completed in early spring and launched in La Rochelle's Les Minimes harbor with us being present, as we had come down to see the launch and to get some of the optional equip-

ment fixed, mostly at the masthead. This was to be installed by John Beale, from our anchorage at Mylor. He worked on all the Brooks & Gatehouse equipment, installed a single-sideband radio and a VHF radio. He enjoyed his week of work away from home and spent much time in the bosun's chair up the mast.

Meanwhile we were selling *Intsholo II*. We had left her in M. Montagne's boatyard in Toulon. I couldn't predict the difficulties to come. When we wrote to him instructing him to sell, (he was also a registered yacht broker), we had a charming letter back, obviously very pleased for the opportunity. It wasn't long before we

On the hard

had another letter saying that he had sold the boat for the price asked, and where should he deposit the money. We gave him the name of our English bank, and waited and waited, but nothing ever came. We decided that on our next trip to La Rochelle, we would go down to Toulon, and find out what was happening. On arrival we found that the boatyard was closed down and locked up. M. Montagne had declared bankruptcy and was nowhere to be found. Not knowing what to do, we called on a lawyer in the city, to be told, "C'est tres difficile, Monsieur." We knew that already, and when we arrived home we hired a lawyer in England to pursue the matter. The boat of course was long gone with its new owners. After much legal expense, we found that M. Montagne had not put the money in the bank, declared a sale, or even transferred the boat's passport. He had claimed the money he had received for *Intsholo II* as an asset for himself. After perhaps a year, we received a small payout and heard no more. We had lost quite a lot of money, but realized how hard it is to learn life's lessons even in one lifetime.

We were now in Penzance, with the business and the house sold. Cars were accounted for, furniture passed on, sold, or crated for delivery to the other side. In fact, all the arrangements for a move across the Atlantic were complete. Lorna was to stay in college in London to complete her course. Gaere was to accompany Alex and me on our last journey to La Rochelle, where *Intsholo III* lay ready for our greatest adventure. We went on the ferry from Plymouth and went out on deck to see England slip away behind us, as we left the

Gaere, leaving England

port. This was not without emotion, and I certainly remembered the last time I left England for Canada in the Aquitania, 32 years before.

We landed in Roscoff, France, and drove down to La Rochelle, were we put the final touches to the boat, and unloaded a car full of supplies of all kinds. We took Duty Free stores aboard and stored a huge amount of wine and spirits in the bilge area. The crew was to follow in a vehicle driven by John and Pam Davis, Alex's sister and brother-in-law. The crew list for the first leg of the journey about to start was Tristan (skipper), Alex (mate), Gaere everything that needed doing plus David Eddy, Ian Hicks, John Harvey, and Philippe Engelhard from France.

Alex and Gaere on the ferry

Before welcoming the crew, Alex, Gaere and I decided to have a celebratory meal in La Rochelle, a city famous for its restaurants, seafood in particular. We chose Andre's which specialized in lobster and shellfish. On arrival we noted the cart with all sizes of lobster and crawfish , each marked on a claw or the carapace with the price. In due time, we had the pleasure of a visit from the cart and a chance to choose the victim. Gaere picked the largest crawfish on the cart. My thoughts were how long would the money last? He ate the lot.

The plan was to sail across the Bay of Biscay and down the Spanish and Portuguese coasts, stopping only in Lisbon for a couple of nights. Then to Gibraltar and into the Mediterranean, visiting all of our friends in the Isles des Embiez, before our crossing. I can't finish this chapter without remarking on the tremendous sendoff we received from all our friends in Cornwall. There were parties, lunches, dinners, and a wonderful show of friendship.

In La Rochelle with the crew

24 LA ROCHELLE TO ISLE DES EMBIEZ

At 10 am on May 7, 1979, the *Intsholo III* slipped her moorings bound for the Mediterranean and a last visit with friends. This was also to be a shakedown cruise, for the boat was completely untried, as we had previously put her under sail, but the wind would not cooperate. We came out of the bay and the weather was glorious. We motored for a time, raised sail at 7 pm and were able to sail at about 5 knots, with a preventer on the boom required to counteract a good swell. I note in the log that by 11 pm a fair wind with main, mizzen, genoa, set with the wind from the north at Force Three to Four with an almost full moon. What a great start.

Boat trial

At 7 am the following day, the wind decided to quit, and the "mechanical topsail" was started. By 10 am, we had made a good 146 miles. The engine on this boat was a Perkins 6-236 and at under 1500 rpm would move the boat at 6-plus knots very quietly for a diesel engine. It was a good thing we had a good engine, because the Bay of Biscay decided not to live up to its reputation. There are entries in the log: weather fabulous, lunch in cockpit, dolphins all around, days run 158 miles. In the afternoon, Gaere broke the barometer with his head, while passing a cup of tea up to David. The barometer was much more damaged than Gaere's head! We came abreast of Cape Vallero lighthouse at 8:30 pm on the ninth of May, exactly six years and 1 and 1/2 hours after passing the same light in *Intsholo II*.

The dawn of May 11 brought no more wind and although we continued with the sails raised, they were not working and the engine was on. The run for the day was 199 miles up to 10 am. No more wind came for the day. At 3 pm, we rounded up into the Tagus River and Lisbon, clearing customs using a taxi to the office. The customs officer insisted that we had never left, as *Intsholo II* six years before had not checked out on leaving port. There were no recriminations, and I drove back to the boat in the taxi, to find Tony, the skipper of *Decca Navigator* on board. He was attempting to fix our auto-steering system, and the wind speed indicator, but he was unsuccessful in both cases. As it happened, the electronic equipment would not get fixed until we arrived in Gibraltar, where we met a remarkable man, not for his abilities, but for his verbal additions to our vocabulary.

We moved to a more suitable dock with some other yachts in the basin, so we would feel safer leaving the boat while we went out to dinner that night. Dinner took the form of a prawn starter, followed by a large crawfish each and seven bottles of Vinho Verde, followed by brandy and coffee. We came back to the boat at 2 am, and sat in the cockpit talking and drinking until 3:30 am, a very hot night.

Next morning Phillipe and I went shopping for a few supplies. The shops were of poor quality. The high spot was meeting a fisherman on the way home, from whom we bought a large fish.

It was decided by all that we should leave Lisbon and head to Gibraltar, after lunch. We cast off at 12:15 pm into a beautiful day but still with no wind. The night followed suit with a full moon to add to the beauty of an absolutely still night. Next day was the same story as we passed Cape St. Vincent, Cape Sagres, and Cadiz harbor lights. We changed course to pass by Cape Trafalgar, and we were abeam of the Cape by 1:30 am, with an increasing wind from the E.N.E.

As we opened the Straits of Gibraltar the wind increased to Force Eight and any hopes of making it through the straits were finished. After a couple of fruitless tacks very close hauled in the night, with stormy skies, I decided to make for the beach at Terifa and anchor. We were directly under the headland on which Terifa Light is placed. As soon as we entered the bay, all the pounding and spray ceased, and we set anchor in 4 fathoms on sand. The wind was still blowing hard off the beach, so we set an anchor watch for safety. We all had bacon and eggs for breakfast as Gaere took the first watch.

We made a radiotelephone call to Phillipe's office, to tell them of his inability to get home until the 15th at least. In fact at 9:30 am, the wind had subsided so we upped anchor and motored and sailed around into Gibraltar Bay and into Algeciras Harbor, where, without touching shore, Phillipe leapt for the dock, clutching his bag. He was sorry to leave and we were sorry to see him go, as this was the third delivery he had participated in and it was to be the last. Not all that long after, he left his wife of many years, and sometime after that died of cancer. I missed his wisdom of the sea, and never saw or spoke to him again. His ex-wife and family are still good friends.

We sailed over to Gibraltar only a few miles away, where we anchored in Shepperd's Marina. The Spanish Coast Guard never did know that they'd had visitors. Later on in our stay in Gibraltar I was stopped by a gunboat for windsurfing into their territorial waters, and they proceeded to shadow me back to Gibraltar. These were tense times between Britain and Spain over who should own the Rock. The dilemma was resolved by a referendum of the people, who resoundingly voted to stay British.

Our arrival in Gibraltar Harbor was the first leg of the journey to Les Embiez. The log read 901 miles and it was the 14th of May so with a day in Lisbon, we had taken seven days to do 901 miles. I think the trip was successful but not as a sailing trial, as we had only a few hours under sail. What was a success was the navigation by sextant that Alex and I had learned in night school the previous winter. We took many sights and reduced them to positions, and they were very accurate.

Now we had the problem of getting the pieces of gear fixed, and we did not realize that this would be a near impossibility on the Rock. As previously mentioned, we somehow or other made contact with Mr. Dudley, who was a man of medium height, dark complexion, and with the most terribly undershot jaw we had ever seen. Gaere would swim around pretending to be Mrs. Dudley, who would have needed an over-shot mouth for any contact he made. Well, Mr. D. visited us and took our autopilot away with him. He stated clearly that he would be unable to do anything about our wind speed indicator. He recommended a mechanic to look after our generator, and the mechanic said that it was not something he could do, as we needed a marine electronics person. The marine electronics person came, and said that it needed an Onan dealer. There was not one on the Rock, so in disgust we decided to sail up to Porto Jose Banus a few miles up the coast, and get back to Gib and Mr. Dudley for Tuesday.

This we did very easily the following morning, mooring beside the billionaire Adnan Kashogi's yacht (200+ feet). He was not on board but his crew of seven or eight were, and they explained how they had to prepare breakfast, lunch, and dinner for 20 every day. If no one showed up, they ate what they could and the rest was thrown away. This Arab-owned port was full of suited little men with briefcases full of cash. Kashogi ended up in jail for his financial manipulations and illegal dealings. Still, we were in brilliant company. With an option to visit many of the bars around the harbor, we had a drink or two. David in particular enjoyed this. I must here give credit to Gaere, who spent most evenings, even when we were underway, cooking. His range of food was imaginative to say the least, and whether he had fresh or canned ingredients, a delicious meal would follow.

The next day we decided to sail over to Ceuta in Morroco. The winds were light and variable and we had no trouble getting into the harbor, where we moored up alongside another English yacht. We walked around the city, from where the Spanish Civil War started in 1936. General Franco is well remembered there. Otherwise it was a dull city, and we were not sorry to go back to Gib. We found the solenoid for the Onan had arrived, but the electronic guy didn't show up. Mr. Dudley said that the circuit board of the autopilot was burned out due to "negative feedback." This term is still used in the family to describe any technical hitch. We phoned John Beale in Mylor, England, and he promised a replacement part and a new part for the wind speed indicator by next-day air. It arrived three days later, and I was able to fix the wind speed. Mr. Dudley was unable to fix the autopilot. Surprise, surprise!

Sadly both David and John had run out of time, and returned to England by the 3:15 plane on the 24th of May, leaving just Alex, Gaere, and me to sail the 778 miles to Embiez.

With the help of no one, I put the new circuit board into the autopilot, which was going to be an important factor, now that we were a crew of three. We headed out of Gibralter at 9:15 am on June 8, to resume our journey. We had obviously lost a lot of time, 22 days in fact, and achieved almost nothing. In fact, the only really successful thing was the fabrication of four stainless brackets to hold the two windsurfers we were carrying. The autopilot was working when we left Gib, but for how long? Our first stop Malaga was reached at 6:15 pm. We had dinner and a short sleep and started again at midnight for Almeria. The autopilot broke down at 7:15 am, so we were back to hand steering for the remainder of the voyage.

Arriving at 4 pm in Almeria, we found the harbor filthy with no facilities for yachts, so we sailed the next day for Alicante. In this leg of the voyage, we had great sailing weather. For the first time we could find out what the boat would do. We set the cruising chute, main, and mizzen sails, finding the chute did better without the mainsail, so we stowed the main and held the chute all the way to Alicante, arriving at 9 am, not too tired after a long sail. We anchored off the harbor and had a swim and slept all afternoon. I have made a note in the log that, "Alex isn't happy about anything."

At 5:30 pm, we went into the harbor and moored stern to the quay, next door but two from Charles and Kate Buckley on *Isolde*. We had met him years before in Penzance and a couple of times afterwards in Alicante. They were both looking old and tired like their boat. They had been moored in the same place for nine years. He had once said that I would have first option on *Isolde*, but by then, it wouldn't be an option I wished to pursue—the boat had grown to the bottom of the harbor.

After a shopping trip to the market with Charles, we said our good-byes and headed out to sea and a port we had never been to, Javea. We had difficulty finding it in the daylight with no lighthouses to give us an indication of its whereabouts. This part of the coast of Spain is so built up with highrise apartments, condominiums, and hotels that it is really hard to tell where one town starts and the other ends. We made it into the port at 6:45 pm and tied up alongside another English yacht.

This was just an overnight stop and by 10:30 am on June 13 we were on our way to Sitges, a town that we had visited before. This was a trip of about 30 hours. We had only been sailing for a few hours when the mizzen halyard blocked and wouldn't move up or down. I went up the mast and freed it despite a considerable swell running. Alex was really unhappy by this time, and she said that she wanted to leave the boat. Gaere and I both remonstrated that this night passage would be different, but she insisted, so I altered course for Valencia.

A few hours later, and I realized that this was not going to be an easy passage. At 10:30 pm, we were doing well under all plain sail, but it was so dark we could see nothing coming. At exactly 10:30, it came in the form of a thunder, lightning, wind, and rain storm as severe as the one we had experienced previously. Regardless of the wind, the rain came down so hard it flattened the sea, into which plunged bolts of lightning literally feet away from us. The sea boiled alongside as the lightning struck the water. Needless to say, the thunder was immediate. Gaere and I stowed the sails while Alex steered, and we were soaked to the skin in seconds. We were all so in awe of the display of nature surrounding us, we didn't think to be frightened. As quickly as it had arrived, it left us; the wind went down, the rain stopped, and the lightning strikes were behind us. We looked at each other, and thought how lucky we were to be in a boat that had lightning conductors, and was rock solid in the storm.

The wind changed after the storm, and went dead ahead of our course for Valencia. Gaere and I put the sails back up, and Alex steered our original course for Sitges. I never heard another word from Alex as to her wanting to get off the boat. I think this was the first of many times that we would realize how mutually dependent on one another we had become. We made harbor at 1 pm, after a 26-hour passage. We all talked that evening about our experience, and agreed that sailing a boat that size with three people was inadequate, and we should make shorter daylight hops wherever possible. We only had one more potential long passage to do, that was across the Golfe de Lyon.

I phoned John Beale from Sitges, and told him of our continuing problems. He was sympathetic, but obviously could do nothing to help us until we reached somewhere we were going to stay for a while. We had noticed a loud harmonic sound coming through the hull and dismissed it several times, but on this last leg where we were sailing fast it became very apparent that it was the fairly large three-bladed propeller that was causing the trouble. After some thought, I decided to order a folding prop, which would give us more speed under sail, and hopefully cure the noise. The downside would be much less propulsion under engine, and more difficulty maneuvering. I wasn't going to tackle this until I was ready to leave the Mediterranean.

The following morning, we headed out to sea for the comparatively short trip to Arenys de Mar. This was a harbor we had entered a number of times, and the yacht club welcomed us as old customers. We phoned our friends Fenita and Diana Muir. Fenita's husband had died since our last visit. We told them we were in the harbor, and they said they would come round for a drink at 8:30 pm, and would we like to come to their home, La Encina, for the whole of the next day? Unanimously this was accepted—all three of us had been to this paradise in the hills before. Our visit was wonderful and totally relaxing after many weeks on the

Diana, Fenita, Lorna and Alex

boat. A walk in the hills with Spotty, their dog, then a great curry dinner and home to the boat, stopping for a gin and tonic in the yacht club before we went down the dock. Fenita was fascinated by our plans, par-

ticularly our intended flight across to the U.S.A. to establish our residence in the country and to buy a house to become non-residents of Britain. She gave me the name, address, and phone number of her niece, who lived near Westport, Connecticut, and was a realtor. As we were intending to buy a house in that area, we took good note.

Top of the mast

Our next steps were small ones to round the Bay of St. Sebastian one harbor at a time, to get into the Golfe De Lyon where there was a mistral wind raging. So with a collection of early starts from June 18, we made Palamos, Estartit, Cadaques, and Port Vendre, where we picked up a German cyclist complete with bicycle. We finally stopped in Canet,

Down wind

where Bernard the cyclist left us after lunch. We were going to stop in Canet for a few days, so John Beale and his assistant could fly to Montpelier, and solve all of our problems. Before their arrival we had unwelcome visitors in the form of two customs officials. They searched the boat, and said we had too much liquor aboard. They were pleasant, but firm, charged us 220 francs and took a bottle of whiskey, which they put on the table and it exploded with no explanation. They came back the next day and refunded us 20 francs, saying they had overcharged us. Having sailed many times from one country to another, and never having been searched or charged for anything on board, with one exception in England, I had serious doubts over whether they were customs officers at all.

John and David arrived at 9:30 pm on the 20th, and said they would start the repairs the next day. After two days of work, the steering, hydraulics, autopilot, wind speed and many other electronics niggles were all working so it was decided to do sea trials to Gruisson a few miles along the coast. This was also the town where we had arranged for M. Duhammel to fix the generator, so the trials were useful in two ways.

Everything worked, John and David were away on the 7:20 am bus back to Montpelier and home. M. Duhammel and the mechanic were on board in the morning and resolved all the problems of the generator. So, for the first time since we picked up *Intsholo III*, everything was working. The only problem remaining was the noisy propeller.

We left Gruisson for Sete on a beautiful sailing day and made a fast passage, ending the day with a swim outside the harbor, then entering this old port, on the Canal du Midi in time for a celebratory dinner on the quayside. The next leg with little drama was to Marseille and a mooring outside city hall. Overnight there and on to Port Miou, just two hours later into the harbor and grilled sardines. On the 28th of June, we sailed the last 74 miles to Embiez and took up our old berth next to our friends. We had covered 1663 miles, seen good and bad weather, had troubles and some triumphs. Now we were ready for some fun and our trip to the United States.

25 U.S.A. AND MAKING IT LEGAL

On our arrival in Embiez, we saw our many friends there, but the first thing we had to do was to fly to the U.S. to follow the provisions set by the immigration officials for aliens with entry visas. This clearly stated that if granted a visa, you must enter the country within six months. It would be six months at the end of July 1979, and we had booked flights for Alex, Gaere and me from Marseille to London arriving in plenty of time to catch the British Airways flight from London to New York. Lorna was booked on this New York flight as well, and it was our intention to fly back to the boat as a complete family, after about three weeks. There followed a sequence of events that were completely beyond our control. The plane from Marseille to London was delayed for several hours—in fact, as we landed, we saw the plane we should have caught taking off. Lorna was on board, on her own. We went to the British Airways desk and explained our situation, and they promised to put us on the next flight, which would bring us to New York about eight hours after Lorna. On trying to explain that our daughter was on her own, the girl said she would be sure to contact the flight and also the terminal at JFK. The message Lorna received in flight and on arrival was, "Your parents won't be joining you in the U.S.A." Lorna had no money and didn't think to call my father in Westport to see what he could suggest. After refusing help from a couple of stewards from her flight, she sat on her luggage, cried and waited, not believing the message she had received. When Alex, Gaere, and I saw her sitting on her bags, we rushed together, and soon were on our way to Westport, where my father, who had been expecting us, wondered what had happened.

The next few days were a rush of activity. We met with Fenita's niece, who very quickly sold us a nice Salt Box House on Tulip Tree Lane in Darien, a nearby town. Seeing the color it was painted inside, predominantly orange, we decided to repaint to make it more attractive for a would-be renter. We rushed to the hardware store and bought various more muted shades, brushes, roller pans, and all the other equipment to make painting easier. At the same time, we phoned for delivery of the container in which our furniture and things were stored. This was in Bergen, New Jersey, less than 100 miles away. On arrival, the truck driver insisted that I pay him in cash or by certified check $2,500, which was the fee for storing the container and delivering it to Darien. No payment and he would drive back! I found the money and we started to move the furniture into the large basement of the house. The driver explained that he was not allowed to help. Let me explain my annoyance at this $2,500 charge, as the moving company in England had come to the house, packed everything in boxes, moved all the furniture and boxes into a container, and then shipped it to the U.S.A., all for the cost of $2,500. It reminded me of the shakedown so many immigrants to the U.S. in the previous 150 years probably had endured. We didn't have time to complain and the truck driver was obdurate in his attitude.

We went on with the painting, all pitching in, and the house was transformed inside of a week, the only vestige of orange left was the carpet. We were told that the previous owners, whom we never met, were in the movie business and liked bright colors.

While we were doing all this work, our future next door neighbors, came over to say Hi. Their first question was to ask, "Who are you with?" Alex and I looked at each other nonplussed. We really didn't know that they were enquiring as to which corporation we worked for. Not working for any corporation, I think our status diminished considerably.

Before we left, the same realtor rented the house for a year, to a couple who worked for Exxon, so I'm sure the neighbors were happy with the stability this provided. We of course were allowed to keep our possessions in the basement. All we had to do was pay the taxes.

As we had allowed three weeks for our visit to the U.S.A. and had finished all the chores attached to the new house, we decided to take our rental car to upper New York state, for a visit to the Adirondacks. We found a cabin to rent at Blue Mountain Lake, where we spent a few days canoeing and hiking in that lovely area. Next we moved to Alexandria, New York, where we rented a motorboat for a day and cruised through the Thousand Islands region. It was beautiful weather so sun bathing on the rocks and picnicking were perfect. That night we all went out for a meal at a fancy restaurant, and both Gaere and Lorna ordered an appetizer of smoked salmon, followed by lobster. Neither could finish their meal, and we reminded them of this fact when they got carried away in the future.

As we were now fairly close to Toronto, we drove the rest of the way to see my sister Wendy and her husband Ernie. At least two of their girls were at summer camp, so the following day we all spent the day with them. I remember that once again the weather was fabulous and we all had fun in the lake and other facilities. Very soon afterwards, we had to return to New York for our flight home to the boat. The trip had been an eye opener for all of us, and gave us a taste of all the things we were going to enjoy in the U.S.A.

We flew back from New York to Marseille as a family, and took the train to Toulon where we transferred to a taxi to Les Embiez. Quite an adventure in itself, but we had satisfied the immigration requirements of one country, and the emigration requirements of another. Here, we were on our boat, and, it seemed, stateless.

A few words about the Isle des Embiez. It is a limestone outcrop, the highest point being 200+/- feet with an old abandoned hotel on the top, and a more modern hotel built around the marina, which was constructed in a natural bay facing approximately north toward the towns of Bandol and Sanary, perhaps 3 miles away. Behind these towns were the beginnings of the Alpes Maritime. The bay in which these two towns lay also contained the two islands Embiez and Bendor. The islands had been purchased by Paul Ricard. He was the maker of the Anisette drink, Ricard. He used the island of Bendor as his summer home, built a small harbor to keep his large boat in, and built a many-roomed mansion around the harbor. The island of Embiez he developed as a commercial enterprise, with the marina, hotel, and several restaurants. About a mile long and a half-mile wide, covered with pine trees, many beaches and trails, made it perhaps an ideal destination for boats or just tourists. No cars were allowed on the island, adding to its attraction. There were about 80 boat slips in the marina, and to get a place you had to be recommended by an existing slip owner. In our case, this was Renaud and Yola Mueller. We had several very wonderful summers there, and made a number of friends.

Before we get back aboard *Intsholo III*, let me describe the boat a little. She was a ketch-rigged 47-foot fiberglass boat with laid teak decks, a 57-foot main mast and a proportional mizzen mast. Her main sail was fitted with roller reefing. The foresails clipped by hanks on to twin headstays. She had two crosstrees and two backstays, making her a very stoutly rigged yacht. The deck and cockpit was completely flush so any water that came over the very flared bow would be diverted by high coamings that made a false cockpit. On each coaming were two large Lewmar winches to handle the foresails. The sail locker, accessed through a hatch in the foredeck, contained a cruising chute, a Number One and Number Two genoa, a regular jib and a storm jib. We also carried a colorful staysail and a mizzen staysail.

Down below, reached by a fairly steep companionway, was a large salon with a banquette to port, a table with two temporary stools on the outside. On the starboard was an inside steering position, with a hatch to view the sails, over the tall stool, which doubled for use with the navigation table which was alongside the inside wheel. To round out the accommodations in the salon down two steps on the starboard side was the galley. You might say the perfect galley for an ocean-going yacht, it wasn't too large, so you could wedge yourself in place in a seaway. There were numerous lockers for food storage, and a refrigerator and freezer locker, which was not efficient, but was altered later. A two-burner propane stove with an oven on gimbals rounded out the galley.

Aft was the master suite, to which you gained access by a passage on the port side, which also doubled as engine access. The passageway was about 6 feet high and opened into a large cabin, which was under the cockpit and afterdeck. In it was a large circular bed, which proved great for the crossing, as you could sleep on it in any direction, depending on what tack you were on. There was a reasonable sized bathroom with shower, basin and toilet within the cabin. Emergency exit was achieved by a large Goiot hatch over the bed. Two opening portholes on each side provided light and air when in harbor or sailing in calm weather.

Forward of the salon were two cabins, one on either side of a central bulkhead. Each contained two bunk beds with lee cloths for bad weather. Each also was furnished with a wardrobe with shelves and cupboards for stowing gear. Ahead was a fairly large bathroom with all the amenities, leading to two more bunks, which were largely used for sail and gear storage. In the peak of the bow was a large chain locker and rope storage.

Altogether a very seaman-like rig and we were super confident it could fulfill our quest of an Atlantic crossing and a great cruise to the West Indies and beyond.

26 ISLE DES EMBIEZ TO FLORIDA, PART 1

At 0900, August 13, 1979, log reading 1780 miles, weather forecast "beau temps, brise par le cote", it was time for all four of us to start the greatest adventure of our lives. After many goodbyes and the blowing of horns, we motored out of Embiez Harbor, and into perfect weather. The object was to return to Gibraltar, with a short stop in Marseille for parts. There was really no hurry, as we had until the beginning of October before we needed to leave Gib for the Canary Islands, so we would enjoy a relaxed cruise down the French and Spanish coasts, and sail across to the Balearic Islands, which we had enjoyed previously.

On arrival in Marseille, we picked up our parts from the Dufour agent, and despite a number of friends in the port, decided to continue our voyage. It was not easy to pull in and out of Marseille, because the yachts lay at anchor stern to, in front of the town hall on a beautiful esplanade. There were constant distractions and much to watch. I have a note in the log: "Lorna depressed." I can't remember why, but as I know Lorna then and now, it couldn't have lasted long.

We set course across the Golfe de Lyon in fabulous weather and sailed a steady six knots with the autopilot, now named Dudley, working really well. For the first time in many crossings of this long stretch of open water, the weather was kind, and we pulled into San Felieu de Guixhols early in the morning, with the crew all sleeping in the aft cabin. San Felieu is a large harbor devoted to fishing, but there is always room and a welcome for yachts. It is the kind of harbor that you could swim in and we did, not leaving until the following day at 10:00 am.

We had a great sail down to Arenys de Mar and our friends previously mentioned, Fenita and Diana. We made contact with them and arranged to go sailing with them the next day, and for this we were rewarded with dinner at the Mas Nadol in San Andres de Llaveneras, in a setting that is rare to non-existent. The building, which is hundreds of years old, nestles on the side of a pine-covered mountain, with a view of the Mediterranean a couple of thousand feet below. Fenita had a special association with the restaurant as she had the water rights for the whole mountainside. I'm sure we would have had a great meal without this leverage, but the spectacular dishes kept coming, as did the wine of the region. We all stayed the night with Fenita and Diana, and they delivered us back to our boat the following morning.

At noon, giving ourselves time to sober up, we set sail for the island of Majorca, with a good forecast that didn't last long—within an hour and a half, it was blowing a steady 25 to 30 knots. I made the right decision to alter course for Barcelona. Under Albert's jib, a reefed main, and mizzen, we just flew into Barcelona Harbor by 8 pm. We tied up at the Real Club Nautico de Barcelona, with a free mooring and a wonderful welcome back. These Spanish yacht clubs are full of hospitality and good will. Because of the bad weather in the Golfe, we decided to spend the day in Barcelona, never a hardship, as there is so much to do and see. With a short stop in Sitges, the following day was all about sailing, arriving and leaving on the same day for Ibiza, our departure time being governed by the expedient time that would bring up the island in the dark. Once you see the lighthouse you are looking for, you can make corrections to your course if needed, and proceed to enter the harbor in daylight, which is a much safer option than making your way through approach buoys in the dark. At this time, all of our navigation was done by dead reckoning, the use of the sextant being reserved more for open-ocean passages. Basically dead reckoning comprises assessing speed and distance covered on a compass course, making allowances for wind and current—an inexact science, but surprisingly accurate. Of course with GPS, just a push of a button lets you know where you are. Alas, it had not yet been invented.

As we pulled into the lovely island of Ibiza, we were greeted by two yachts that we knew well. On board one of these yachts was a couple, Roger and Kay Hughes, who exclaimed, "Are you really Tristan Mac-Donald?" My fame was spreading across the cruising world. We had a number of drinks with my "fans," in the beautiful bay of Portinaix. Plenty of swimming and windsurfing as the whole family was now proficient at this sport. In fact, the boards were only brought back on board if we were ready to sail, or at night. After a couple of nights in Portinaix, we sailed in ideal conditions to the town of Ibiza, to do odd jobs and order self-steering gear to supplement the autopilot that worked erratically. More about the self-steering gear later.

The town of Ibiza was the Key West of the day, particularly crowded at night, by people of every kind of persuasion you could imagine. Being moored stern to on the main town quay was a wonderful vantage point, as the parade of gays, transvestites, cross-dressers, and the like continued long past our bedtime. The town itself is a Mediterranean gem:

beautiful old buildings, a maze of small alleyways, and colorful flowers in window boxes and hanging baskets everywhere.

After we were satiated by this promiscuous display, we headed out to Espalmador, one of the smallest islands in the Ballearic group, and definitely the least visited. In our previous cruises we had visited, sailed around, and spent time on all of these beautiful islands. Our favorite I think was Minorca, with its wonderful harbor of Port Mahon, where Nelson and his fleet of 50 or 60 great sailing ships could enter the harbor and be completely safe from the weather and the enemy. In the Napoleonic Wars, these islands had belonged to Britain, who used them for a base of operations against the combined fleets of France and Spain. One thing that the English had left behind was the distilling of juniper for gin. There were several varieties, but our favorite by far was Rives, which only came in litre bottles and cost about £1. At that time and because it was expedient to use local products, we drank nothing but gin and tonics.

With the log now at 2171 miles, we begrudgingly left the islands for the mainland, to continue our progress towards Gibraltar. Because of headwinds, we were forced once more to go into Javea. I made the note in the log, "Tied to the wall, crummy town, went out for an inferior dinner." After shopping and fueling, we left for Altea, but it was not to be. After a terrific sail down the coast, we went into the harbor, to be told there was no room, so, frustrated, we motored back to Calpe, a miniature rock of Gibraltar. Feeling very unsafe in this anchorage with very strong winds and poor holding, we left at first light. We brought up at Alicante, and decided to spend a few days in there, and to try to get our refrigerator fixed, which we accomplished. Meeting many friends old and new, including a boat named *Esperance*, which was to play a very big part in our lives for many months to come. On board were Dave and Trish Webb, a couple from New York who were planning an Atlantic crossing in the next few weeks. They proved ultra-sociable, and we spent many hours with them.

Over the next several days, always headed westward, we were in the company of *Esperance*—their destination was also Gibraltar. We kept in touch by VHF radio, and as we were the faster boat we would find a good harbor and good moorings and tell them where to go. In this way, in pretty rapid succession we stayed in Garucha, Almeria, which proved difficult to find, Motril, Fuengirola, Marbella, Estapona, and finally Gibraltar. A lot of these passages were made under perfect sailing conditions. We found out a lot about *Intsholo III*, and the four of us became a close team, able to change sails quickly and efficiently. One thing we did find out was that few 47-foot boats sailed faster, as we had such a range of sail options for almost any conditions. All we had to do in Gibraltar was to get all the bugs out; i.e., the propeller, the autopilot, the fridge, fit a new self-steering system to supplement the autopilot.

All the time we were approaching Gib, we began to meet new boats, with a similar itinerary to ours. Perhaps ours was more intense, as we still

Going west

had so many problems to address. On arrival in Gib, I called the company which was making our new folding propeller, and asked that it be shipped air freight as soon as possible. It arrived in a couple of days, and it was so beautifully formed you could easily have placed it on a mantelpiece as an ultra-modern decoration. There were three interleaving blades, which closed to look somewhat like a ducks bill when not in use. When put under power, the blades opened and drove the boat in forward and reverse almost as effectively as the original prop. It was not as good in tight maneuvering, as it did not have the torque of a fixed prop. I

brought it home and immediately put on my diving gear to see how it would fit. With the aid of Gaere in the dinghy alongside, I took the old one off and got the new one fitted in a couple of hours. We stowed the old one for refitting before we entered the U.S. waters, which would require lots of maneuvering.

The next major job was to fit the new self-steering gear, which arrived by air a few days later. For this job some expertise would be needed. It came in the form of our fifth crewmember, Richard Checkley. We had met him before on a delivery from Marseille to Le Havre, on a motor boat that his father was buying. In the interim period, he had opened a boatyard in Newton Ferrers, Devon, England, and of course was very familiar with boat work of all kinds. He had asked us to include him in any Atlantic crossing we might make, which we were glad to do. In the end, he stayed with us for six months, falling in love with Lorna in the process.

The day after his arrival we all set to work on the deck to unpack and sort the various components of this piece of equipment. We had chosen a Hydrovane, as we had used this model before on *Intsholo II*. The only reason we had not fitted the boat with a self-steering system before now was our confidence in the electronic autopilot. After sorting and laying out the templates for the holes needed in the stern, Richard drilled away with a confidence I would never have felt. Gaere went down in the depths of the stern, and as the bolts were passed through, he placed wooden backing plates behind. The nuts were tightened over the backing plates and later glass fibred over. All the gearing of the unit was put in places and finally the windvane that would tilt if the boat went off course, activating the supplemental rudder, which was on a stainless steel post suspended from the bottom of the steering unit. The main rudder was locked while using this device, and if the sails were balanced correctly, it stayed on a good course. With all these jobs and other

repairs completed, we were ready for some relaxation and having a good time in all the night spots of Gibraltar. Gaere, now 19, Lorna, about to be 18, and Richard, 19, certainly made full use of the many bars and hot spots. During the day, we all swam and windsurfed. We also walked around the Rock, or thought we could, until

Richard, Lorna, Alex and Gaere

we found a military blockade in the tunnel, which takes military traffic into the very center of the Rock and out the other side, We must have looked a forlorn group, because an army truck came along and the driver said, "Hop in, mates." We did, and got a privileged view of all the installations inside the Rock. We, of course, all went to the top of the Rock and visited with the very aggressive Barbary apes that have had a colony there for hundreds of years. On the 15th of September, 1979, we celebrated Lorna's 18th birthday at the Holiday Inn on Main Street, quite a night, as it was now legal for Lorna to drink.

As our intended departure date of 7th October approached, I don't think any crewmember didn't feel a little sadness at leaving the Rock. We only had one crewmember still to pick up. That was Renaud Mueller, in the Canary Islands, where we would head when we left Gibraltar.

27 ISLE DES EMBIEZ TO FLORIDA, PART 2

The log read 2585 on October 7, 1979. We pulled up anchor in Gibraltar ready to face very open water for the next 600 miles to the Canary Islands. Our plan was to cross the straits to Tangier and to stay overnight. Alex, Lorna, Gaere and Richard had never been to Morocco before, and I had described it as a fun place from previous visits. In perfect sailing weather we crossed in company with *Rondalay*, a husband, wife, and two daughters plus Tosca, the dog. We were to get to know Walter, Lee, Lynn, and Ann very well in the next ten days. However we didn't know this at the time. We pulled into Tangier in a strong wind with all sails up and drawing, not knowing that these winds were the precursor of Hurricane David, a hurricane that was to cross the Atlantic and do billions of dollars worth of damage to the Caribbean islands and then mainland U.S.A. By midnight, the wind was blowing 60 mph, and any thought of continuing to the Canaries at this time had to be dropped. We had previously arranged to meet Renaud, the sixth crew member, in Los Christianos on November 6th, so we still had plenty of time.

Tristan in Tangier

The next ten days were spent in a whirl of Moroccan fun, accompanied by the Hawleys on *Rondalay*. We covered everything Tangier had to offer. One of the high spots was a visit to Restaurant Hamadi, an authentic ethnic restaurant, complete with music from all kinds of exotic instruments. We all had a chance to play these at one time or another, and at the end of a very long dinner we posed for photos with the musicians. Ann and Lynn had culture shock in the open market, where every kind of food was on display, both alive and dead. Bread was put out on the sidewalk for you to choose, while chickens, alive and plucked, were hanging by their legs awaiting their fate. Meat of all kinds was hanging with an attendant cloud of flies. As Walter observed, these two American girls were unaware that milk comes from cows, not supermarkets. We visited mosques and carpet factories, where we saw young children sitting at looms, weaving and knotting carpets of great beauty. Alex, Lorna, and the girls required a male chaperone at all times, but gradually after some days, we became "the yacht people" who were waiting for the weather. Solicitors of all kinds stopped harassing us, market people let us alone to make our choice, and the atmosphere was congenial.

One evening Gaere, Richard, and I were walking in the Casbah, and a man sidled over and asked us, "Would you like to buy a diamond ring?" We really hadn't given such a purchase much thought, but thought it might be a good idea to take a look. He produced this enormous apparent diamond from a velvet sack, and it was in a beautiful setting. He proceeded to demonstrate its authenticity by cutting glass with it. All kinds of fears raced into our minds, including that this was stolen property, and after making the sale to us, he might report us to the police. Then we would spend a number of dreary years in jail. So we declined, and for the next few days, we kept seeing him. Each time, he would renew his offer at a lower price. Each time we declined, and, of course, sailed away from the deal of the century, or was it?

It was the 17th of October, and ten days had been spent in Tangier. Both the Hawleys on *Rondalay* and the crew of *Intsholo* were ready for sea. At 11 am and 2619 on the log, we both motored out of the harbor bound for Santa Cruz, Canary Islands. For the first two days and three nights, the winds were favorable and the boat was making a steady 6 and 1/2 to 7 and 1/2 knots. At 10 pm on the first night, we blew out the number 1 genoa. We needed to be more careful in the future, and look for oncoming gusts by studying the sky. I made a note in the log that there was a very high swell running, probably left over from the hurricane. It was enough to make Richard seasick, but he still stood his watches all night. Our watch system was two people at night, doing two hours on, two off. In the daytime when it was easier to see what was going on, we had one person on for one hour and four hours off. I had taken out the sextant again, and found that we had a considerable error in our first night's course. I thought we had made more than 170 miles, but the sight taken at noon on the second day reduced that to 148 miles. By midday on the 18th, the wind dropped to nil, and we had to resort to motor, never comfortable in a big swell. As there was no pressure on the rudder from the sails, we put on the autopilot and it almost immediately broke down. What's new? At 7 pm, we turned it on again expecting nothing. Eureka! It worked, so Dudley steered the night watch.

The 19th saw a light wind and an overcast sky, which turned to light rain, with the sky becoming more and more stormy. We were rolling along at a steady 4 knots. As darkness fell, all the crew was feeling comfortable and happy. We really felt everything was going well, and Gaere served up a delicious chicken curry.

By 4 am, on the 20th the wind and swell both disappeared completely, and we were left on a glass-like sea with lightning flashing all around. It was very warm, or should I say hot. During this still period, the first of many birds landed on deck, presumably for a rest. On close inspection, the little birds had no usable legs. They just flopped around. They are called Mother Carey's Chickens, and just ply the oceans, taking rest where they can find it.

I was able to get a good fix at noon on the 20th and to everyone's satisfaction we had made 160 miles in the previous 24 hours. This left just

First fish

235 miles to our destination of Santa Cruz. All day we played with the sails trying to get a little more speed. I had noted 25 sail changes in the 24 hours.

The night of the 20th/21st was a brilliant starlit night with only one ship sighted and a flat calm sea, with negligible swell. Needless to say we were under motor and doing about 6 knots. It was Sunday; we had a scrambled egg and bacon breakfast, and prepared pork chops for dinner. The pork chops went back in the freezer when, at 3 pm, we caught our first fish, a 4 and 1/2 pound bonito. There was great excitement from Gaere and Richard who had been working hard at this since the beginning of the voyage. I must explain that our fishing equipment was not of the rod and reel variety, but a huge reel fastened to the pushpit of the boat, complete at this time with 50-pound test line, later changed to 200-pound test. The reel had a progressive brake on the drum, which could be cranked down to a stop. A handle on each side made it possible for two people to reel in a fish.

This was the 21st of October and it proved a relatively busy day, apart from the fish and egg breakfast. Showers for the whole crew from a bag of water suspended from the mizzen boom. The sighting of a cruise ship *The Black Prince,* which we called on VHF, resulted in an exact position, which was the same as ours. This put us just 92 miles from Santa Cruz and a certain landfall the following morning. By this time, we were getting some wind from the northeast and once more much experimentation with sails. We settled into a pattern of main, mizzen staysail, and cruising chute, the latter being of enormous size and requiring a boom for stability. With this rig, we were able to keep up 9–10 knots, which was our maximum hull speed.

Bath time

Pulling into the harbor of Santa Cruz at 6:30 am on the 22nd we realized that this harbor had nothing for us at all. I made the notation, "Harbor foul in every respect and no space available", so the decision was made to sail the 45 miles on to Los Christianos, which was to be the departure point for the actual crossing. It proved a good decision, and we arrived under main and cruising chute at 4:30 pm. The harbor was very exposed from the southwest, and the swell was a constant nuisance. We were in good company, because apart from a number of yachts doing the same as us, some years earlier Christopher Columbus had made his first of several crossings from Los Christianos.

Our voyage from Tangier took five days and three hours, the log now registered 3238 miles, a distance by log of 619 miles, but with the Canaries current's assistance we had covered 702 miles. On arrival the dingy was inflated, and Gaere and Lorna went ashore for shopping and a look around. The remainder of the crew and captain went to sleep or even died! We made a small side trip from Los Christianos to Los Gigantes, a resort complex with a harbor that must have been designed by someone who knew nothing about the ocean. The swell coming around the breakwater was at least 10 feet high, and all the floating docks were rising and falling in a snake-like action. This was accentuated at the ends of the docks, which acted like whips. To tie up to one of these was dangerous and the backwash created a turbulence resembling a washing machine. We found a place in the corner of the harbor, which was relatively quiet and went to the hotel to make contact with our friends Ian, Ann and Suzanne Long. They were the owners of a restaurant near Penzance that we often visited. They had offered to bring out our mail, when they came on a holiday to Los Gigantes. There was a lot of mail, but we put this aside in order to invite them to lunch aboard. This proved impractical as Ian felt seasick, so we transferred to the shore and had a pleasant visit. It was obvious that it wasn't going to be safe to spend the night there, so at 3:30 pm, we left at full speed out of the harbor. I was very concerned that we could be picked up by one of the swells and dashed against the harbor wall. I asked Ian to stand on the end of the wall to time the swells, and to tell us by shouting how far away the next one was. This worked and we just missed being dashed to pieces. About two hours later, we were safe back in the Los Christianos harbor, anchored next to *Escape* with Alan and Elaine Jeter from Charleston, South Carolina. They would become good friends along with people from the many other boats anchored in the harbor.

Our biggest disappointment was the non-appearance of *Rondalay* and the Hawleys, who turned up several days later. It transpired that they'd had trouble with their steering and returned to Tangier for repairs, losing several days in the process. It was now the 26th of October and we had little to do other than swim and windsurf in the vast open anchorage that was Los Christianos. We did have quite a few stores to buy, in particular wine, which was stored in every conceivable crevice in the bilge. It is impossible to know how many bottles were on board, but I do know only one was broken on the voyage.

One incident is worth recounting. We were all swimming off the boat in the early evening when one of us noticed a tremendous confusion in the water behind us. In seconds we were surrounded by a large school of bonito, and in the midst of the school came a huge swordfish thrashing with its sword. The bonito were being thrown feet in the air by the swordfish. The whole event was over in a few seconds, but was a near miss for us, as I'm sure the swordfish would in his feeding frenzy not have noticed us swimming amongst his prey. A few minutes later the swordfish cruised back past the boat, gulping down all the injured or stunned bonito.

All we were waiting for now was the arrival of Renaud to complete our crew, and even more importantly, the arrival of the easterly trade winds that would carry us across the ocean to the Caribbean. The log read 3251 miles.

28 ISLE DES EMBIEZ TO FLORIDA, PART 3

On November 6, 1979, Renaud arrived on time and persuaded someone on the beach to take him out to *Intsholo*. After the initial greetings and introduction to Richard, who he had not met, he asked, "When are we leaving?" To be quite honest, we hadn't thought too much about it, and, after a little pause, he said, "How about the day after tomorrow?" So we were set on a date of departure being the 8th of November. Gaere and I had repaired the damaged number 1 genoa, and a fellow yachtsman and sailmaker was repairing the cruising chute. This had been torn coming around the end of the island of Tenerife, by a sudden and very heavy gust of wind that put us on our beam ends for a few moments. He said he would have it finished the following day. With the last loading of stores and wine complete, and all sails in their locker, we were ready to sail.

What a bunch

On the morning of the 8th of November, 1979, having celebrated Alex's birthday the night before, and with the full crew now assembled, we said our goodbyes to the anchorage and made ready for sea. We pulled up the anchor at 5:30 pm, with the log reading 3265

Leaving the Canaries

miles, took the dinghy aboard and deflated it, stowing the outboard on the aft rail. With a clear sky and confident crew, we headed out of the anchorage to the blowing of many horns and whistles and ringing bells of the remaining boats, all of whom in their own time would receive the same sendoff. It was very moving, and helped compensate for the complete lack of wind outside the harbor. With the engine running at 1400 rpm for the next 6 and 1/2 hours, it gave us 5 and 1/4 knots in fairly calm seas. Gaere prepared pork chops, and everyone felt ready for the watch system to begin, two on at night for three hours, until 8 am, when it was one on for one hour each until 8 pm. The watches were Renaud and Gaere, Richard and Lorna, and Alex and Tristan. This proved a fine system, until the clock caught up with us, as I'd had the idea of sailing on Greenwich Mean Time all the way across the ocean. As we proceeded west at just over 150 miles a day, every 3rd day or so we should have put our clocks back by one hour. Not doing so created a situation where lunch was at breakfast and so forth. The original idea came from a thought that would make navigation easier, never having to make allowances for how far west we had sailed. Having scrapped this system, life became more regulated.

At 12:15 am, the first signs of the easterly trades were felt, and all hands were on deck to take advantage of the wind, which slowly increased to 12 to 15 knots. At this time we were steering a southerly course towards the Cape Verde islands in order to pick up stronger trade winds, which are stronger in the southerly latitudes. By morning, having made several adjustments to the sails, as the wind continued to rise, I made the decision to steer a course more or less directly for Barbados, our first destination in the Caribbean. It proved to be the right decision as the wind continued to rise, until we didn't need it any stronger by going further south. In fact, the log book shows continued activity in sail changes to find the right balance. The self-steering vane was working well, which took a lot of pressure off the watches. Day two resulted in a day's run of 156 miles, with the log showing 3397 miles. As night descended Gaere and Renaud took the first watch after dinner. It was a bright starlit night and *Intsholo* roared through the water at 6 and 1/2 to 7 and 1/2 knots, with the wind on the port quarter.

Sailing hard

Day three, with all the crew resting well, I made a few notes in the log that we were on the "bus," so to speak. Flying a poled-out genoa and altering the course slightly to reduce the amount of roll from a heavy swell, nothing changed. Toward evening, the wind, ever changing, decided to reduce enough for us to try flying the chute on the starboard side and a poled-out number 1 genoa to port. This is the classic rig for trade wind sailing, with no other sail up to steal the wind from the two foresails. Gaere unfortunately got a rope burn on his hands from the halyard while raising the chute. After an adjustment over a period of 45 minutes, we finally had it right and were able to have dinner in the salon with the wind vane doing the work. At midnight on day four, I noted our best day yet of 162 miles, with Lorna and Richard on watch on a beautiful night and still running wing-and-wing, i.e., chute and genoa.

Day five produced another 160-mile run and a catalogue of sail changes throughout the day, with the wind increasing and a slight course change necessary. This had been caused by the nearly two days of east northeast winds slowly putting us closer to the Cape Verdes than necessary. At 9:30 am, we took the chute down and an intermediate jib was raised, and that evening we had a whiskey and a chat in the cockpit before a dinner of spaghetti bolognaise—yum!! This was the first time we had felt comfortable enough to socialize and have an alcoholic drink all together. By now we were at latitude 21 degrees north and it was quite hot. Our standard clothing was a swimsuit and a light coverup for night watches. I had made a rule that shoes should be worn on deck to avoid injury to feet, etc. This rule was broken shortly after it was announced. Similarly, we had all agreed that smoking should be only on deck, but it wasn't very long before a cigarette was enjoyed after dinner and then at any time anyone felt the need. I wasn't smoking at the time, but I had to start again in self-defense. We had another good day's run of 160 miles, with no untoward incidents. Our position at noon was 20 degrees 56 minutes north latitude, 23 degrees 43 minutes west longitude, and sailing at a steady 6 and 1/2 knots day and night.

Six and a half knots had become our standard expected speed; if it fell below, adjustments to the sails were made. As day six started, we realized that this was to be a busy day. The wind came up and went down almost as quickly. Then it blew from the starboard side, and we had our foresail poled out from the starboard side. This required moving the pole to port, not an easy task with the sail full and the roll of the boat. Then of course the wind changed to the opposite quarter and the whole thing had to be repeated. If the wind was immediately aft, the two foresails would be raised on their own separate poles. At 6:30 pm, there was a notation (not in my writing) in the log: "Freak wave broke over port quarter swamping skipper's wife, who dived to keep Tristan dry. It came through the main hatch and washed the salon for us."

There was a growing or should I say a "ripening" problem aboard *Intsholo* by day six. Before leaving the Canaries, we had ventured into the countryside in search of a banana plantation. I bought a stem of bananas weighing 48 pounds, figuring that the fresh fruit would be welcome. We stored them forward on the port side and by day six, with the sun shining mostly on the port side, the whole stem was beginning to ripen in unison. What to do, as this was a valuable food source. The answer was simple. Each person when coming on watch had to eat a banana. I must explain that a Canary Island banana is smaller than those we have become accustomed to. Occasionally I would catch a transgressor of the banana rule, and there was chastisement of some kind or another.

The sixth day had a day's run of 164 miles and a distance from the Canaries of 676 miles; on the seventh day at sea, we got off to a bad start. At 3 am, with Lorna and Richard on watch, *Intsholo* made a very heavy jibe and broke the shackle of the kicking strap. This was replaced and a preventer was attached to the end of the main boom. It was taken aft to one of the winches and secured. A jibe is when the main boom comes across from the port to the starboard side or vice versa, uncontrolled. If serious enough, it can break backstays or other equipment. This jibe had been caused by a slight wind shift that caught our self-steering vane by surprise, and it didn't correct the boat's course in time. At 5:30 pm, after a really fast day, I took a sight with the sextant which showed a day's run of 174 miles. This day was not over by any means, and at 9:30 pm the wind was increasing. The auxiliary rudder of our self-steering vane snapped off at the end of the shaft. This meant hand steering for the remainder of the voyage. In order to make steering easier, we flew two foresails with two poles to stabilize them as much as possible.

Navigating

As day eight opened it was obvious that the weather, despite the clear skies, was getting windier with occasional line squalls hitting us. At 3:15 am, Alex was hit in the shoulder by a very small bird, which fell into the cockpit at her feet. It was unable to stand so we wrapped it lightly in a cloth and it stayed for quite a while. Also, a good sized flying fish landed on deck, which Richard cooked for breakfast. We all had boiled eggs and bananas, as well as the fish. The sea was building and there were house-sized waves following us. On the top of each wave, the boat accelerated to

10+ knots and then was held back as it climbed out of the trough, sometimes losing the wind completely. Still running under the twins and going very fast, I decided to trail two 100-yard lengths of rope, to slow us down and avoid a broach. This

Renaud eating a carrot

can occur if a boat is traveling at the same speed as the wave system, and the wave takes hold of the boat and turns it sideways to the oncoming waves. These ropes created a much better motion and a greater ease for steering. The day's run was a record to date of 181 miles, with a total distance of 1156 miles.

November 16 dawned with massive seas, the height of a two-story house coming up behind and then passing us by, dropping the boat into the trough. I decided to trail two more 100-yard ropes, and all four of them could be seen behind, trailing on the surface and breaking up the waves before they came down on us. We decided to change the night watch system to two hours on and four off. This made it easier to hand steer, because it required a lot of concentration especially at night when it was not possible to see what was coming up behind. I made the notation that all the crew were rested and well, and still eating bacon and eggs for breakfast. We had a little trouble with the engine not starting that day. The engine was needed for generating electricity. After bleeding the fuel system, I was able to start it. I think the fuel had been so stirred up in its tanks that an air bubble resulted. After an excellent lunch of home-pickled herring, we pulled aboard one of the trailing ropes as the sea had gone down quite a bit. By 5:30 pm, all were sleeping except Alex and me. The evening sight gave me a day's run of 180 miles, distance covered 1336 miles. At 6:30 pm, we had a rain shower with more to come, generally a very murky night with a fairly comfortable swell on the starboard quarter.

Saturday the 17th of November dawned cloudy, but with a much reduced sea, allowing us to pull in the other three trailing ropes. On trying to start the generator, it wouldn't, and the same with the main engine. I bled both fuel systems, and had them running within an hour. The next disaster was that the freezer was no longer cold. With daytime temperatures in the 80s and 90s, we had little choice but to cook up all the meats we were storing for the remainder of the voyage. By 3 pm, all meats were cooked and in the refrigerator or in our stomachs. We found the new motion of the boat very restful, rolling along at 6 and 1/2 knots with 20 knots of wind dead aft. This was sailing at its best. We were flying a genoa and a large jib, both poled out. At 5:30 pm, I took a sight and the day's run was 210 miles with the log at 4443 miles.

Sunday, the 18th of November at 9:30 am, I turned the chart over and could see the Caribbean side of the ocean, instead of the African side. We had a double bacon and egg breakfast to celebrate. Showers or rather salt water baths were taken on the aft deck, using a gallon jug suspended from the mizzen boom. We had a plastic bathtub that we gallantly filled for the ladies. Richard was in charge of getting the water by the bucketful. He lost two buckets and the ropes with which they were supposed to be attached in quick succession. I couldn't teach him how to do it, because we had no more buckets. The best alternative we could find was a canvas bag made by Albert Willoughby many years before. A new piece of rope was attached to one of the rope handles, and the art was to throw it in so that the bag scooped up water. Richard nearly went over with his first bag full. I still have that bag, which we used for the rest of the journey. I managed to get the freezer restarted and we proceeded to refreeze all of the cooked meat and fish we had thought we would never be able to eat in time. Gaere cooked beef burgers in the evening on the grill attached to the pushpit. At 8 pm, the chute was reset with a pole and the number 1 genoa on the opposite side. We tried to rig windsurfer sails under the two to catch a little more wind, but it didn't work very well. We would try again the next day. I wrote in the log that the distance run at 5:30 pm, was 161 miles.

The 19th of November, day 12, started badly when I tried to start the engine at 12:30 am—no go. Throughout the night we spent a lot of time raising and lowering different sails to try to keep the speed up. In fact, there were 29 sail changes in the 24 hours. I repaired the engine by 2 pm and we had to use the main engine for generation from there to Barbados, as the generator was no longer serviceable. At 5:30 pm, our day's run was 155 miles, so we were still keeping up a good average despite much reduced wind. At 7:15 pm, we saw a tanker on the horizon. I raised them on the VHF. He confirmed our position, and we made a small correction to the south. We had a long talk with the radio operator, finding out that the vessel was the *Golden Sunray,* registered in Singapore, with an empty tank, going to Beaumont, Texas to fill with oil. He mentioned that he had seen two more yachts going in the same direction a couple of days before.

The 20th of November, day 13, was mostly the same scenario, a continued struggle to keep up a decent speed with the light winds from the east northeast. At 2:30 am, we spotted a single white light a good distance off. On calling on the VHF we immediately knew it was Alan and Elaine Jeter from Charleston, North Carolina in *Escape*. His southern accent was so recognizable! We swapped stories with him, particularly about fishing, in which they had been very successful. Up to this point, we had caught only one fish. We had lost a lot of lures, but I think we were sailing too fast to catch fish. In the morning, there was no evidence of *Escape* and although we left five days after them, we had to wait three more days for them to arrive in Barbados. At 5:30 pm, we had a day's run of 149 miles, which put us just over 700 miles from Barbados. Each day's run was increased by the favorable west-flowing Canary current, which would give as much as 25 miles that the log would not record.

Lorna

Wednesday the 21st of November, day 14, saw us making a good speed of 6 knots throughout the day and night. Both Alex and Lorna were not well with a stomach upset. I was able with the much calmer seas really to concentrate on the generator and the main engine. Gaere, Richard, and Renaud also had a repair day, and by the end of the day, everything was running for the first time in 14 days. This was cause for a small celebration as we headed into the night. Distance run for the day was 154 miles and a total distance of 2038 miles.

The 22nd of November was day 15. The most exciting thing to happen was that two whales were very close on the starboard bow. They frightened Lorna when they suddenly blew right beside her. She was on watch at the time. At 3:45 pm, we caught our first fish, a mahi weighing 2.2 pounds. Guess what was for dinner that night? We all went to bed feeling well, and pleased with the day's run of 136 miles. At 8:30 pm, the wind changed, allowing us to fly the chute once more as the wind had shifted more to the starboard quarter. A quartering wind was our fastest point of sail.

Mahi

Friday, the 23rd of November, day 15, started with an all hands on deck at 1:30 am. The problem was a huge squall with a lot of wind and rain. We just managed to get the chute down in time, then retired below and let the autopilot, which had suddenly begun to work again, do the steering for the next hour or so. I must mention that for a while we used the autopilot to allow us all to have dinner together. The autopilot didn't seem to mind this light duty. We saw another cargo vessel at 5:30 pm, but no answer on VHF or single sideband radio. The day's run was 143 miles, which put us about 350 miles from Barbados.

Saturday, the 24th of November, day 16, was another light wind day and very hot. We were now on latitude 13 degrees north, well inside the tropics, and we were sailing with the chute and a number 1 genoa at 5 and 1/2 knots. The genoa was badly frayed on the foot, where it came over the pulpit. This would be a repair job when we got to port. We had moved into such a comfortable routine that none of us was looking forward to landfall. Although land was upwind of us, we could all distinctly smell the familiar smells of life. I suppose it was because of the incredibly clear air we had been breathing. Throughout this passage, there were two pieces of music that will forever remain in my mind. The first was "Country Roads" by Olivia Newton John, sung continuously by Richard. The second was, "I Wonder Who's Kissing Her Now," which was the plaintive cry of Renaud, who was missing his wife, Yola. Strangely only a year or so after the voyage, Renaud left his wife and children for another woman. Perhaps someone was "kissing her now." The day's run was 133 miles and the distance run 2471 miles.

Sunday, 25th November, day 17, brought engine trouble again. It started but the alternator would not charge the batteries, either domestic or engine. At breakfast it was decided to keep the engine on, for fear of our not being able to restart it without battery power. By 10 am, with the chute and genoa winged out with poles, we were making good time.

At 4 pm, I made the notation of squally weather with rain and very heavy wind. We made ten sail changes in the hour between 4 and 5 pm. At 5:30 pm, the day's run was 148 miles with a distance run of 2752 miles. As night came on, the excitement built, and the competition to be the first to see the lights of Barbados began. Gaere won with the sighting of the loom of Ragged Point lighthouse dead ahead at 11 pm. Incidentally, this was the exact point that we had been aiming for.

November 26th, day 18. At 1 am, Ragged Point light was abeam and we were still sailing fast, with the wind on our starboard quarter. At 6:57 am on that Monday morning, we dropped anchor in five fathoms of water off the beach known as the careenage. Since those historic days when ships would be hauled up on the sand and laid over for bottom cleaning, it has been renamed the Esso Dock.

I have made the notation that, "Immediately on arrival a magnum of Piper Heidsieck was opened and a celebration ensued." There was no need for that comment, because none of us will ever forget the feeling of achievement, despite the many difficulties from equipment that often failed. But here we were 2836 miles from our starting point, all healthy and happy. I think that as a family we could never have been closer, and of course I include Richard and Renaud in that feeling.

29 CRUISING THE GREATER ANTILLES

After our crossing of the Atlantic in 18 days—a record by a sailboat under 50 feet in length—we took a little time to settle down to life at anchor and not having to dash up on deck for sail changes or other emergencies. Our most immediate disappointment was when Renaud announced that he was leaving on our day of arrival. By 10:30 am, he was on his way to the airport, just over three hours after arrival. He would not be dissuaded, despite the proposed celebratory meal at the Holiday Inn down the road. Perhaps his ditty, "I Wonder Who's Kissing Her Now," had become real to him. I think he was very jealous.

I suppose the most exciting thing that happened to us over the next several days and weeks was the arrival of our sailing friends, each with their own particular story of their crossing. I think perhaps the person whose visit gave us the most pleasure was Fred's. We never knew his last name, nor anything much about him. He sailed in a wreck of a boat, and came across to see us in a half-deflated dinghy, to say hello. His had been a harrowing journey of 35 days, with only one other completely inexperienced crew member. They made it. I don't recall ever seeing him again in any of the other islands.

We made several land contacts; some were from my father's stay in Barbados, and other acquaintances that we made on shore. I must mention Ian and Mary Dowding, who had been my father's closest friends. They took care of all our incoming mail. We wanted to avail ourselves of their auto rental business, and the car that everybody wanted to rent was the "Mini Moke", a Caribbean version of the Mini that was popular at that time. After a few days in the anchorage, we realized that security was not too good. Leaving the boat unattended was asking for trouble. Indeed, Alan and Elaine's *Escape* lying next door was broken into and a number of items were stolen. When the police turned up to investigate, the very black policeman wearing heavy boots was told by Alan not too subtly, "I could smell that damn n…. as soon as I came aboard." Like most crime in the Caribbean, this and others went unsolved, so it was decided we would always have at least one person on board. The consequence of this was that we saw much less of the island than we would have liked.

Meanwhile, repairs went on at a rapid pace. The ailing engine and generator had professional attention, arranged by the Dowdings. All the sails that had chafed on the voyage were repaired by the crew. The most important repair was to the auxiliary rudder for the self-steering vane. This was taken on by Richard, who borrowed the workshop of Val and Alan Knowles, who lived nearby. He proceeded to graft a new piece onto the stump that was left. With careful reinforcement, this rudder was a lot stronger than the original.

Shopping in Bridgetown was undertaken by Alex and Lorna, with a male companion to help carry the groceries. After stocking up our now-working refrigerator freezer, we thought about leaving for the islands to leeward. Our choice, and everyone else's, was to make for Bequia. At a wonderful party at Alan, Val and Debbie Knowles' house on the beach, we were introduced to goat roties and other Caribbean specialties.

We set sail on the 17th of December for Bequia, to celebrate Christmas and the New Year in beautiful Admiralty Bay. There was plenty of room for anchoring, and we chose a spot near Dave and Trish Webb on *Esperance*, founding a friendship that would last for the whole trip. Spending Christmas in Bequia included two walks across the island to see Walter Bino—first to order lobsters, and second to collect them. These made for a feast on Christmas day. Walter was an interesting man, being a member of a family of albino blacks. The whole family led a life of seclusion on the windward side of the island, whether by choice or exclusion we were not to find out.

The Frangipani bar and restaurant was too full to include us on Christmas Eve, but we made a reservation for New Year's Eve. This was always the happening place, and not many nights went by that they didn't host a "jump up." This was the Caribbean name for a party, which originated from a wedding ceremony, where the bride and groom had to jump over a broom.

After Christmas and before our New Year's reservation, we decided to sail over to the island of Mustique. We had company on the voyage, Carl and Priscilla Poster on *Galaxy*, who wanted to come too. Of course it resulted in a race—they took the passage to windward, and we took the leeward. They won by five minutes. I was completely disgusted by our performance. We anchored in 20 feet of water in Grand Bay. We had never experienced such a beautiful tropical place before. We all went ashore to a bar right on the beach, and a short walk to the store.

The next day was spent snorkeling and swimming in the beautiful, clear water of the anchorage. I had to take myself to bed, as a cut on my leg had become septic, and the poison was spreading up my leg. I started taking antibiotics, but it wasn't until we went back to Bequia the following day that I was told by our friend Alan Jeter of *Escape* that I had a serious infection, and that I must stay out of the bacteria-filled water for two weeks. Alan was a doctor, and our friendship came in handy more than once on our voyage.

After a day off in Mustique, which everyone except me enjoyed, we set sail for St. Vincent to do some shopping, and arrange a barbecue on the beach in Cumberland Bay for Dave and Trish from *Esperance*. The event was Trish's brother's and would-be sister-in-law's wedding. The shopping was easy. We pulled into Kingston Bay and tied up to the dock, with a walk ashore where there were good shops and markets. To arrange the barbecue was much more difficult. We sailed in tandem with *Esperance* up to a bay on the west side of St. Vincent that fit the description on the chart of Cumberland Bay. On sailing in close to the shore, all kinds of watercraft came out to meet us, and the people tried to clamber on board to sell us something. We were very concerned, as a very famous yachtsman had lost his wife on one of these bays just a few months before. The scenario was dreadfully similar. He had said he didn't want to buy anything, and the people who had boarded his yacht had turned ugly and shot his wife. He got away by starting the engine and motoring out, with the killers bailing out as he left the bay. No charges were ever brought.

We found by deduction that we had gone one bay too far, and motored down to the real Cumberland Bay. We anchored off the beach, rowed in and spoke to the chief about Dave's requirements. He was very confident that he could put on a wonderful goat roast on the beach, with vegetables, salads and desserts. Looking around, I certainly had my doubts, but Dave, being a confident New Yorker, handed over a $100 bill, and said he would be back. We rowed out to our two boats, upped anchor, and sailed back to Bequia for our New Year's celebration. After a great meal at The Frangipani, we saw in New Year 1980 on board *Intsholo III* with a large group of friends. I do remember that people kept jumping over the side, either to cool off, sober up or have a swim.

January 1 was a day to sober up; the next day, we sailed back to St. Vincent, where we tied to the dock. Foolishly, I decided to walk the few hundred yards to town. I hadn't got off the dock before I realized that I had someone right beside me. I felt a knife in the small of my back, and the man said, "Keep walking," which I did. I could see a corner ahead, and it was my intention to break for it, with a sharp left turn. As I approached the corner, a policeman came around it, and on seeing the situation, he shouted at the man, "Get out of here!" He did, and I breathed a sigh of relief. I had no money, watch or anything of value on me at the time. I went straight back to the boat, and we cast off with Dave and Trish for Cumberland Bay and his barbecue. We had a fast sail up the island's lee shore and put in to the correct bay this time. We anchored close to shore, and took ropes back to the palm trees on the beach. For some reason we both took a rope in, and then doubled it back to the boat so that we would be able to pull them back to the boat without having to go to shore. This done, we all climbed into our inflatables, and made for shore, where a number of people were congregating. We thought it was in preparation for the barbecue.

There was a fairly large swell running, large enough to get everyone wet on landing. Dave found the chief, and asked him about the barbecue preparations. He looked vaguely at Dave, who immediately became combative. It transpired that there was no goat or anything else. Dave told him, with many expletives, that he better come up with something, and fast. The whole village was in a turmoil of activity as we sat on the beach waiting. We had some wine, until the goat turned up, freshly killed. A fire was lit and the cooking proceeded. As you may imagine, this took some time. We were tired, Dave was angry, and the villagers were belligerent. Eventually the goat was served, but no one had much appetite for it, and there was little else supplied.

As the darkness closed in and the fire burned down, we couldn't help but be aware of a circle of black faces, with glittering eyes like tigers in the night, surrounding us. All of them were sitting on their haunches, and it looked like trouble was coming. Dave picked up the goat, and threw it at them, with more expletives. They descended on it. We all looked at each other, and moved toward the inflatables on the beach. We got everybody launched into the surf, and the chief came down to ask for his money. You will have to imagine the conversation between Dave and him. Dave had no intention of paying another cent. We all arrived back on our boats, and hauled in the lines around the palm trees as the locals took to their boats. Dave came out with a gun, and they retreated. We spent a very restless night, with a guard on each boat as we swung to our anchors. It is impossible to sail or move at night because of unmarked hazards and reefs everywhere. So, that was the wedding feast that never was.

On the morning of the 3rd of January, we thought we might like to see some more of the Grenadines, so by mid morning we were sailing fast at

8 knots for Canouan and Mayero, catching a large barracuda on the way. At that time, we were unaware of the saguaterra poisoning you could get from eating this fish, especially large ones. When we arrived in the beautiful anchorage of Canouan, a fisherman rowed out and offered us eight lobsters for 21 B.W.I. dollars, perhaps $7 American. The purchase was made, and after a good lunch and swim, we headed to Mayero and Salt Whistle Bay, an idyllic Caribbean bay. The bay was almost completely land-locked, with a sandy beach and palm trees all around. We all took a walk up the one hill on the island, and met the Roman Catholic Curé who had a small mission on the island. From the top of the hill, we had a wonderful view down to the south to Union and Carriacou islands, and beyond to Tobago Cays. The water in these islands is crystal clear and between 10 and 20 feet deep, making for wonderful anchorages. The five of us easily ate the eight lobsters that night, and all agreed that the next day should be devoted to snorkeling, swimming, windsurfing and just relaxing.

After a thoroughly restful day, we sailed off the next morning for the Tobago Cays. Because of the extremely shallow water, we thought that a voyage of exploration via dinghy would be sensible. This completed, we sailed back to Canouan for the night and on to Bequia the following morning, where we were reunited with *Esperance* and *Prana*. The whole crew except Lorna was sick the next day, probably from the barbecue we'd had the night before.

By the 13th of January, we thought we should be heading north to Martinique, to meet my sister Wendy and her husband Ernst, so, sadly, we left Bequia that morning. We stopped off in the Blue Lagoon, on the southern tip of St. Vincent. This was the nearest thing to a marina since we left Gibraltar. The depth of the entrance was really not sufficient, and both going in and coming out the next morning, we skipped across the bottom. We were in for a hard sail, as there was a big sea running and plenty of wind. We laid a course for Vieux Fort on the island of St. Lucia, but soon realized that we weren't going to make it. We let off a bit of sail, and headed for Castries, the capital, passing a very prominent feature called the Pitons, on the way up the island. I made a note in the log that the wind was blowing hard from the east northeast, with big seas and lots of water on deck. We had lost contact with *Esperance* as they were far behind. They changed their minds, and went for the milder but longer route to leeward of the islands.

By 5:30 pm that afternoon, we dropped our anchor in Vigie Cove, only to be told we had to go over to the main harbor to get clearance—in other words, to pay a fee. After formalities, we went back to the cove and waited for *Esperance* to show up, which they did just after midnight. They had experienced a very bad passage indeed, and were very tired. It was their intention to leave their boat in Castries for a week or two, while Dave went on an assignment for *Time* magazine. On seeing the harbor and the state of the people onshore, they suggested that Gaere, Lorna, and Richard could sail their boat north in tandem with *Intsholo III*. This was an extraordinary vote of confidence in the abilities of all three. We agreed, and the following day, they set sail for Fort de France, Martinique, on their own, as we wanted to get a burst water tank welded. We said we would catch up with them in a week or so. As soon as they had left, Alex and I set to work dismantling the dinette to extract the water tank. We hoisted it into the dinghy and went into Castries, where we found a taxi that could take us to a welding shop. After several attempts, they had it repaired, and after getting it out of the dinghy and onboard, we reinstalled it. There were five separate water tanks onboard, which were all interconnected, so if one leaked, they all leaked. This repair cost under $20 and took most of the welder's day.

On the 21st of January, 1980, Alex and I rented a car for a day and toured the island of St. Lucia, revisiting the Pitons and several volcanic sites. It was a wonderful drive through tropical forests that neither of us had experienced before. At the end of the day, we stopped off at the airport where we were to meet Richard Bate, one of our partners in The Bear Essentials restaurant. The plane arrived, and sometime after every passenger had left the plane, we enquired at the terminal whether he was on board. We were told that, yes, he was a passenger, and one of the flight attendants went back on board to find him. He was sound asleep, and didn't know they had landed. We got back to the boat and he settled in very fast. The following day, it was decided to go south to visit Marigot Bay, a lovely small bay almost completely enclosed, with a restaurant-bar on the side of the hill overlooking the bay. The restaurant was called Dr. Doolittle's, and proved to be a great place for a drink (pina coladas), a meal or an ice cream (papaya). Alex became very enthusiastic about pina coladas, and we both enjoyed the papaya ice cream so much we spent another day lying around eating and drinking. Richard was always exceptional company on this and other visits he made to us.

While lying in Marigot Bay, we were swimming in the rather landlocked waters, and a young lady came across in her dinghy to advise us it was unsafe to swim in the bay. We thanked her for her advice, and continued swimming. We didn't know at the time that Hilary and her husband Derek from *Summerun*, registered in Cape Town, South Africa, were destined to play a major part in our future lives.

After leaving Marigot Bay, we returned to Castries harbor, and spent a few days in town and touring the island. As Gaere, Lorna and Richard had left for Martinique, sailing *Esperance*, the guest Richard, Alex, and I were able to fit into a rental car, and we toured volcanic sites on the island's west side, and its incredibly lush rainforest.

The darker side of this paradise was displayed afterwards when we returned to the boat and went to bed. In the middle of the night, a gunshot woke everyone in the anchorage. After looking around, seeing nothing of interest, and exchanging a few words with our next door neighbors, the Hawleys on *Rondalay*, we all went back to bed. The next morning, we were awakened by a scream from next door. We hurried on deck to find Lyn, the oldest daughter, looking down at the body of a black man. He was floating face down beside their boat. After Lyn's father had pushed it away with their boat hook, it floated around for a bit. We reported it to the police. A launch came to pick up the body and made off. Shortly afterwards, policemen arrived to ask questions, but received no answers as to who had fired the fatal shot. I never did find out who it was. Everyone sailed away, and the case was closed.

January, 25, 1980, was the perfect day for our proposed sail to Fort de France, Martinique. The wind was blowing on the beam, and with main, mizzen, and genoa set, we roared across the straits separating St. Lucia and Martinique at over 8 knots. We sailed right up to our anchorage beside *Esperance*, with Gaere, Richard, and Lorna aboard. We were reunited with drinks, barbecued pork chops, and coffee in the cockpit of *Intsholo III*. The three of them had many experiences to tell of their voyage to Fort de France. I think that Alex and I had more than a touch of pride in these three young people, who had learned so much about boats and responsibility in the months since leaving home and Europe.

Wendy and Ernst arrived on the 31st of January, and left on the 7th of February. By then, Ernst had become a proficient windsurfer. We sailed out of Fort de France on several day trips to bays on the leeward side for recreation of different kinds. They left with all of us feeling sad at their departure, but another guest was due on the 12th. Gerald Waldron came in from St. Lucia to stay for an indeterminate period. After refilling the wine cellar from the plentiful selection available in Fort de France, and storing up generally, we thought we would move on to Dominica. Gerald had visited us many times in the Mediterranean and was accustomed to sailing. He seemed very sluggish and was of no help on this trip, there being only Alex and I to do all the work of sailing a 47-foot boat. It was only when he returned from this trip that he discovered he needed triple bypass surgery. We were rather upset that we had been less than civil to him at times, never realizing that he was unwell.

We pulled into a small bay just south of Rousseau, the capital of Dominica, after a fantastic sail from Fort de France. In the bay was a small hotel, the Sissefrou, which was very sailboat oriented and had mooring posts on the beach in front of the hotel. We anchored in about 15 feet of water and tied the stern to one of the posts, which cost $2.00 B.W.I. Upon going to the hotel, we found that the following morning they were running a safari inland to see the jungle rainforests, hot springs and waterfalls, which are features of Dominica's geography. Unfortunately, a couple of months before Hurricane David had destroyed much of the vegetation of the island. There were places where all the trees had snapped off at about 6 feet above ground. Houses and buildings were likewise devastated. The safari was very successful. We visited Trafalgar Falls where two waterfalls met in one pool, after a drop of about 200 feet. One of these falls consisted of hot water and one cold. This synergy resulted in a pool of water at exactly bath temperature, where we lounged around for some time. This was a rainforest, and throughout our tour it rained constantly. Alex was wearing an emerald toweling dress, which throughout the day got progressively longer until it was almost ankle length. We bought a carved totem from one of the natives for $20 B.W.I., which we still have upstairs in our adventure room.

The next day, I was invited by two Germans, Jergen and Ellie, who were lying alongside, to dive on Scots Head. The Sissefrou Hotel had a compressor and happily filled my tanks, which had not been used for pleasure during the whole voyage. We dove to about 150 feet, following the enormous rock to its base. The whole rock was covered in the most amazing coral formations I had yet seen. We also saw one very large lemon shark and numerous huge manta rays about 20 feet across. After the dive, we all went into downtown Rousseau to watch the Carnival Parade. I don't think we had experienced anything so colorful and innovative. The costumes were made of anything they were able to get hold of. Necklaces were made of the ring-pulls from cans, cans of every make of beer and soda were put together to make dresses, etc. Throughout all of this display, we couldn't help feeling the spirit of welcome from the crowd and participants. They would pose for a photograph, or wave and smile. In the press of the crowd down the main street, we were a few of the only white people. This was very different from our experiences in most of the islands to the south. The next day, Dave and Trish returned to their *Esperance*, and we regained our full crew. Gaere and I went off for another dive with Gaere borrowing bottles from Jergen. This time we saw no sharks or rays but beautiful underwater scenery. A reunion party was held aboard that evening, as Dave and Trish were sailing for Antigua the following morning. Gerald burned himself quite badly on a hot dish of Pan Haggarty, but numerous glasses of rum punch dulled the pain.

The following morning with Dave and Trish gone and Gerald's burn a lot better, we could see no further point in staying off Rosseau, so we weighed anchor for the northern end of the island. This proved to be a great decision, as there was a lot less ocean swell, a huge fortification left over from the Napoleonic wars, and a river up into the surrounding jungle. This river, known as the Indian River, was the major source of income for the people of Portsmouth. They offered boat trips up it, but we didn't see much point in paying to do something we could do in our own dinghy. This caused a great deal of resentment in the village, and it looked as if we might have some trouble. The latter was assuaged by a gesture that occurred quite by accident. We had noted a lot of activity in the bay, with small boats and youngsters diving off them for an unknown reason. On closer enquiry, we found that they were diving for a shell called by them a lambi, which resembles a cowrie. They would make perhaps ten dives for one lambi in about 20 feet of water. I reasoned that where we were lying in close to 40 feet of water, very few lambis had ever been collected. I put on my scuba gear, and soon had the dinghy full. We offloaded them onto the small dock and suddenly the entire village loved us. We learned that these shells were a major source of food, and the shells, when polished, were sold to tourists in Rousseau.

This left Napoleonic ruins yet to be explored. We spent a day up on the headland, and could quite understand what a dominant point it was. There were still cannon and shot lying around, as, of course, the timbers had all rotted. The stonework was beautifully crafted from indigenous stone. No one could tell us from whence it came, or how many times the fort had changed hands. All we knew was that the English had held it at the end of the war. This was probably a bad outcome for the islanders of Dominica, because the French-dominated islands immediately to their north prospered and became part of France. The English islands languished in poverty for another 150 years. Indeed, on visiting a school there, we were appalled to see the students still writing on slates.

On the 23rd of February, it was time to leave Dominica and all the friends we had made there. We gave a t-shirt each to Oswald, Eric, and

Cyprien, for which they rowed out four jerry cans of water and 12 loaves of bread. We were off in a fresh easterly wind, to the Bourg des Saintes, the first of a string of French islands. The first anchorage off the town proved to be untenable, so we moved to Pain de Sucre, which proved about as bad. The following morning, we moved to the Islet de Cabrito and on to Basse Terre, where we were able to shop for the first time in many days. With groceries stowed, we went on to the Anse de Borgue, which proved to be a high point with great swimming and snorkeling. Dinner was taken in the cockpit, then early to bed. The following day was Gerald's birthday and we sailed in the afternoon for Deshayes Baie, where we had a celebration dinner, once again in the cockpit. The menu was lapin aioli, banana cake, and Gerry's chocolates with coffee, all delicious, and so to bed.

The next morning we made an early start for Antigua, a long sail with plenty of wind. We pulled into English Harbor, and settled in to what was to become our favorite Caribbean anchorage. After entry formalities were conducted by a Sgt. King, who also conned us out of quite a few E.C. dollars for a sponsored walk he was doing, we saw that we were surrounded by the boats of all the friends we had made recently. Alex and I went into the Admiralty Inn ashore where we made our first acquaintance with a daiquiri, which we were unable to pronounce. Alex liked them a lot. This became the unofficial meeting place; it was impossible to go ashore and not meet a number of friends.

Shortly after arrival, we met a young marine engineer named Cap Green. He ran a very successful business helping yachtsmen, such as ourselves, to solve their problems when campaigning their yachts on a voyage. The first discovery was that there was a space on the slip the following morning. So we hauled *Intsholo III*, repainted the bottom, fitted new anodes and a new echo transponder, while Cap fixed the wind speed monitor. The crew completed all of that work in one busy day. Gerald left us the next morning, just as we were being lowered back into the water, so he received rather short shrift, but our friendship survived.

Cap suggested that rather than trying to repair the benighted refrigerator freezer, we invest in a new Grunert system. On the 6th of March, we bit the bullet and ordered the most expensive item that we bought on the entire trip. When fitted a few days later, we never had trouble with the refrigeration again.

A shopping trip to St. John, the capital, was accomplished by local bus. This was a hectic ride, with the driver pushing animals off the road with his bumper, and between times reaching speeds far in excess of any limit that existed. While in town, we met Carl and Priscilla Poster of *Galaxy*, who were anchored in the harbor. They suggested that when we were finished at English Harbor, they would accompany us north to the island of Barbuda. This was agreeable to us, and we said we would call them on the VHF when we were finished all the work on *Intsholo III*.

On the 14th of March, we cleared English Harbor for Barbuda at 7 am. The arrangement was to pass St. Johns where Carl and Priscilla were still anchored, and then sail north with them. In fact, they were already out of St. John's as we came abreast of the harbor, so we came alongside, transferred Richard to their boat as an extra crew, and the race began. After the chain on the tack of our number one genoa broke, causing a long tear on the luff of the sail, we put up the number one jib instead. With this, main and mizzen, I described in the log book the sail to Barbuda as "phenomenal."

Getting through the reefs surrounding the island depended on the sighting of a Martello tower on the shore. We eventually spotted it, and made our way very carefully through the narrow coral-strewn entrance. We dropped anchor, to see *Galaxy* making its way with apparently no consideration for the reefs whatsoever. We tried the VHF, but no one answered, and as we waited for the crunch, they went through un-scathed. We asked them how they had made it, to be told, "We didn't know about the reefs." We re-named the reef Galaxy Reef.

On the beach

We found ourselves off one of the most beautiful beaches in the world, and it wasn't long before a boat put out from a small resort hotel further down. The message they had to deliver was unfriendly, basically that we couldn't anchor off the beach or land on it. I was able to tell them truthfully that the Prime Minister of Antigua and Barbuda had told us to anchor there. We'd had lunch with him a week before, with reference to the possibility of our investing in a failed hotel on Antigua. With this information, they went off to tell their employers that we were there on the invitation of the PM. We heard no more, except that we were not welcome at the hotel for any purpose. We proceeded to have a fire on the beach, and grilled lobsters, which were so plentiful that we caught 144 of them. Lastly, we congratulated ourselves that we were having a much better time than the residents of the hotel.

After a couple of days, we moved around to the leeward side of the island, where there was no sign of human habitation, with a beach formed of millions of crushed shells. As the sun set, the whole beach turned a beautiful pink hue. From here we could carry our dinghy across to the lagoon, launch it on the other side, and head the mile or so over to the village of Codrington. The village was named after an admiral in the Royal Navy, who owned the whole island. His use of the island was to breed slaves for sale in the U.S.A. He imported the very finest black people from Africa, and set up a breeding program that lasted well over 50 years. The results were obvious when one moved around the town—these were some of the finest looking people in the world. We had a wonderful reception from everyone. The kids liked to have their pictures taken, and were only disappointed when they couldn't see the pictures immediately.

We had lunch in the only restaurant in the village, where one sat in the front room of a very small house, and had whatever they were serving that day. On the way back across the lagoon, we caught some lobsters for dinner, and prepared to leave Barbuda for Antigua the following morning. The Barbuda experience has probably stayed with our family more than any other. To us it did, and still does, represent the perfect Caribbean island. The beauty of the ocean, looking down from the rocky highlands 210 feet above sea level, could only be described as exquisite, and the perfect sand beaches and the people added up to an unforgettable experience. I understand that all the pristine shoreline, off which we anchored, is now full of resort hotels, and chic bars and grills. This is the sort of "progress" to which we have become accustomed.

On the return sail to Antigua, Richard, who had been part of our family for six months, told us that he felt he had to return home. Lorna, who I am sure had been in love with him for some time, was very upset and depressed at his news. I have never found out, nor asked her, if she knew of his decision prior to the announcement.

On arrival back in St. Johns, we had a last supper, rather grim and sad, and that night at midnight we put him on a flight back to London. The atmosphere on the boat was funereal for several days, as Alex continued to set the table for five, instead of four, and his absence was felt by everyone. Our last few days in Antigua and the Greater Antilles were spent going from one anchorage to another, looking, perhaps, for what was missing in our lives.

On the 4th of April 1980, with 6229 miles on the log, we left English Harbor for St. Barts, to the northwest.

Lorna

30 CRUISING THE LESSER ANTILLES

At 6 pm on April, 4, 1980, we hauled up the anchor and waved goodbye to Cap. We had all loved Antigua and were sad to leave, but we all knew that there were a lot more islands and adventures ahead. The passage between Antigua and St. Barts was clear of any hazard, so we would sail at night. In fact, we brought up the island at first light, sailing between the Isles des Saintes directly to the main harbor of St. Barts. It was Easter weekend, so the small town was packed with people shopping. While ashore, Gaere noticed that a backgammon tournament was scheduled, and he was allowed to enter. He had been playing the game regularly for the previous few months, and he made the semi-finals before he was knocked out, winning a small monetary prize. A slow sail took us from St. Barts to Philipsburg, the capital of St. Marten, where we met up with a large charter yacht, *Windseeker*, with Ken and Marianne Buzzard aboard.

This meeting started one of the most hilarious nights of our lives. Ken invited us over for drinks at about 5 pm, at least an hour earlier than we were accustomed to. We toured their boat, as he had no charters at the time, and we were very impressed. Meanwhile, a 70-foot sailing yacht, *Shangri La*, had pulled in nearby. The boat and its crew were known to us, and we exchanged shouted pleasantries from afar. A while later, a fast dinghy put out from *Shangri La* and approached *Windseeker*. The question was, "Can you cook two ducks for us?" The answer from Ken and Marianne, "No, we only have a microwave." We piped up that we had a propane oven, and would be pleased to cook them. For this, we all got an invitation for dinner, which Ken and Marianne declined, and the ducks are handed up to Gaere, who shortly thereafter made off in our dinghy. When he got to *Intshollo III,* he lit the oven, did everything necessary to the ducks, then returned to *Windseeker*. Perhaps an hour and a half's drinking time later, Alex returned to *Intsholo III* to find that the oven had gone out, and the ducks were still raw. In a panic, they loaded the ducks back into the dinghy, and returned to *Windseeker*.

Marianne obligingly put both ducks into her microwave and started to cook them. This was going to take time! The answer as to what to do with that time was obvious—keep drinking. Ken had a heavy hand when pouring a drink, and by that time, they were getting to us. At about this stage it was proposed, by whom I am not sure, that *Windseeker* and *Intsholo III* should race the following night over to St. Croix, and the challenge was accepted. After two hours or so, the ducks were looking a bit cooked, and Gaere said he would take them back to *Intsholo III* to brown them in the oven. Into the dinghy went the two anemic looking ducks, and Gaere put them in the oven. This time the oven stayed on, but it took an hour or so. What to do with the hour? Keep drinking! At last, the ducks were done and Gaere proudly bore them over to *Shangri La*. We followed as a second load, and climbed aboard the magnificent 70-foot sailboat with a huge salon and drinking table in the middle. At the table sat this extraordinarily beautiful young woman, who was introduced to us as a top British model. She of course had done nothing to further the preparation for dinner. Her fiancé was racing around in the galley completely out of his element. Eventually all the food, including the ducks, was on the table, and the host poured each of us a tumbler of vodka.

As the meal progressed, so did our lack of sobriety, and by the time ice cream was served and eaten, it was 4 am. I made the bright suggestion that four o'clock is the time for tea. Everybody shouted, "Back to *Intsholo* for tea." We all fell into the dinghy, theirs being larger than ours, which took all except the model and me. She and I, alone in the inflatable, started to try to find *Intsholo III*. Soon the crew of *Shangri La*, plus Alex, Lorna, and Gaere, started screaming around the bay at top speed, shouting and waking the entire bay. I couldn't find *Intsholo III*, so the chase continued for a while, with various boats shouting at us to be quiet. Eventually I found our boat and helped the model aboard. I must admit that she was even more attractive wet. The rest climbed aboard and we really did have a cup of tea. The next morning, we saw the model and a crew member going ashore, and she was carrying a suitcase. We on the other hand had to sober up for the race, which was scheduled to start later that day at 4:30 pm. Ken on *Windseeker* would not postpone, and insisted on that start time. That will always be known as "Dinghy Ducks Night."

A not-quite sober and very hung-over crew weighed anchor at exactly 4:30 pm. The wind was northeast, perfect for a sail to St. Croix, so we raised the chute and boomed it out. Before long, we realized that we could raise another foresail, which we had bought from *Flying Swan*, a racing boat. It was a large Hood genoa that they had surplus to their requirements, and this seemed the perfect time to use it. It was duly raised and then poled out to give us the fastest hull speed possible. We arrived at Christianstad, St. Croix, at 8 am, with *Windseeker* not even in sight. This meant that Ken had to buy dinner that night for the whole crew, and we chose the Chart House, which had just reopened after being burned down by restless islanders. The following day was spent in a hired car, touring the island. We visited the Great Whim house and museum of the sugar industry, and the beautiful beaches that make St. Croix a must-visit island. Afterwards we saw *Kramer vs. Kramer*, our first movie in many months, then went back to *Windseeker* for a dessert of mud pie, a Chart House specialty.

The 13th of April, we were up early to return the rental car, and to do some serious grocery shopping at Pueblo. We were unable to exit the marina until noon, as the customs officer was too busy to complete our paperwork. We made up for it by having one of the most wonderful passages of the entire trip. With our new, now-christened Flying Swan genoa, the main, and mizzen, we flew across the straits to Great Cruz Bay on St. Johns in four and a half hours. On arrival, we contacted my half-sister Angela, who would join us aboard on the 22nd of April. With nine days before we had to be anywhere, we all decided that those days would best be spent visiting all the other bays, anchorages and islands in this amazing and historic chain. The wind was always constant, and a great sail was guaranteed. A visit was made to St. Thomas, easily our least favorite island, to clear customs. After a short stay, we moved east to Christmas Cove in company with friends new and old. As we moved from place to place, we were joined by other boats we knew.

A quick list of destinations might serve to jolt the memory of people who have cruised in the Virgins: Sopers Hole on Tortola, visiting Poor Richards restaurant, an interesting place with a cabaret by the owner. His main song, "Me and My Little Piece of String," which was a takeoff on the ownership of the benighted Seagull outboard, was hilarious, particularly if you had ever owned one—and we had. From there to Roadtown, Tortola, a small, quaint town that epitomized British colonialism. From Tortola, we went on to Little Dix Bay on Virgin Gorda, and then on to Gorda sound, where the Bitter End Yacht Club is situated. After exiting the club bar, we were walking down the dock towards our dinghy, when one of us heard a faint voice. Looking around, we could see no one, but eventually, looking down into the water, we saw a hand on the dock and the face of a very overweight man looking up at us. We hauled him up onto the dock, and he explained that he had been in the water for some time. He could not swim, nor raise himself from the water. I believe he would have drowned if we had not come along. As usual, we closed the bar down, so there would have been no more potential rescuers.

After a terrible night's sleep, because of a very rolly anchorage, we sailed to the famous Baths, another very rolly anchorage, certainly not suitable for a night's stay. After exploring these amazing granite rocks for several hours, we headed back to Tortola and Roadtown. Alex and I repaired the genoa halyard that had parted that morning. A quick splicing job at the top of the mast was all that was required. We didn't spend the night in Roadtown, as in the early evening we moved to Little Harbor, Peter Island, a private island with a sumptuous house on the cliff looking down on the anchorage making sure we all behaved. It was the first time we had seen pelicans diving for their dinner. They plummeted down from 50 to 100 feet in the air, and even with their natural buoyancy reached the depths where the fish were. We were upset when one dived and broke its neck.

The following morning we were loathe to leave such a nice spot, but having promised Dave and Trish on *Esperance* that we would meet them in Christmas Cove, we had to go. They were to leave for the U.S. the next day and would not return for a while. Dave had another assignment with *Time* magazine. The next time we saw them, we were in London Airport returning from South Africa some years later. We were killing time before our flight, and they were next to us in the duty-free shop. Trish's remark was, "I would have known that voice anywhere." We had a drink together, and parted. We have never seen Trish again, but Dave did turn up once more in Florida.

After our parting, we were to greet Angela, my half-sister, and Patrick Nugent, her husband. They were due to fly into St. Thomas the next day, so from Christmas Cove we sailed into Charlotte Amalie, the name of the town in the prettiest part of the tourist-filled island. We moved into slip number 701 in the first marina we had been in for many months. It was miserable, crowded, and noisy, but the best place for meeting guests. They duly arrived at 6 pm, and after a terrible dinner at the Sheraton, we all went to bed. The only thing St. Thomas was good for was shopping, and if there were cruise ships in the harbor, one had difficulty getting into the shops. The following day, we decided to go to the south side of St. Johns, and anchored off in Caneel Bay, where our guests had been before, staying at the resort on shore. We thought that Roadtown, Tortola, would be a better experience, so after clearing customs, we sailed on to Trellis Bay on Beef Island, where the nightly entertainment of "Me and My Little Piece of String" was once again entertaining. Unfortunately, Patrick was afflicted by an Irish complexion, and was horribly sunburnt as a result. We definitely had to cut the sailing to a minimum, or he would be a hospital case. We thought we would revisit the Bitter End yacht club, where we could take advantage of the facilities ashore. The following day, we were greeted by torrential rain, but sailed anyway.

On arrival, we went ashore after dinner and had coffee and cognac, so everyone was feeling better by the time we went back to the boat. Angela and Patrick's visit soon came to an end, and we once more returned to St. Thomas, where we dropped them off and picked up Richard Bate, our restaurant partner. He complained that we were late, as if we were on a train schedule. As always, Charlotte Amalie's harbor was very full, and finding an anchorage was really difficult. In our tour of the harbor, we spotted a familiar boat, and sure enough it was our friends who had picked up the chickens in Penzance some years before. We had not seen Leo and Phylis for a long time, and did not know they were on another cross-Atlantic trip. We had a rowdy reunion with them aboard *Brabo,* finished by Leo serving Bananas Foster, which had always been his

Leo and Phyllis

specialty. They were sailing on next morning for their home port of Camden, Maine, so it was our first and last meeting on this voyage.

After messing around in the Virgins for a few more days, it was the 6th of May, and time to go north toward the U.S., as hurricane season was approaching. Our first stop was Culebra in Puerto Rico, where, after clearing customs, we spent a couple of days in a beautiful, quiet anchorage, with no other boats. On to Isla Marina, where to our surprise, we were forced to clear customs again. The customs office was in town, and required a long walk in both directions. On arriving in Ponce the next day, as we moved across the south side of Puerto Rico, once again we were forced to clear customs. Was this to be indicative of the bureaucracy we would encounter in the U.S.? We made a visit to Ponce Yacht Club and had dinner there, noting as we signed the register that the previous three boats had been the Carruthers on *Rafiki*, the Jacobs on *Summerun*, and another couple, whose name I forget, on *One World*. This meant we had friends ahead of us sailing in the same direction. I must explain the very civilized practice, adopted by yacht clubs worldwide, that if a visiting yachtman and crew are members of a bona fide yacht club, they would find a welcome and help from almost any reciprocating yacht club. We belonged to the Royal Cornwall Yacht Club, and found this to be useful many times. We flew their burgee throughout our voyage, and presented it to the St. Augustine Sailing Club on arrival there.

Out of Ponce on the 11th and heading westward to the Bay of Borqueron at full hull speed, it was a unanimous decision to only spend the night there, and sail across the Mona Passage the following day and night. We had been worried about the long and unpredictable stretch of water that lies between Puerto Rico and the Dominican Republic. It was about to live up to its reputation. After a promising start with two poled-out genoas and doing 8 knots, the wind did a 180-degree switch to dead ahead. Within an hour, there was no wind, and so for the remainder of the day, we changed sails as the wind came and went. The direction of the wind boxed the compass. Just before midnight, we sighted the Engaro Point light on the Dominican Republic eastern shore, and changed course northwards by 35 degrees to avoid approaching the shore too quickly. At 12:30 am, there were two distinct bumps on the bottom of the keel—we were touching something, perhaps coral heads or a whale. I quickly altered course to an even more northerly direction, and noted that the echo sounder showed more than 300 feet under the hull. It was navigationally the most frightening event of the whole trip. I took a running fix on Engaro Point light immediately after the event, and it showed us 4 miles from shore. Since then, I have often wondered what it was we hit. I reported the instance to the Hydrographic Office in London, and received a polite reply.

The night was far from over, and the continued wind changes in strength and direction made for a very tiring passage. We sailed into Samana Bay at 10:30 am, a 24 hour trip of 145 miles, and we were all exhausted. Six customs officers boarded and proceeded to search *Intsholo III* from stem to stern. After a breakfast/lunch, we all went to sleep and didn't awake until early evening. We walked into town, and then returned to bed. This was the 13th of May, the log showing 6664 miles.

The 15th of May, 1980, one day before our 21st anniversary, might well have been my last day on earth or sea. Gaere and I quietly raised the anchor at 5:20 am, and came out of Samana Bay, headed east for Porto Plata. The autopilot was set and working well with the main and genoa set on a broad reach. All of the remaining crew were on deck by 8:30 am. After breakfast, we just got on with the day's jobs, sailing at maximum speed with a cloudy and stormy sky. At 2:50 pm, the fishing reel on the stern pushpit started screaming as the line was taken off the reel so fast as to create smoke from the brake. After applying more brake, we were able to slow the fish down, and we were at this time sailing downwind with both poles out on two foresails. Seven to eight knots was our estimated speed.

Slowly, hand over hand, three of us, Gaere, Richard (still aboard), and I wound the reel, regaining line a foot at a time until the fish, now recognized as a marlin, was brought to the stern of the boat. The question was what to do now, and how to get it aboard. I had the bright idea to go over the stern with a winch handle, and hit it as hard as I could. We were towing the inflatable dinghy at the time, and I was soon in position to render the death blow. I hit it, and watched for a split second as blood spurted from the fish's head. Its reaction was not as I had predicted. There was no surrender—instead, with a flip of its powerful tail, the dinghy was turned upside down with me in it. I had plenty of air, because of the cavity between the seats, but I was holding on to one of the side ropes with one hand, and the winch handle with the other.

As a companion, I had a very large fish, which was being dragged at the same 7 to 8 knots as I was being towed. I could see blood flowing out of the fish's head and leaving a trail in our wake. My first thought was that sharks were prevalent in these waters. I decided there was no future in holding on, so I released my grip and surfaced, giving quick directions to Alex and company on deck. I was now alone, 8 or so miles from shore, in a very rough sea and feeling very lonely. I saw *Intsholo III* fast disappearing downwind. Alex threw a life ring over the side as *Intsholo III* departed, but I was unable to find it, as the sea was too rough. I was treading water, trying to stay in the same position for a reciprocal course to be set for my recovery. As always, Alex did all the right things, and she got a reciprocal course, but not until she and Lorna took the two poles off the genoas and took down the sails. Meanwhile, the engine had been started for the return to my position.

Miraculously, I saw *Intsholo III*, with no sails, reappear on my limited horizon, getting bigger by the minute. When she was alongside, someone spotted my head and my hands waving. I was pulled back aboard. Alex made the casual comment, "There is the life ring," and I immediately jumped back overboard to retrieve it. This was the worst thing I had done in a day of stupidity. Alex was the most furious I have to this day ever seen her. During all the time I had been waiting for rescue, I had held on to the winch handle, and it came back on board with me.

After finally getting the fish on board, which had drowned in the ensuing time, we were soon underway with all sail set for Porto Plata. At the entrance to the harbor, a huge lightning and thunderstorm hit us. Visibility was down to a few feet, and we had to stand off for a while. On finally entering the harbor, we docked alongside a wall, where there were, perhaps, a hundred people, excited about the fish on the afterdeck. It was carried, with great ceremony to the customs house, where it weighed in at 74

White marlin

pounds and 7 feet 4 inches, and was declared to be a white marlin. The natives proceeded to butcher it on the steps of the customs house. We were given a small piece, while the rest was distributed to the general population. We had a delicious dinner that night.

Talking of fish stories, *Rafiki* was also in the harbor, and we heard Bill's story of poisoning by Sagatura, outside of Ponce a few weeks before. He had hooked a good-sized barracuda and cooked it. He offered some to the cat, who refused it. His wife Sue was a vegetarian and daughter Pasha didn't eat fish. Bill tucked into it, and had a really good portion, but soon afterwards he contracted stomach pains. These were only the precursor of things to come, and he soon began to hallucinate, then to lose the mobility of his limbs. He was still at sea with his wife and daughter, and the entrance to Ponce was extremely hazardous, with many reefs to be negotiated. Sue did the best she could with Bill slipping in and out of consciousness at her side. Unfortunately, at 3 am, the boat struck the reef outside of Ponce harbor. The Coast Guard came out and took Bill off to the hospital, and Sue and Pasha, much shaken, to the hospital as well. Bill remained there for more than two weeks, and meanwhile the Ponce Yacht Club previously mentioned for their hospitality, set about refloating *Rafiki*, taking it into the harbor, slipping it for repairs, and completely repairing it, with no charge to Bill and Sue. Bill was very lucky to survive this poisoning—a few years later, a restaurant in Jacksonville, Florida, served barracuda, and five customers died as a result. Bill, Sue, and Pasha aboard *Rafiki* followed in our wake all the way to Palm Beach, Florida.

For our 21st anniversary, we spent the day exploring Porto Plata, and took the funicular railroad to the top of Mount Isabella Torres. A very large and beautiful botanical garden was spread over the mountain top. For dinner, we treated ourselves to lobster at an eatery in town. Yum!

The Carruthers and the MacDonalds felt that two days amidst the poverty and squalor that was the Dominican Republic at that time was quite enough. During the day of the 16th, we made plans to sail on to Grand Turk, in the Turks and Caicos group of islands. The importance of timing this voyage to arrive in daylight was the crux of the plan. The distance of about 160 miles must be covered, including crossing several reefs, with a schedule that would allow us to be able to see the reefs before possibly going aground on one. Anchors were raised at 6 pm, and after untangling ourselves from *Sunseeker's* anchor chain, we left the harbor with a fresh breeze and 7 and 1/2 to 8 knots on the log. At 1 am, feeling we were going too fast, we reduced sail to achieve 5 knots. By 6 am, we sighted land on the port beam about 6 to 7 miles off. Altering course to pass south of what we took to be South Rock, *Intsholo III* came into the lee of South Bay. We anchored in 16 feet of crystal clear blue water, over sand so white it could have been snow. This was perhaps one of the most fabulous spots in which we ever found ourselves. There was no sign of habitation—just a clear beach with the reef in front. No navigation aids, just eyeballs to go through. We radioed *Rafiki* our position, and told them the coordinates to follow through the reef. They turned up a couple of hours later, and we all decided we deserved a day off in this paradise—this against the instructions of customs officers in the Dominican Republic.

On the 19th, we sailed the remaining distance to Grand Turk, a hard beat up the narrow channel between two reefs, to the town. The customs officer was British, and was most helpful. He gave us a lot of advice as to when and where to sail within the islands. There had been several incidents of piracy related to the drug traffic going north to the U.S.A. In most cases the boats were taken, the crew killed, and the boats abandoned or wrecked after the drugs had been dropped. We listened to his advice carefully, as the next steps north were through this corridor.

It was time for Richard to leave us, as he had been with us for nearly a month. He was able to arrange a flight out the next morning. We made contact with Hugh and Gwen Layton, who were the representatives of Cable and Wireless in the islands. We had never met them, but he had trained at the Cable and Wireless center near Penzance. His best friend was David Kendal Carpenter, who I knew well; he had played rugby for Cornwall and then England. Before our departure, he asked us to be sure to look up this couple. We were glad we did, as we were all invited to their home for dinner, where it was good to sit in a real chair for a change. They told us of the intricacies of life on a band of small islands, with an almost illiterate population. The mess and filth was so bad that we had to wade through tin cans and the like wherever we walked.

One thing that sticks in my mind was the near loss of our inflatable dinghy. I noticed it floating away downwind, and picking up speed. I dived over the side, and started to swim to catch up with it. Eventually I succeeded, but was too exhausted to get the motor started for a while. This happened again in the southern Bahamas a few weeks later. We never did discover the person who was tying the bad knots. We had all had rigorous training in the art of knots, which consisted of being blindfolded and given a piece of rope with which to tie each knot faultlessly. We must have forgotten the lesson when it came to the securing of the dinghy.

May 21st, after clearing customs from Grand Turk as early in the morning as was possible, we sailed up to South Caicos Island, and had to enter customs there. This was the only way they could keep track of boats for safety purposes. The best part of South Caicos was that it was a safe anchorage, with plenty of conch and lobster immediately under the boat. We took advantage of this, and put quite a few in the freezer. Cockburn, the capital village of the South Caicos, was at best a scruffy mess, with all kinds of litter in the streets and many empty lots. The customs man told us we shouldn't stay there long, as we would attract attention. We, along with *Rafiki,* decided that an early start to Providenciales would be a good idea. It was a long passage, so we left Cockburn at 6 am, and were rewarded by a good wind on the beam, with both boats doing 7 and 1/2 knots. There were to be many course changes, and numerous reefs were between us and our destination. As we approached Providenciales, a huge thunderstorm came over and obscured the break in the reef that led to the Meridian Club. I radioed them on the VHF, and they gave us coordinates to follow. Once inside the reef, all was peace and tranquility, and anchoring in the just over 3 meters of water seemed preferable to going through the cut to anchor in their marina. Our log read 6945 miles.

We settled in to a pleasant evening with the Carruthers and went to bed at 11 pm. On awakening the following morning at 6 am, instead of facing the shore, we were facing out to a very angry sea, and it was time to move into the marina, as waves were breaking over the reef a couple of hundred yards away. Inside this very protected lagoon, the mosquitos were vicious, but there was no wind or sea. At 7:45 pm, we had to go below with screens on every opening. This was a new experience, and one we would soon get used to as we traveled further north.

After a snorkeling and a diving trip to the reef the following day, and catching many more lobsters, all of which went into the freezer, we talked with *Rifiki*, and were told that they had been offered a job of managing The Meridian Club. They were to be interviewed that day, so they opted to stay behind. Their job interview was successful, and they were scheduled to start work in three months, so they made the decision to accompany us to the U.S.A. and then return.

On the 28th of May, with 6969 miles on the log, we both sailed for Mayaguana, the southernmost island in the Bahamas chain. Mayaguana is a wildlife preserve, and you could only go ashore with a permit, which was only available from the officials in the Acklin Islands further north. We broke the rules slightly and went on the beach, to see the myriad sea birds. The center of the island was the location of the main rookery, which we didn't disturb. Even with a major reef to seaward, this was a rough and windy anchorage, and as it was not possible to explore ashore, we decided to sail for the Acklins the following morning.

Gaere and I got up at 5:15 am to make an early start, and we saw that *Rafiki* was making similar preparations. With difficulty we raised the anchor, which was embedded in coral. The weather was heavy with squalls and the wind was strong, but in the right direction for a good sail. When we were abeam of Eastern Bay and sailing over 8 knots, I decided to change course to pass between the various islets and make a passage to the Acklins, saving many miles. Hardening up the sheets to allow for a wind that was now just ahead of the beam, we accelerated to 9 knots with little or no sea.

Avoiding some very vicious looking rocks and endless small reefs, we popped out of this narrow channel in no time, making for a lighthouse on the northeast point, which was marked on the chart as being on the southeast point. As we came abeam of this lighthouse, a particularly heavy squall with rain and heavy wind hitting us hard, the sea became very rough, caused by the shallowness of the water. Suddenly at 2:30 pm, we could see the harbor dead ahead, and sailed inside with a positive gale blowing. *Rafiki*, meanwhile, was still out there, and we finally talked them in by VHF about an hour and a half later.

On looking to seaward, we spotted two more yachts obviously also looking for an entrance. After convincing them we were not pirates trying to wreck them on the reefs on both sides of the channel, they agreed, on VHF, to follow our instructions to make the entrance. They were doing all of these maneuvers with only their engines running, and consequently they were being thrown around in the maelstrom. It was obvious from the conversation on that radio that these were very nervous and worried sailors. When, finally, they were in and anchored, they both came over to thank us. Over drinks, they told us that this was the end of their adventures. They were two American couples who hadn't researched the difficulties of an upwind cruise through the Caribbean.

The following day, with the same weather in place, we decided to explore Acklin. The village of Attwood was more than 2 and 1/2 miles away, and not worth the walk, except to meet the people. The main street was a straggle of small houses and empty lots, neat and clean, but subsistence-level living. There was no store of any kind, and bread was unavailable. We did, however, meet Mistress Cox and Mistress Johnson, who served us a soda, and filled us in regarding the history of the island's population. They, along with the rest of the black population, had been expelled with their masters for loyalist sympathies at the end of the American Revolution, as the British call it, and the War of Independence as Americans call it. The few white people left on the island were what remained of the masters, and a motley looking lot they were. The black population seemed healthy and happy, with the use of old English language and terms as part of their culture.

We walked back to the harbor, to an invitation from *Ursa* and *Everfair*, the two boats we had helped the previous day. This was our first experience of the American 5 pm dinner. After spending the remainder of the day snorkeling, we had dinner with them, and went to bed late.

The next few days, as we worked our way north along the Bahamian chain, we spent our nights in peaceful crystal-clear bays, sometimes named on the charts, and often not. Our first landfall that had a village attached to it was Clarencetown, which had a store where we were able to order bread. We had gone aground on the way into the small harbor, but on close inspection there appeared to be no damage. This did leave us with the worry of getting back out to sea on leaving. The log read 7115. On the 3rd of June, we successfully exited Clarencetown, and with no wind for the first time in many months, motored up to Rum Cay, catching a nice dolphin fish on the way. We decided that we couldn't miss dinner ashore at Delores Wilson's Bahamian Restaurant. I made no notation of what we ate or drank, but I do remember the cloud of mosquitos that followed us from shore back to the boat. An expression Gaere coined that night has remained with the family ever since: "Shall I spray out, Dad?" This meant using bug spray to make the area below habitable. We suffered badly through the Bahamas with the "noseeums" and mosquitos, as the former were able to penetrate the screens.

Moving on to Conception Island after a day's rest, there were three other boats in the bay apart from *Rafiki* and *Intsholo III*. We all got together and had a fish and vegetable curry, with numerous mosquitos and drinks. By this time, we were almost self-sufficient for protein, as catching fish was very easy. Vegetables were at a premium, so a vegetable anything was a treat. Our menus read like a seafood restaurant, with lobster and every kind of fish except barracuda. It was in Fernandez Bay where we had our first Bahamian pineapple, $1 apiece, and they were like no other I had ever tasted. We learned that pineapples had originated in the Bahamas and that the Hawaiians had come over, stolen the plants, and started the pineapple industry in Hawaii. A movie was made showing this early example of agricultural espionage.

From Cat Island, we moved on to Little San Salvador, catching a large grouper and several dolphin on the way. I probably should say that all the fish were caught without lures or bait of any kind. We took the hook and swivel, and wrapped it in a plastic bag—preferably colored—frayed out the plastic, and towed it at whatever speed we were sailing. That night in Little San Salvador, we had nine boats aboard for dinner. As we were closing in on the mainland of the U.S.A., there were more and more boats in the anchorages, and the marinas were crowded. Having been used to anchoring and unaccustomed to paying for the privilege, we almost always anchored.

Cape Eleuthera was the next destination and the sail there was with little wind and much frustration, leading to seldom displayed bad temper. On arrival we were surprised to find only a marina, so we fueled up and did some shopping and prepared to cross the Bahama Bank the next day. With the 7-foot, 6-inch, draft on *Intsholo III*, this promised to be an interesting passage. This vast, flat, and shallow piece of ocean is about 30 miles across and only 8 to 9 feet deep. That water is so clear that every coral head is clearly visible, and it took little imagination to think that you could hit one. In fact, we hit nothing, and the lowest reading was 1.7 meters under the sounder. The feeling of imminent disaster was increased by the brisk wind, and a speed of 7 to 8 knots across the bottom, which was so plainly visible.

After successfully crossing, we made for Governor's Harbor, a quaint and pleasant town, with a large shop for food and drink. The lasting memory will be the number of chickens, walking and pecking their way down all the streets. This was truly a free-range poultry island. I phoned my friend and lawyer, Graham Calderwood from there, and received news that the case of *Intsholo II*'s sale was then in court, and would be settled shortly. Governor's Harbor was the first real customs point in the islands to date, so we started to chase this elusive individual, until an appointment for 11 am the following morning was made. At 12:30 pm, he still hadn't shown up, and we realized this was an example of "island time," which we had better get used to. After much questioning and searching, we were cleared, then had lunch in The Blue Room after a beer at Ronnie's. The menu was predictably chicken and chips, conch and chips, etc. After lunch, it was rest for those that needed it, and wind-surfing for those who felt so inclined.

I think it is time now to mention money concerns, not necessarily the lack of it, but the terrible time we all had getting our hands on any. Before leaving Britain, I had obtained from my bank an International Letter of Credit. Armed with this and a checkbook, I was supposed to be able to get money at any bank. This just did not happen, and more often than not we were scratching together enough of the local currency to buy bread. If we'd had credit cards, not then in general use, it might have been easier. The wait for even a small check to clear our bank in Connecticut was one or two weeks. We did not have one to two weeks anywhere, and if we thought it was bad in the islands, it was about to get worse on mainland U.S.A. More on that later.

Our next anchorage was Hatchet Bay, where we were warned of very poor holding ground in this duckpond of an anchorage. As we came through the narrow passage, we selected a spot well away from the few boats anchored there. It was to no avail, as a particularly strong squall sent us flying across the pond, into a boat named *Molly Brown*. We didn't hit her, but somehow got her anchor rope between our fin and skeg. After much grunting and pushing, and with Bill's help, we kedged off using our second anchor. No damage was evident, except to our pride. We invited *Molly Brown* aboard for drinks and dinner, but they declined, so we ate the whole 8 and 1/2 pound grouper with Bill, Sue, and Pasha.

The next day was the same weather, so we stayed in Hatchet another day and did lots of small jobs, like oil changing, checking all ropes, etc. This time we had two anchors out and when the squalls came, we had no worries. A shore party was mounted to visit some caves 3 miles north of the settlement, which proved to be very small caves compared to some we had previously seen.

On the 13th of June we set out for Nassau, with *Rafiki* and another boat, *Whisper,* all headed in the same direction. All plain sail was set by 8 am, and we headed for the Porgee Rocks. The wind picked up after a while, and we left first *Whisper* behind and then *Rafiki*—as I have said, no two boats going in the same direction can avoid a race. Arriving in Nassau, we anchored off the Nassau Harbor block in 13 feet. This was a city by comparison to any recently visited, and we made the most of it, shopping and sightseeing. The same occurred over the next three days. On the 17th, we started to move out of the anchorage at 8:00 am, and at 8:05 am, we were hard aground on a clearly visible sandbank to our starboard. After trying to reverse off with no success, we rigged a line from the top of the mast to *Rafiki*, who pulled *Intsholo III* on her side, so lessening her draft. She gently came off, and we were on our way to The Berries. While in a quiet anchorage in 9 feet of water, I changed the folding propeller for the three-bladed one, in preparation for our arrival in Palm Beach, Florida.

After the prop change, we motored over to Little Harbor Bay and moored over what amounted to a conch garden. Gaere and I were over the side in moments, and we picked up enough big ones for two meals for the seven of us. It was an amazingly calm anchorage, more like a swimming pool than the ocean, and we stayed in the water to keep cool. Our next and last step in the Caribbean was to sail to Great Isaac Light and anchor in 6 meters off the lee side of the very small island on which the light stood. This was perhaps the most isolated of our many anchorages. It was spooky as the light flashed into our cabin all night. That morning, we brought aboard a 22-pound dolphin, which was enough for dinner and much more.

The course was set for Lake Worth Inlet, allowing for 40 miles of drift northward from the Gulf Stream. There was little wind except in the squalls, so we motored. Having caught en route one 28-pound, one 22-pound, and one 12-pound dolphin, we stopped fishing! As we approached the entrance, a huge squall hit us, with winds registering over 65 knots and plenty of lightning. We looked over to see Sue wearing her Wellington boots, in the certainty that it would help with the lightning. In fact, we were all soaked and would have made wonderful lightning conductors. We entered the inlet with a feeling of great pride at 4:30 pm on the 20th of June, 1980, and anchored under Peanut Island. The log showed 7853 miles.

31 REFLECTIONS ON A FAMILY AND A VOYAGE

I think it appropriate at almost the end of this mission to bring a family and a boat across nearly 8000 miles of ocean, to add up all the benefits that our family gained from the experience. As we were nearing completion of the voyage, Alex and I sensed that our children needed some space from the close confines imposed by living for several months on anything 47 feet long and 13 feet 6 inches at its widest point. Gaere expressed his feelings by walking down the dock of the marina in which we took up temporary residence, and falling in love with the first girl he met. Lorna, on the other hand, found a job as a waitress in the restaurant at the end of the dock, thus regaining her financial independence. This had never actually been removed, as we had made an arrangement to pay both of them an allowance, but this plan became unnecessary very quickly, when we all realized that we lived and worked so closely together that a communal pot of money should be available to all.

By far the greatest benefit to us was the reliance on each other at all times of the day and night. We needed to do what was required, without question, and at times what might not have seemed to be the best thing. Afterwards, questions could be asked, and perhaps a different solution might have been reached. This reliance on each other created a bond of trust, which has held to this day. I feel it absolutely in our current relationship, and it goes well beyond platitudes into expression of our love for each other. For me, this has been one of the hardest adjustments to life in America. I was so unused to any terms of endearment from parents or relations during my childhood that it did not come easily for me to give the constant reassurance needed by my family. I know that Alex and I have always loved our children, as frustrating as they can be at times, but I know that the experience that was just drawing to a close made all of us realize how much we needed and loved each other. I remember sad times on the journey, such as when Richard went home, but we were each sad for different reasons. We enjoyed the happiness that only this type of freedom can give, and we got through the sad times together.

Of one thing I am perfectly certain—that neither of our children, nor Alex and I, have regretted for one minute the decision taken as a family across the dining room table, so many months before. We embraced America as enthusiastically as all immigrants had done before us. There would be many frustrations in the upcoming months and years, as we tried to get established in a new life and country, with lots of adjustments to a new lifestyle. Lorna adapted most easily, and was indistinguishable from her peers very quickly. Gaere, on the other hand, could still be taken for an Englishman or a very recent immigrant. Both have very strong work ethics, which have brought them great success. I hope that this was learned partly from the example set by Alex and me throughout this shared experience.

MY THIRD QUARTER

32 IMMIGRANTS TO THE U.S.A.

As we dropped anchor under Peanut Island, our first anchorage in the U.S.A., it was with a lot of pride that we raised the United States courtesy flag, and the yellow quarantine flag to denote that we were in U.S. waters, and had not been cleared by Customs and Immigration. It was to be the last time that *Intsholo III* was to raise such a flag. She was a British-registered boat, and, as such, was in American waters by courtesy only. We had raised the courtesy flag in the same manner 42 times before, as we entered and sailed within the waters of each country. Due to our late arrival in Palm Beach, we knew it would be to no avail to go to the customs officials that night. We stayed aboard, and drank the remaining bottles of Piper Heidseck that we still had, plus had a dinner of dolphin caught on the trip that day.

The following morning, Bill and I dinghied over to the customs dock for instructions, and were told to be over at the dock in a half hour. When we returned, he boarded, and, because of our immigration status, made it a formal visit of welcome. He issued the boat a six-month cruising permit, which was never asked for again. In front of us, moored to the same dock, was a fishing boat in appalling condition, flying no flags at all. We were told that this was one of the Haitian boats carrying immigrants from that benighted country. The immigrants had been removed, and were in temporary custody and quarantine. The boat was a sad looking wreck, and it was hard to believe that anyone would have entrusted their lives to it to cross over to the U.S. for a better life. The customs man said that after acceptance of the crew and passengers, the boat would be taken out and sunk. He also said that they had at least one of these boats per day.

After returning to our boats, we went in search of a more permanent berth. We found it at the Sailfish Marina, where they had dockage for $10 per day, plus electricity. The two sailboats looked a little incongruous next to the high-rise fishing boats, the like of which we had never seen before. We were welcomed by them all, and realized that their owners all came with the prefix of Captain before their names. We still didn't think of ourselves as captains, although Bill and his family had sailed *Rafiki* from South Africa, and we had sailed from Europe. They were a very good natured lot, and we quickly realized what hospitality meant in the United States.

The next few days were spent in a whirlwind of hospitality from all quarters. Polly and Joe Nugent, the parents of Patrick, my sister Angela's husband, lived about a half mile away in a condominium. This was the first time any of us had ever heard the word "condominium," so we were not sure where we were going. Their request for all of us to come to dinner in an hour's time was a bit unexpected. However, Gaere, Lorna and Pasha declined, so just four of us set out to walk the very short distance. We were plied with drinks of enormous alcoholic content, and then wine with dinner. By the time we were ready to go home, we had another drink, and so on. Getting home was another matter, as we got hilariously lost in the maze of condominium buildings and roadways. These were interspersed with fountains, which Sue insisted on jumping into. Needless to say, the noise of all this attracted considerable attention. We finally made it back to the road leading to the marina, and it was a truly celebratory evening.

As soon as we arrived in Palm Beach, we realized that living aboard with the heat of the summer was going to be impossible. Without the cooling breezes of the anchorages, the temperatures would reach 100 degrees F. or better every day. It was decided to fit a central air conditioner in the rear locker. This was done very quickly by an engineer from Spencer's Boatyard. Meanwhile in the evenings, there was a round of entertainment laid on that was hard on our digestive systems.

On arrival, Bill, Sue, and our family had $23 between us in cash; this was not enough for everyday living, let alone other expenses. We hired a car for $69 per week, with unlimited mileage, using a credit card from my Connecticut bank. There was a clause in the rental agreement saying that the car was not to be driven out of state. Having not been told, we chose to be ignorant of this provision. The car was in constant use by both families and for daily trips to the bank. We had chosen to obtain funds for both families from our respective banks. The answer was always the same—nothing yet. This was our first experience of non-national banks, and it was not very encouraging to find out how difficult it was for one bank to talk to another to make a transfer of funds. Our meager $23 was slipping away quickly!

Bill and Sue decided that they wanted to go up to Prince Edward Island to visit with Bill's parents in Charlottetown. We had finished all the work on *Intshollo III*, and were ready to move north to our new life. Meantime, we gave instructions to the realtor in Darien, Connecticut, to sell our Darien house. This she accomplished in just over a week, leaving us without a home, and the furniture still in the basement. Fortunately, a fairly distant closing date was agreed upon, letting us off the hook for the time being.

We left the Sailfish Marina on the 12th of July, without Gaere, who had decided to stay with his new love. Alex was very unhappy about this, and she begrudged every mile we traveled north. Lorna came with us, leaving her job at The Galley, which she had really enjoyed. She had proved her ability to find work in her new country. We pulled into Fort Pierce after a long and tiring day motor sailing up the coast. The following day, we decided to go by Intracoastal Waterway for the remaining distance to St. Augustine, our next objective. After trying to enter the marinas in Titusville and then Cocoa, going aground in both entrances, we finally found an entrance that we could get through in New Smyrna. We liked the small town and decided to rent a car and go to Disney World and Epcot the following day. This was obviously much more than we could do in a single day, so we stayed over, leaving Intsholo III alone for the first time ever.

We only had to travel a short distance north to St. Augustine, and it turned out it would be our journey's end. Alex would not be persuaded to leave Gaere any further behind. He had found a job in a boat yard in Palm Beach, and was living with Donelle, his new girlfriend, quite happily. We pulled into the city dock in St. Augustine, where subsequently Lorna would find herself a friend. At that time, St. Augustine had an A&P supermarket within walking distance, and it seemed a good place to stop and take stock.

Bill, on his return from Prince Edward Island, handed the car back with in excess of 6,000 miles on the odometer. The car rental company was not amused, and asked how it was possible to do that many miles in Florida in just two weeks. I don't know how he explained that!

33 STARTING LIFE IN ST. AUGUSTINE

On arrival at the city dock in St. Augustine on the 17th of July 1980, Alex, Lorna and I knew that this would be the end of the voyage of *Intsholo III*. Apart from already being several hundred miles from Gaere, we were ready to stop and see what life ashore in the U.S. was all about.

Very shortly after our arrival, we spotted The Anchorage Motel, just across the Bridge of Lions. There were several vacant docks, and we felt we would have more feeling of permanence there than at the city marina, which was designed for transients. We walked across the bridge and inquired as to availability and price. We were given a great deal, and said we would move in a few days. Phyllis, the manager of the motel, made us feel very welcome, accepting mail and phone calls on our behalf until we could get set up with services on the dock. Our next door neighbor, a construction supervisor named Tom, became a friend immediately. He seemed to be of indeterminate age, but with a collection of very much younger women friends, who visited on a sort of rotation system. We settled down to a life, closer to shore life, but still subject to the vagaries of living on a boat.

One of our first visitors on the dock was a maverick character named Dan Holiday. He introduced himself, said that he had an English wife, and invited us to join them for a Bahama Blues party the following night. We accepted, and walked to his house a few blocks away, to be greeted at the door by Dan in a very bright Hawaiian shirt, with an automatic rifle in his hands. His remark was to be classic Dan, "Welcome to my world." We were led into the swimming pool area, and served blue drinks in glasses with palm trees all over them. I never did know what the contents of this cocktail were, and I think it better not to know, because I didn't wish to repeat the effect. Other guests were soon falling into the swimming pool, and making the usual cocktail conversation. Dinner was eventually served, huge portions of protein cooked by Dan on his grill. We were glad to be walking home, although several people in a similar state offered us a lift.

We have been friends of Dan's ever since, despite his divorce from his wife Andrea, who is a sister of a now-close friend. We didn't know it at the time, but Dan would become a key player in the struggle for the

MacDonald family to make much headway in the business community of St. Augustine. At this time, St. Augustine was a small town with the very strong urges of its residents to keep it that way. Basically, it could be explained that they had reached a status quo, and didn't want any newcomers to upset this.

Some days after Dan and Andrea's party, we walked into town and visited with Pierre Thompson, who was the Century 21 realtor in town. He took us around several different real estate opportunities, but we weren't excited by any of them. I had the feeling that he was trying to find out how much money we had, rather than selling us anything. We walked a block back to a less pretentious realtors office, that of Emmet Pacetti. He proved to be a sound advisor with regard to real estate in St. Augustine. At the time of our enquiry, the old brick Y.M.C.A. and a secondary wooden structure, which had been a gym and indoor basketball court, was for sale. It had occurred to us that its proximity to Flagler College just over a block away and also on Valencia Street, would make it suitable for student housing. The buildings had been constructed during the Flagler era—1880s to 1900. The brick building required a lot of work, as the façade was leaning outwards and would need to be tied back. The wooden building was only fit for demolition. The land could then be used for parking and the construction of further apartments. We made an offer on the two buildings subject to an architect's review of our ideas and the building's suitability.

We had heard through the boating grapevine that our friends Derek and Hillary Jacobs had arrived in Ft. Lauderdale, and were looking for something to do. We got in touch with them, and they arrived at the same dock as us at the Anchorage Motel within a few days. They went to work immediately on a feasibility study, while we pursued the change-of-use permits necessary from the city of St. Augustine.

The first City Commission meeting was held to a packed audience of protestors, all of whom were, of course, against the closure of the Y.M.C.A. or its change of use. The Y wanted to move their facility to a different site, one more central to the population. We realized that we had stirred up a hornets' nest of dissenters, and were rather relieved when Derek and Hillary, both very competent architects, advised us that the building was unsound and wouldn't stand up to the structural changes required. The buildings were both razed, and the college used the land for a tennis court complex. That is the end of that story, but certainly not the end of St. Augustinians' protesting against anything we might want to do.

In our walking around town, we had discovered a semi-detached light keeper's house underneath the St. Augustine lighthouse, and set in a grove of old live oaks. It really was in a perfect setting, but had been badly damaged by fire a few years before. The fire had been set by vandals who were squatting in the building. There was a For Sale sign on it, so we decided to make enquiries into its purchase. Our business plan was to convert it into a restaurant, despite its rather poor location. We felt the old lighthouse would be a sufficient landmark for potential customers. We were completely unprepared for the firestorm that the proposal would create. Despite three years of vacancy and a roof that had been burned, allowing water to destroy most of the interior, people were completely unwilling to let two foreigners take over and renovate this gem. I even received a verbal threat of dire consequences if I were to proceed with my offer. I let the offer stand, and waited while the county reviewed the plans and architects drawings showing what we intended to do with the building. Derek and Hillary Jacobs had done a wonderful job of producing these in a very short time. I suppose, in retrospect, that our proposals, all of which were turned down by public opinion, were the catalyst that started to get the city and county to do something with the building. It is now a museum—and is in almost every detail as Derek and Hillary had drawn it.

Meanwhile, we had an option on two pieces of land immediately over the Bridge of Lions, and we felt that both pieces of land would lend themselves to the construction of low-density town houses, with a pleasant view of the bridge and the waters beyond. Derek and Hillary proceeded to draw site plans and renditions of our proposal. By this time there was so much work going on that we had rented Room 29 at the Anchorage Motel as an office and headquarters. The motel staff removed all the furniture, and we placed the necessary desks and drawing boards in the room.

On completion of the presentation material, we applied to the City Commission for approval. This time we hired a lawyer, John Bailey, to help us through the procedural side. The town turned out in force to state their opinion and feelings about the plan. One of the objectors, in his dissertation, stated, "They only live on a boat." This brought forth a roar of approval. A dissenter, Dan Holiday, immediately jumped to his feet and said, "Their boat cost a lot more than your house." This further angered the crowd, and it was time for the City Commissioners to cast their votes. It was almost unanimous—one voted "yes" after consultation with associates. We were back to square one.

After this blow, we went back to the rule books to see if there was anything we could build on the land. One piece was zoned for a motel or inn, so we drew further plans and renditions for that use. The other piece of land was zoned for an office building. We decided to propose an office condominium on the site, so plans were drawn and a presentation was prepared. The night of the City Commission meeting came, and once again the hall was packed with angry St. Augustinians. When John Bailey pointed out to the Commission that the use of the land was within the code in both cases, they were aghast. The City Attorney was called over, and the zoning was changed immediately from Commercial Intensive to Multi-Family for the motel site. The office site already had a large concrete structure on it, and we were told that this would have to be incorporated into our building plans, because it was an existing structure. This was obviously impossible, as we planned to build a modern office building, which could not incorporate something that had been built and abandoned in the 1930s.

At about this time of complete desperation, and against the advice of Mary Lou McEver, a real estate agent working for Emmett Pacetti, we bought a house at 242 Argonaut Road. The advice was that we should choose a better neighborhood, and this proved all too true later when we were burglarized.

At this stage, we decided to abandon the purchase of the two parcels of land and to try to find something else to do. We notified the owner of the land, and he decided to sue us for non-performance of the contract. After pointing out that we had done everything we could to find an acceptable use for both pieces, he persisted, and we went to court, with John Bailey as our lawyer. The judge found in our favor, and for the first time since our arrival, something seemed to be working for us.

We went back to Emmet Pacetti, who was very aware of our disappointment in everything we had tried. It was the 15th of September 1980, and Lorna's 18th birthday. As a family and with a few friends, we decided to celebrate at the Casa de Espania on San Marco Avenue. During the meal, which was served by a waiter who insisted that he wasn't a waiter, I made the comment that someone should take this place, and make it into a really good restaurant. I did not realize what a prophetic statement that was.

On the day after the party, we visited Emmet again, and he, knowing of our restaurant experience in England, told us that the Casa de Espania was for sale and the sad story of its decline. He pointed out that no one could stop us from buying and reopening the building as a restaurant, because the zoning was in place. We mulled it over, and pointed out to each other that most of our restaurant experience came from eating in them, and we had little experience in the administration side. We rationalized that a restaurant is like any other business, and could be made to work by sound business principles. We went back the following morning, and made an offer of $95,000 for the land, building and equipment. The offer was turned down, but an agreed upon price of $96,000 was reached the same day. We were restaurant owners!

34 GETTING INTO THE RESTAURANT BUSINESS

It is often said that immigrants go into the restaurant business because serving the food of their origins is the thing they know best and miss most. This was certainly not so in our case. Our knowledge of the business was mainly from eating in restaurants, and the little we had gleaned from owning one, but with no involvement in the day-to-day operations. There was another strike against us, which was the poor opinion that most of our potential customers had of British food. In defense of British food, it had fallen into disrespect during the shortages of the World War II. This was the time when many American people had been exposed to it. We had to design a menu that would have more appeal than roast beef and two vegetables, or bangers and mash.

When we closed the purchase of the restaurant a few weeks later, the menu was considerably down the list of priorities we were considering in our new commitment. First on the agenda was to clear out the detritus left by the former owners. That ranged from freezers and refrigerators full of food that was all rotting, because they had turned off the power, to all kinds of rubbish, from old clothes and furniture left in the upstairs, where the owners had lived. I believe the only thing salvageable was a bread warmer, which gave us many years of service after we finally opened on August 28, 1981.

An inspection of the building was done by our new partner and contractor, Charles Clifton, better known as Charlie. Charlie was a contractor who Derek and Hillary had met in Fort Lauderdale. He suffered from bipolar disease, and his wife Cricket had just left him. He was in a particularly dark mood when he arrived in St. Augustine, which was coincidentally his home town. After much discussion, it was agreed that his contribution would be to supply the contractor skills and time, and we would supply the labor, or a good part of it, and the money required for the very extensive renovation needed on a building that had been neglected for many years.

The premise of the partnership was that neither Alex and I, nor Charlie, were to receive any remuneration for the work we were about to commence. The partnership divided the business 50/50, and we were to be paid seven percent interest on all the money invested.

After the inspection of the building and a review of the plans that Derek and Hillary had drawn, permits were sought to commence work as soon as possible. These were in place by December of 1980. Meanwhile, Gaere had rejoined us from Palm Beach with his girlfriend. He agreed to come on staff and work with me on the renovation. Alex, meanwhile, never one to care about getting her hands dirty, joined us in the demolition stage of the project. Every bit of the old lath and plaster in the building had to be stripped, the studs cleaned of nails, etc., and all carted off by wheelbarrow to the area behind, which was to become the parking lot. This work went on in unrelenting monotony for several weeks. Coinciding with work on the old house, Charlie was busy laying out and preparing foundations for the very extensive addition that was to be built on the north side of the building. The old kitchen was found to be so rotten it had to be completely torn down and rebuilt with a larger footprint. This went on for many weeks before it began to be put back together again.

After removing all the lath and plaster, Gaere and I started to remove the many layers of paint on the outside siding. This was achieved by the use of a blowtorch and scrapers. There was always the danger that we would start a fire in the century-old cypress siding, but this was averted many times by the use of a hose to put out a smoldering board. We started to repaint it on the outside as the extension, with its many windows neared completion. It had been decided to put the bar upstairs, with a piano, and a back stairway for direct access from the parking lot. Downstairs there would be three dining rooms, with a staircase turned around from the original direction for inside access to the bar. I had decided that in order to obtain a full liquor license we should have 150 dining seats, instead of having to pay for a license that wasn't currently being used.

Meanwhile, Richard from the Bear Essentials, our restaurant in England, had arrived to take charge of the planning and installation of the kitchen. After many frustrating weeks of vacillation regarding the equipment needed and the layout necessary for the menu, which was still not complete, we made the decision that Richard was not up to the job, and let him go.

His replacement was Philip Grainey, the other partner in our English enterprise. Philip did not take long to develop a plan, and the equipment was ordered and installed in due course. The menu proved a little more difficult, as we really were not sure what our customers would like to eat. Finally a menu was agreed upon, which landed the new restaurant somewhere in the middle of the Atlantic, as far as the choice of food was concerned.

Toward the end of July 1980, as the building neared completion, the problem of what to call our new business arose. After much deliberation and many ideas we all decided on Raintree. The logo was created, and the sign was ordered. It was now time to start hiring both kitchen and dining room staff.

For the kitchen, Philip was basically in charge of the selection from a very large pool of applicants. For the dining room, Alex and I were responsible. Charlie, whose name had been given to the bar, was responsible for the selection of staff there. Alex and I were very lucky to have a group of young people from Flagler College available to us at that time. Over the course of a week or so, we hired some of the best young people a restaurant or any new business could hope for. People like Ted McLemore, Tom Schelfoot, David Arnold, Frank O'Rourke, David Bradfeld, Buddy Schroder, Mark Simpson, Breck Sloane, and many more. These and others became friends and in many cases we are still in touch with them. All have gone on to great success in their lives, and we follow them with interest.

The next stage was training. We started a rigorous schedule, where we tried to make servers who didn't seem programmed, as was the case in so many restaurants at that time. As opening day approached, we were confident that we had a good team, who had some knowledge of what they were selling and serving. This was a tall order where wine was concerned, as we had decided on a very extensive wine list, which they were encouraged to know something about, without drinking up too much of the inventory!

There was growing apprehension on our part as each of the many hurdles and inspections were carried out, and we were given the appropriate piece of paper to open the Raintree Restaurant. Were we up to the challenge? Did we have enough money to sustain us during the hard times to come? Had we the right menu mix? All of these questions, and many more, were to be answered in the immediate future. Gaere had rejoined Philip in the kitchen of the Raintree instead of Bear Essential. Lorna, after much argument with Charlie, had been allowed to join the staff as a cocktail waitress. She had worked first at the Conch House, then the Chart House, and finally for Charlie Knight at the Clam Shell. She had gained a lot of experience in the restaurant business in America, and we were not allowed to exploit this knowledge, because Charlie thought there were too many MacDonalds in the business.

Finally, in the week leading up to the Labor Day weekend, we received our final Certificate of Occupancy. We set our first night for August 28, 1981, just days before the Labor Day weekend.

Raintree Restaurant

35 OPENING DAY AND BEYOND

On the 28th of August, we rose early, perhaps because it was not possible to sleep. We were all at the Raintree by 10 am, which was to become a habit for all of us. Preparations were made for our first meal period, which was lunch. The staff were ready, and our National Cash Register (N.C.R.) Advisor, Mike, was there for the point-of-sale system, which we had purchased. He was ready to help with each transaction as it took place. This was the first installation of a point-of-sale system in Florida, so we were treading new ground. As the first orders were taken for lunch items, the new waiters would proceed to the terminal, and with Mike's help punch it in. The order ticket would appear in the kitchen, where Philip was ready with his staff to prepare the dish. This all seems pretty commonplace now, but 30 years ago, and with a new and untried system, it didn't work as well in actuality as in theory. Drink orders that were supposed to go to the bar went to the kitchen, and vice versa. All in all, with a little over 30 lunches served, it went pretty well.

We immediately were aware of a problem that would continue for some years—the demand for separate checks at the same table. This was something we hadn't experienced, and N.C.R. hadn't thought about. The misunderstandings and delays caused by this problem would haunt us for years.

The dinner session yet to come was a whole different ball game. We realized by the number of phone calls that were coming in that this was going to be a mob scene. As opening time arrived, a crowd had gathered to see how the newest restaurant on the block would be able to cope. Well, the answer was soon apparent. We couldn't cope with the number of people, nor the food and drinks they were ordering. The kitchen cooling system broke down early in the evening, the hood system failed, and the temperature over the grill and stoves soared to the level that plastic material melted! The point-of-sale system, even with the corrective work between lunch and dinner, was flawed. I will say for N.C.R., and Mike especially, that he hardly left the building for three weeks, as we tried to sort out all the problems. At the end of the dinner session, we had served just over 150 people, and it felt like 500. Probably 50 would have been a better number to start with. Meanwhile, Charlie, upstairs in the bar, was blissfully unaware of the mayhem downstairs. He came down when he was hungry, and asked for a dinner to be prepared for him. The bar was a lot slower to take off, as most people didn't know it was there.

Slowly we ironed out the problems, and refined the menu. We made several menu changes in the first six weeks. Very few people in St. Augustine thought that we would survive, and the most commonly asked question on the telephone was, "Are you still open?" The first six months, apart from being hard going, was a period when we made very few friends in the local market. This was very stressful, knowing that we needed their confidence for referrals.

A few weeks after opening, with the bank balance still sagging, I made a rule that Charlie, Alex and I had to pay cost for any food or drink we consumed. Charlie took that very hard, and argued that he didn't have money to pay for his and his wife Cricket's meals or drinks. Cricket had turned up shortly before opening and was busily inserting herself back into Charlie's life and our business. In fact, at the Grand Opening, you would have taken her for an owner. We resented this a great deal, and told Charlie so. He assured us that she had no designs on a position in the business. Knowing that was probably not true, we felt very aggrieved at the next bombshell that Charlie threw into the struggling business. He, or she, had decided that Charlie should receive a $25,000 contractor's fee for the work he had done on the restaurant. This was definitely not in our partnership agreement, and by that token we should be paid for the thousands of hours that we had worked. Charlie was unmoved, and the friction between partners grew, until it was unworkable. He announced that he would leave the management of the restaurant and bar to us, and that he and Cricket would go to live in Ft. Lauderdale. He insisted on receiving his $25,000 before he left. Alex and I discussed it, and thought that it would be better to have a sleeping partner than one who had a personality so unsuitable for the hospitality industry. We paid him his money, and were glad to see the back of him.

After a Thanksgiving and Christmas season, the restaurant was beginning to show signs of survival, and with the help and moral support of the opening crew and friends, we became a little more confident. In March, when the restaurant edition of the Florida Trend Magazine was published, to our astonishment we had been named one of the top ten restaurants in Florida by Robert Tolf, the editor. This definitely had an impact, and more reviews followed from other papers and magazines, mostly favorable.

Seeing the way ahead that would some day lead to profit, we started to rethink Charlie's position in the corporation. Both Alex and I felt aggrieved at the idea of his ever benefiting from operations for which we were wholly responsible. We decided to visit him in Ft. Lauderdale, and offer to buy out his 50 shares. The four and a half hour trip down there was very tense, and on arrival I painted a dire picture of our progress to date. Charlie, knowing the reason for our visit, kept Cricket out of the picture, and negotiations commenced. He had decided that he would sell us his shares for a further $25,000. I was obdurate in my refusal of that sum. We left and started to drive home very disappointed.

Fortunately Alex argued that there never would be a less expensive time for the buyout, and the cancer of his presence would be gone forever. Taking her council seriously, I turned around and drove back. He agreed to the sale and purchase, and we drove back to St. Augustine knowing that it was expensive, but we had done the right thing. It was a huge weight removed from our shoulders, at just the right time.

Lorna and Gaere were both still working in the restaurant. Lorna was taking more and more responsibility for the bar, wine lists, and service. They helped us immeasurably with the day to day toil that is the restaurant business. Gaere was in the kitchen with Philip as his number two, and was already responsible for the menu and quality control. We had a strong team, and a continually expanding business. The first year, we showed a small but significant profit, which was mostly swallowed by further improvements to the business, but we had turned the corner.

Tristan, Lorna, Gaere and Alex

36 THE RESTAURANT: IS THIS A LIFE SENTENCE?

After the initial flurry of opening and becoming successful, our lives, and I mean those of Alex, Lorna, Gaere, and I, settled into a very structured existence. It consisted mainly of work, starting for me with a cycle ride from home to the Raintree, arriving about 10 am. Alex would follow a little later by car, in time for the lunch period. We took turns after lunch to go home for a quick shower, and then went back for the dinner period. The same applied to Lorna, who was by now definitely our right-hand person. Gaere had it a little easier, as he and Philip switched about, and had more spare time. Philip was still living with us at 242 Argonaut Road, about 4 miles from the restaurant.

We hadn't really thought of a method to take any time off. The *Intshollo III* was languishing in the nearby marina at Camachee Cove, needing constant maintenance and not getting it. We certainly had no time to go sailing or to use the boat for pleasure. We had decided, after the excitement of voyaging for many months, that we found little pleasure in sailing in circles around the bay. We should, at that point, have made the decision to sell her and get on with our restaurant lives. We did not do this then, but sold her a couple of years later.

In the late spring of 1982, Alex and I finally thought we could break away for a five-day R & R in Nokomis Beach on the west coast of Florida. We had visited there previously when we still lived in England, and we remembered the clear blue water and white sand full of shells. We left St. Augustine and were excited about the prospect. We hadn't gone 20 miles before we had a speeding ticket. It didn't matter. When we got there we booked into a small motel unit right on the beach, and it proved to be everything we had remembered. It became our escape hatch for some years to come.

Most of our opening staff stayed with us for several years, with the occasional addition of equally memorable servers. One in particular deserves mention. Mike Wilson arrived one afternoon, and was insistent, even though we had no places open. He said, "Boss, you will never regret hiring me." He was from California, and we took him in. He worked for us for several years, and was tragically killed in a car accident north of St. Augustine. There were two other members of the staff in the car, and they were upset for quite a while. The death cast a very sad shadow on us all. Alex and I still think of him frequently, as we had become his surrogate parents.

In the early days, we had a very close relationship with the staff, and many became really good friends. In that regard, I must mention Marianne (Minouche) Palermo. She was the ex-wife of Paul Palermo, a prominent young chef in town. She came with a lot of talent and good humor to the Raintree. Lorna and she teamed up, and rented a house on the beach together. We are still good friends, and look forward to her visits from Pennsylvania, where she now lives with her new husband, Walter Brown.

It was in the first year of business that I cycled into town, leaving my bike at the bottom of the back stairs while I went up to the office to get the bank bag. This was the bike I had ridden thousands of miles on in Britain, and had been custom made for me. When I came down after no more than two minutes, the bike was gone. I made appeals in the press and on radio, but never saw the bike again. Shortly after this theft, Alex and I went down to Daytona Beach to a food show, and on our return we said, "Let's go to the movies," just up the road. Alex left her purse on the chair in the hall, and we left with all the doors locked. On our return, we thought the purse had somehow fallen off the chair, as the contents were scattered on the floor. It soon became obvious that this was a burglary, and that the perpetrators had exited through the sliding glass door at the back of the house. They had thrown a concrete block through the glass door to gain access and exit. On closer inspection, we found that all of Alex's jewelry was gone, all of the silver, and many other items. They were in the process of removing the stereo and TV when we disturbed them.

On walking in the downtown area of St. Augustine some time later, we noticed a silver christening mug in the window of an antique shop. It turned out to be mine, and the owner admitted to the police that he had received several other items at the same time, but they were all sold. The leader of this ring was a jeweler in the town, who had a van with a crucible for melting gold and silver in the back. He paid these youths to break into houses to steal jewelry, etc., which was immediately melted down after the stones had been removed. A few days later, after the arrest of the jeweler, the police stopped a car with a youth in it. In the back of the car was our pillowcase with a silver mug in it. The jeweler went to prison, from which he escaped a few weeks later. The boys were ordered to pay restitution to Alex and me. This was hardly compensation for the loss of some items that meant a lot to both of us. This, I think, was the low point of our lives in America. We felt the loss very personally, and we talked of selling up and going back to Britain. We received no items back, and a few dollars of restitution money were paid. Case closed.

The other concern at around this time and one that lingered for some time, was the lack of friends. We were both gregarious people, had always made friends easily, and usually kept them for a long time. The combination of the unsocial hours we had to work, and the reputation that we knew a lot about food and how to serve it was a probable cause. This was a deterrent to people not wishing to make a faux pas at home. People actually would say, "I couldn't cook for you." We were somewhat depressed and lonely, with only our own company.

At about this time, a person we met in the restaurant who was building condominiums at Camachee Cove. He suggested, after our recent robbery, that we have a look at those units. We did, and we liked them on paper. They were yet to be built, but work had started on a three-floor apartment block next door. We decided to wait and see how they turned out.

Coinciding with this, Alex had the misfortune to injure her back quite seriously in the restaurant. She was moving a heavy table and ruptured a disk in her lower back. She sought help from various local doctors, with-

Citizenship day

out success, and as the damage spread down her right leg, she could no longer work in the restaurant. One night, talking to a regular customer, Dr. Max Karrer, and his English wife, he suggested that Alex should seek treatment at Memorial Hospital in Jacksonville with a particular back specialist, Dr. LeGrand. An appointment was made that resulted in a successful surgery.

A long recuperation followed that kept Alex out of the restaurant for six months or so. It was beginning to feel like a life sentence. Alex and I have always worked together, and I missed her badly. While she was in the hospital, I came to an agreement with Joe Taylor to buy the best looking condominium in the second phase. I think Alex was a bit startled, but I had to make the decision quickly, as there was somebody else interested in that unit. We lived in that condominium for 15 years.

Joe Taylor was meanwhile becoming our first friend. He was recently divorced, and was in need of company. He put out a very generous invitation for us to come and visit with him in his family's summer home in the mountains of North Carolina. We could only go for the midweek period, when it wasn't too busy in the restaurant. He had lined up a stellar selection of people, with whom we would spend time, and have dinner with each night. For the first time since we arrived in the U.S., we were meeting and conversing with people as equals, and not as owners of a restaurant. One of our side trips was to Biltmore House, at Joe's suggestion. On our return, he asked, "What did you think of it?" Our reply was, "It's very small." Of course, we were comparing it to the houses of Europe. We were to spend several other short periods of vacation at the High Home, as it was called, and enjoyed every one of them. It was our first introduction to canoeing, which became a passion over many years to come. Whitewater rafting on the Nantahala River was also a new experience for us. These were the short but fun-packed vacations of the first several years.

As the restaurant did consistently better, we hired one of our starting waiters, Ted McLemore, to be a floor manager. He was to assist Lorna and ourselves to run the front of the house, and hopefully to allow us some free time. In early 1986, Joe and Tom Taylor approached us to see if we would like to join them and a group of local people to raft down the Grand Canyon. Meetings were held, and a group of 12 people, including Alex and me, were soon looking forward to the late June start. We flew into Phoenix, and rented cars to take us via Sedona and Oak Creek Canyon to the start at Lee's Ferry. This was our first exposure to the western states, and we were captivated to see such different desert scenery. We met up with my sister Wendy and her friend Dean, who were joining us for the trip.

Soon all 12 of us piled into a large blue inflatable with an outboard on the back to navigate down the 190 miles of the river to Lake Mead. Each night, we would pull up onto a beach, set up tents, and have ex-

Rafting in the Grand Canyon

cellent meals cooked by our guides. During the day, we traveled through sublime canyon scenery, and had the added excitement of shooting the rapids. Those ten days started a life-changing love affair with the Grand Canyon, and outdoor adventures in general. We had been named by our friend Andrew Ramsay, "A raft load of wrinklies." This referenced our supposed advanced ages. The name stuck, and the group embraced the name, The Wrinklies, on future trips.

As we approached Lake Mead, more excitement was to come—we were to be helicoptered out of the Canyon and then put on a small 8-seater plane, which would fly us over the canyon back to the starting point at Lee's Ferry. Alex was not sure about the small plane, as we were were buffeted around by the many updrafts, causing her to hold on very tightly. Meanwhile, I was trying to photograph from the air all the incredible features that we had passed through on the raft. This very successful trip made us a group of friends, most of whom we still socialize with today.

For the next several years, we did a trip with the Wrinklies, or some of them, each year. The second trip was to France and a three-week tour of the canals of Burgundy. Alex and I did all the logistics of getting 17 people to Never and other places along the way. Two boats were hired from Blue Line Cruises. We set out rather erratically up the Canal Lateral du Loire, as the boats were very difficult to steer, and getting into the locks was particularly tricky. Our boat contained Charles and Smitty Willis, and Tom and Pat Wiley. The second boat was subject to changes of crew, as periodically they would drop two people, and another two would come aboard. It was decided to rent a car for everyone's use, as this would take anyone who wanted for a day off the boat on a trip to sightsee or shop, etc. We would tell the driver the furthest point in the canal that we would travel. At the prearranged point, we would moor up, and if it was not possible to make the rendezvous, the driver had to follow the canal back to a junction of the canal and a road that the boats had reached. This system never failed, and was used when the car was needed to pick up new participants, or to drop off people going home.

The second boat's revolving crew, was Tom, Nona and Noalani Tayor, Greg, Lillian, Matt, and Erin Baker, Ann and Bill Robertson, and finally Joe and Judy Taylor. Joe and Judy Taylor were on their honeymoon, and met us close to Paris on the Seine. Unfortunately, Joe was a little overexcited on arrival, and, after a couple of glasses of wine, he fell over the side. He hit his hand on the side of the boat on his way over, and injured it very badly. The rental car then doubled as an ambulance for the many trips to the hospital made by him and Tom Wiley, who had landed on his shoulder getting off our boat a couple of days later. Both were treated in French hospitals, and both required further surgery on return to the United States.

This did not dampen the enthusiasm for the ongoing trip, which was plagued by rain to the extent that the canal we were traveling on had to be closed because of flooding. At the beginning of the trip, we had all visited the battlefield and fortress of Verdun, a model of historical re-creation that had every member of our party moved emotionally. En route we had arranged for a visit to Michel Redde's vineyard for tasting and a tour. We carried two cases of wine back to the boat, a couple of miles downhill to the canal.

The end of the trip was to be the apogee of the whole event. Firstly, with several people having left for Paris or hospital, Ann and Bill, Charles and Smitty, Alex and I went to L'Esperance for lunch. This Michelin three-star restaurant is set in a beautiful garden under the hill that is topped by the Cathedral of Vezelay. The food is as famous as its chef, Marc Menau, whose wife took care of the dining room. The six of us had a most memorable experience, not leaving from lunch until after 5 pm. We had traveled the 20 miles in our little car, which had only five seats. Charles being the smallest, volunteered to ride in the trunk. Probably not many clients of this restaurant had arrived and left in this manner.

Finally, we went to Reims, where we met up with the Wileys, and Joe and Judy Taylor. The afternoon was spent on a special tour of the vast caves of the Champagne maker Veuve Clicquot. This had been arranged by us via the Raintree before our departure from Florida. The caves, quarried by the Romans for building stone, were arched inside so the maximum amount of stone could be quarried, while the minimum amount of land was lost on the surface. A small hole at the top of each arched cave was used to extract the stone. We toured the caves, some 16 miles of them, and were able to taste the champagne. At the end of the tour, each of the five couples was presented with a bottle of their grand marc, "La Grande Dame."

This is not where their generosity stopped. They knew that we had all booked a table at Gerard Boyer's Les Crayeres, another Michelin three-star restaurant that was housed in a beautiful 19th-century chateau set in 14 acres of garden in the middle of the city of Reims. On arrival at the restaurant, we were told that Veuve Clicquot had arranged to pick up the bill for their champagne to be drunk throughout the entire meal. All we had to pay for was the food itself. The following morning, we went back to Luxembourg to fly home. I know that Tom and Pat Wiley, and Alex and I, still drink almost exclusively Veuve Clicquot champagne. That was a wonderful trip despite the weather and the resulting accidents.

Another trip was to Montana, to canoe down the Missouri river from Fort Benton for 190 miles. We carried the six canoes and all the necessary equipment on our Ford Explorer and a special canoe trailer with two custom gear boxes on the bottom. We all pushed out into the very swift-flowing Missouri with great trepidation, and were soon on our way to Vergelle, a trading post for well over a century. We camped on the sides of the river, often choosing sites that had been previously used by the Lewis and Clark Expedition of 1809. After Vergelle, there were no more signs of civilization until we arrived at Judith's Landing, where, contrary to most participants' wishes, it was decided to pull in and camp in the Bureau of Land Management campground. The main reason for the choice was a supply of food from a local woman who had picked it up from Fort Benton. The secondary reason was not discovered until later. The campground contained a toilet, which had been denied to some of the women, who were happy to see it. The toilet was in place, but, predictably, not one you would wish to enter. The occurrence that night was a raid on the campground by an armed, drunken and jealous husband, who was convinced that his wife was in a trailer with her boy-

Boundary Waters

Wrinklies in the Boundary Waters

friend. Always in first gear, he proceeded to circle the campground (i.e., our tents), shouting all kinds of expletives and expending an occasional round of ammunition into the air. We had every reason to be concerned for our safety, and were glad next morning to continue downriver with fresh supplies. It was agreed unanimously that we would not stop in any more organized campgrounds.

About halfway through the second part of the trip, a little more than half the participants went off at speed to the finish at the Robinson bridge, where, coincidentally, there was another public toilet. We and perhaps four others continued through the Missouri Breaks, and a chance to visit many of the abandoned homesteads. In some cases, these still had in them all the things that were necessary to live in those hardscrabble days. It was a very special insight into dry farming, so convincingly sold by the railroad companies of the 19th century.

Canoeing wasn't dead after the Missouri adventure. In fact, the next suggested trip was a canoe trip in the Boundary Waters Canoe Wilderness. Those who had not paddled before were advised to learn these skills. Some did not, and found it hard to make a reasonably straight line across a lake. At the very first portage, a disagreement occurred when some people thought it would be easier to do five shorter portages than two longer ones. The two longer ones won by many hours, and the trip descended into a power struggle between participants. The trip was completed, and everyone was pleased to get back to the Chocolate Moose restaurant for a burger, after a diet of freeze-dried foods.

A trip to North Carolina's French Broad River was next. It was our intention to paddle as far as practical on this fairly shallow river. On reaching the end of the deep water, we all went back to High Home, and did some hiking, and, for many of us, our first ride in a hot air balloon. Alex and I were not impressed sufficiently to repeat the experience. We had a very hard landing in the middle of the interchange on Interstate 40 leading into Biltmore.

The group also went en masse to the Abaco Islands in the northern Bahamas. Stephen, a new recruit, Alex, and I traveled down in considerable luxury on Malcolm Shulz's boat. The others flew, meeting at a rented house on the beach on the eastern side of the island. Most of our time was taken up with swimming, snorkeling, and other activities typical of the Bahamas.

There was one last effort to rejuvenate the spirit of adventure in these trips. That was to whitewater canoe down the Rio Grande River's lower canyons. Only a very few of us signed up for this one, as it was ten days of rugged paddling and living in a tent. Alex and I were shown a side of America we didn't know existed. We were excited by the potential for adventure right on our doorstep, so to speak.

The Raintree was running well, and we had the opportunity, with Lorna and Ted's help, to take time off. Gaere was now in the kitchen with Tim Atteberry, who was one of the opening cooks. He was elevated to second chef based on his experience and skills. Philip meanwhile had moved to the Orange Park Mall, and was running Raintreats, a bakery subsidiary we had opened. This business did very well, but fell apart when Philip some eight years later, opened another branch in St. Augustine. I never realized that he had abandoned the first one until I reviewed the figures some months later. I put the Orange Park store up for sale. Philip was most upset with this decision, and thought he had been let down. It wasn't very long before the St. Augustine branch went the same way.

It was in the late 1980s that we decided to open a second restaurant on Wells Road in Orange Park. An existing site was selected, and the conversion from a carpet store to a restaurant was carried out. It was not an unattractive building, and it was located immediately across from the Orange Park Mall entrance. Tim Atteberry went to manage it, with a number of staff from the Raintree. We called it Raintree's Bistro One, and it was a failure from day one, as we never made the numbers necessary to make a profit. After three months, Alex told me that I should close it down, but being as stubborn as I am, I just kept trying. After one year and a loss of approximately $350,000, I came to the same conclusion. It was the worst business decision I have ever made, and sticking with it was even worse. If the Raintree hadn't been as strong as it was, the results might have been catastrophic.

Gaere, Tim, Lorna, Alex and Tristan

37 RESTAURANT BUSINESS, FAMILY BUSINESS

With all the good things that had propelled our restaurant from success to success, there were many family developments that occurred during the same years. We were all working together in a close environment and doing jobs we all enjoyed. While Alex and I were able to take more time off, so Gaere and Lorna's lives also were improving in many ways. As I mentioned earlier, Gaere had come up from Palm Beach with his girlfriend, but this was not to last long after their arrival. They had taken an apartment on Rhode Avenue in St. Augustine, and after they broke up, Gaere had a wide selection of girlfriends. This continued until he was married to Carolyn O. Hall on September 14, 1989. Carolyn, a former Flagler College student, was offered a job at the Raintree. We certainly didn't make her as welcome as we should have, and after a short time she left us, but not Gaere.

Previously while we had Andy and Ann Ramsey with us on holiday from England, Lorna and her then boyfriend Bryan Fraser, came back from a trip to Charleston, North Carolina. Lorna said, "Do you want the

Gaere and Carolyn's wedding

good news first, or the bad news first?" We said we would take the bad first, and Lorna and Bryan announced that Lorna was pregnant. The good news was that they were getting married. They married on the 29th of June 1985, at the Fountain of Youth, which Bryan's family owned.

We had bought a small condominium townhouse in Ocean Gallery on the beach from Walter and Carol Dusseau, who were shortly after-

Gaere and Carolyn

wards to become very good friends. They had a son and two daughters, and the two girls both became wonderful employees of the Raintree. This purchase was an investment, and we rented it whenever we could. We were living happily in Camachee Cove after a short stay in a small townhouse that we rented on the beach during construction. *Intsholo III* had been sold and sailed away with a man I met only briefly, who was planning to sail around the world in her. I never heard from him again. He had little experience of ocean sailing, and I thought back to all the failed adventurers of this kind we had met on our voyage.

After Gaere broke up with Donelle, he came back and lived with us for a short time, before moving to the beach on B Street. He had as his room mate Mike Wilson, until he was killed in the automobile accident I previously mentioned. He was then joined by his new girlfriend Tara, and Buddy Schroeder, who was a waiter at the Raintree. They all lived the lives of the young, and had much good fun; i.e., the surf was very close, and the ability to get into work just on time was a plus. Eventually, when Gaere married Carolyn, he moved into our condo at Ocean Gallery, after Lorna and Bryan had moved out, and then into a house that he painstakingly restored in downtown St. Augustine. After this, a more ambitious renovation came up on St. George Street, once again in the downtown. Finishing Gaere and Carolyn's housing story, they moved into a large house overlooking the bay on a prestigious street in downtown St. Augustine. I must say that Gaere is a perfectionist, as is Carolyn, and all those restorations and renovations were carried out with painstaking care to produce a house authentic to the period.

After getting married, Lorna and Bryan went to live in our Ocean Gallery townhouse, and were happy there until Zach was born on January 10, 1986. Our first grandchild was greeted with all the love and affection that most grandparents feel. The townhouse was too small to house the three of them, so they moved into a townhouse that Alex and I had bought in Camachee Cove. We now lived only a hundred or so yards away from each other. Lorna pretty much kept to her regular schedule at the restaurant until Zach was joined by a sister, Brittany, on June 30, 1987. The townhouse was a little small for a family of four, despite the area under the stairs having been turned into a bedroom for Brittany. In September of 1987, they moved into a pleasant single story house on Valencia Street. In 1988, Bryan and Lorna found that life together no longer worked, so they agreed to split. The children were young at the time, and Bryan continued to visit throughout the separation of three or so years. Lorna had a difficult time during this separation, trying to juggle her job at Raintree with her life as a single parent. We both tried to help her as needed, but Alex and I have never been enthusiastic babysitters, although we loved having the two grandchildren in our lives.

At the time of Zach's birth, we decided to invite Clifford and Kitty Ellis, familiarly called by Lorna and Gaere as Dada and Elly, to visit with us in Florida. They were both very excited at the prospect. Elly had never traveled outside England before, and Clifford only in the army during the Second World War. Their excitement at seeing Lorna's first child was wonderful, and while they were here they visited Disney and other attractions, but there was nothing like Zach for either of them. Alex and I took the two children

Elly in Florida

to England in the summer of 1991 to visit with the Ellises. We were lent a house by our friends Ian and Lynn Hicks on the cliffs overlooking St. Michael's Mount. We will never forget the first morning after our arrival in the dark. The two grandchildren then four and six years old came rushing into our room, shouting, "There is a fairy castle out there!" It was the castle on top of St. Michael's Mount, shrouded in mist, and it was distinctly fairy-like. I don't think that either of them remember much about that trip, but it was the start of many years of their flying out to meet Alex and me at some point in the United States or Canada. This continues to this day, and through these visits they have become familiar with many national parks and areas of beauty in this wonderful country.

After a while, Lorna and Bryan got back together and stayed that way until 2004, by which time they had moved again to 8 Mickler Boulevard on St. Augustine Beach. After 2004 and the final separation, Lorna settled in with Chris Cantabene and his family of two girls, Caitlin and Chelsea. We have observed that Lorna has never been happier in her life than she has been with Chris. They married on October 1, 2006, and have remained so. They have recently joined us in Marsh Creek at 398 Marshside Circle, but that is getting ahead of the story a little.

Meanwhile Alex and I were pursuing our lives with our usual vigor. At the close of the 1980s, we were working, traveling, and adventuring, not necessarily in that order. I took Alex to South Africa, to show her all the wonderful things I had seen some years before. We stayed for a month meeting friends like Ian and Elma Hunter and Derek and Hilary Jacobs, who, after finishing the Raintree, were forced by U.S. Immigration to leave the country. We went to game parks and saw every animal that Africa is famous for, except a leopard. While spending time with Ian and Elma, we all traveled to the Drackensberg Mountains in Natal Province, where we stayed in the Cathedral Peak Lodge, and were introduced to hiking as a means of travel and recreation. Unfortunately, neither of us

Cycle race in South Africa

had boots with us, so we walked 19 miles in tennis shoes. I don't think either of us got over that experience for a while, but it sparked our interest in hiking, which has become a passion.

We were to visit South Africa again in 1996, this time taking our friends John and Nancy McClintock with us. Once more Ian and Elma had organized a trip, to five state game parks in Natal. Before we could set out on this walking safari, it was suggested that John and I should join Ian in the annual Argus Bicycle Race. This testing 106 kilometer ride is through the mountains surrounding Cape Town. I hadn't cycled seriously in a long while, but we had a week in which to train. Derek lent me all of his equipment, as he was unable to compete that year. By the end of the week, we were somewhat fit and were in place to start the race in the 19th group of 1000 cyclists. There were a little over 28,000 entries, and each group started four minutes apart. The time was computed at the finish. Each cyclist had a bar code attached to his or her wrist, which as you went over the finish line was scanned. Imagine my surprise when I came in and found that I had finished first in my age group, and 128th out of 28,000 competitors. John and Ian both finished with good times.

Sailing with Hilary and Derek in Table Bay

I must explain at this time how Derek and Hilary and Ian and Elma had met each other and become friends. As you might remember, Ian and Elma were my hosts on my first trip to South Africa in the 1960s. They lived near Johannesburg at that time, but later when Ian retired they moved to Fish Hoek, near Cape Town. Derek and Hilary, Raintree's architects, had always lived in Cape Town. Ian required the services of an architect on arrival in Fish Hoek, and looked around for recommendations. He was directed to the office of Derek and Hilary, and they didn't realize they had mutual friends until they started talking about previous experiences. When Derek mentioned his trip across the Atlantic and his subsequent employment, Ian said, "Well, you must know the MacDonalds." Of course, Derek agreed. They have been good friends ever since.

John and Nancy McClintock had become our friends over a period of several years. When we mentioned our trip to South Africa, they were keen to join us, particularly as they had never traveled to Africa before, and our itinerary sounded exciting. The plan after the bike race was to

Gold mining in Buffelsfontien, a mile and a half underground at 140 °F

travel up to Durban and pick up two companions, Dirk and Rose. Rose was the organizer of this most extraordinary five game park walking safari. We left Durban with Ian, Elma, Dirk, Alex and me. John and Nancy had to stay behind, as John had a kidney stone problem. We entered the park by a security gate and drove to the most wonderful lodge in the trees. This would be our home for three nights, and although it was rustic in its construction, it had all kinds of sophisticated features. We slept in open cabins with no screens to hamper the outdoor experience. Every morning at about 4 am, we would be awakened by Rose with a cup of coffee, and by 4:30 would be on the trail with our ranger guide. We walked in the bush like this until about 10:30 am. On our return Rose had prepared a huge breakfast, as she did not participate in the walking safari. In this way, coupled by a further walk at 5 pm until dusk, we got close to every kind of animal in a very personal way. The evenings were taken up with an enormous *braaivleis* or barbecue that Rose had first purchased, packed in a portable refrigerator and arranged for the native Zulu porters to prepare. These camps had no wires or fences around them, and were completely open for animals to walk through at any time. The camps were designed around groups of six to eight people at a time, so were very private. Rose had packed large amounts of Cape wine, so we did not go thirsty. After the three nights, we would move on to the next camp, and repeat the experience, usually with a different range of animals. Some of the five camps visited enjoyed nocturnal visitors, including a herd of elephants one night. These cabins were set on tall poles, and the elephants passed underneath. By the way, John and Nancy did catch up—they were at our first camp before us, as we'd had to stop for provisions, etc. This trip was a truly unique experience that few outsiders ever get to enjoy.

As the 1980s came to a close, Alex and I thought we needed to do something special for our 30th wedding anniversary in May of 1989. We chose a destination that both of us had wanted to travel to since childhood. The exotic sound and promise of the Galapagos Islands had always lured us. We organized a trip on the *Isabella II*, a small 32-passenger cruise ship that would take us through the islands in luxury, but still with a spirit of adventure. After flying to Cuzco and on to Guayaquil, we boarded a small aircraft, which transferred us from the mainland of Ecuador to the islands. The airport arrangements at all the South American cities were a free-for-all, and without an agent you wouldn't be able to board the plane. The *Isabella II* was waiting in the bay, and after boarding, we were shown to our very adequate but small cabins. At dinner that night, the Captain introduced himself and his wife, and told us what would happen in the next ten days aboard.

Zach and the Balthazar at our 30th anniversary

Basically the ships' passengers were divided into two groups of 16 with a naturalist for each party. Ours was Jonathan, and although young, his knowledge was encyclopedic. The ship traveled at night, and reached the island we were to visit early in the morning. After breakfast we jumped into a large Zodiac dinghy and were taken ashore for hikes amongst the strange and wonderful birds, animals, and sea life of this place, which had been cut off from the mainland species for millennia. Each day this continued, and each day the plant life or bird life would be different. We were able to snorkel with the fish, who, like the birds and animals, were completely unafraid of humans. It was an experience we have never forgotten, and perhaps would like to repeat.

There was only one close call. We were snorkeling a half mile from the beach, and I turned around to find that Alex was not with me. On closer inspection, I saw her clinging to an exposed pinnacle of rock a couple of hundred yards away. I swam over to her and she explained in a very slurred manner that she was cold. Recognizing hypothermia when I saw it, I immediately started to swim to shore, pulling Alex. By the time we got there, she was completely disoriented and not really able to speak. Some blankets were found, and she walked on the beach in the sun to warm up. Someone else made tea, a driftwood fire was lit, and after an hour or so she started to revive. She told me afterward that if I hadn't shown up at the rock she was clinging to, she would have let go and drowned.

This ended a marvelous and unforgettable trip, on a scary note. On the last day on Santa Cruz, the only populated island, we were returning from the volcanic crater in the center of the island and happened on some boys playing soccer. They challenged us to a match, with their getting a reward if they won. To their surprise they didn't, but we sent them a brand new soccer ball to make up for their disappointment.

38 INTO THE 1990s AND NEW OWNERSHIP

By 1991, Alex and I agreed that we didn't want to spend the rest of our lives as restaurateurs. We contacted Christies Commercial to see if they could find a suitable buyer. They designed and printed a wonderful brochure with all the features of the restaurant itemized. To our disappointment, only three people showed any interest, and they didn't convert into buyers. Toward the end of the same year, Gaere and Carolyn came to us with the proposal that they buy the business, we would retain the building, and they would pay rent fixed to the Atlanta cost of living index. We accepted, and they agreed to a few conditions, one of which was that Lorna would continue to be employed in her current position. The other, and more important, condition was that we could continue to eat at the restaurant, with a 40 percent discount. To all of these they agreed, and on January 1, 1992, they took over the operations of the restaurant. At the staff meeting before the sale, I announced that we had sold the restaurant. Everyone was aghast, and when I told them their new bosses would be Gaere and Carolyn, they felt a lot better. Throughout the next nine years, they operated the business, differently than we had, but with continued success.

I spent those nine years trying not to interfere in anything, or in any of their reorganizing. It was a difficult tightrope to tread, as they were still our tenants, and month by month they paid down the note. In fact, the debt was retired a year early.

In 2001, Gaere and Carolyn decided that they wanted to seek other paths of employment. Gaere decided he wanted to be a contractor, and passed his contractor license easily. Carolyn meanwhile had opened a boutique downtown. The restaurant was up for sale. I didn't want to get another operator in as they might fail after running the business down. Lorna came to us, and said that she would be interested in buying Gaere out, but she didn't have the money to do so. Alex and I designed a deal where she would own 55 percent of the business, and we would own 45 percent, retaining the building. This was agreed to by all parties, and the deal was made, so we were back in the restaurant business, but with no responsibility to work. I would like to think that our occasional advice was welcome.

On January 1, 2002, Lorna took ownership and has run it with even greater success to this day, joined later by her husband Chris. The only day we continue to work is Thanksgiving, and we put up and take down Christmas decorations.

Gaere has made a great success of his contracting business, and has earned the trust of all the clients for which he has worked. He has mainly stuck to the renovation side of building and with his previous experience in his own houses, he has a resumé of success. Carolyn has continued to pursue retail interests up to the present time.

39 AN ALTERNATIVE TO WORK

At the outset of the 1990s we had a taste for adventure, with a rafting trip down the Grand Canyon, white water and flat water canoeing in several locations, and many other opportunities for outdoor activity. We needed to find a means to continue this life, and now that we were retired, not spend all our time at home and flying to various events.

In early 1992 we decided to see what RVing was all about. I must explain that until this time we had wondered what RV stood for, having come from Britain where it is not a customary term or abbreviation. We had passed an RV sales location in Green Cove Springs a few miles away. One morning, we decided to take a trip and find out more about it. As we pulled into the lot, there was no shortage of salesmen to tell us many things about the life. After going through their inventory, I decided that I couldn't live in one of the smaller units for six months at a time. Alex said, "Who said anything about living in it for six months?" We came away none the wiser, but certainly I was determined to find out more about it. By happenstance there was an RV show at about the same time in Jacksonville, which of course we attended, and there was a huge selection to choose from. Having perhaps convinced Alex that we might spend more than weekends on board, we looked at slightly larger units. The Fleetwood Flair at $42,000 appealed to us, and it had a host of things on board that we couldn't imagine would be included in a house on wheels. It was just 28 feet long, and had a gasoline engine. It was available for immediate delivery, so we signed up a few days later at Dick Gore's RV in Orange Park. The salesman asked, "Don't you want to test drive it?" We declined and just drove it away. On the way home, we stopped off at a large parking lot to find out about backing up and turning around, etc. We were just tickled pink about the whole idea.

Lorna had previously bought a pop-up, and we all decided to go camping in one of the state parks. This was the start of all sorts of adventures in Florida and north into Georgia. Both Zack and Brittany loved those weekends. After a while we gained confidence and we decided to go further afield. There was a kayaking trip in Casco Bay, Maine, on offer from the Nantahala Outdoor Center. We piled all our stuff on board, picked up Ann and Bill Robertson in Scranton, Pennsylvania, and drove

Zach, Alex and Brittany

north to Brunswick, Maine, where we parked our new unit in a membership campground we had joined. We did not realize that it was not allowed to leave your unit for several days, and received a sharp rebuke from the president of the association at our lack of thought and concern for others, etc. I wrote back, denying all knowledge of such rules, and suggested that they might try to be a lot less rude in their letters. Shortly afterwards, we left this camping group, and have never joined another.

Our paddling trip went well in Maine, and it kindled an interest in ocean kayaking. This led to a trip the following year to Mexico and the Gulf of California, where we were camped on the Isla de Magdalene and had the privilege of paddling among the Gray Whales that calved in the area. There were nightly spy hopping and breaching shows, which we could observe from the beach, as well as paddling in the day amongst them. Walking across the island produced our first view of the Pacific Ocean, something we somehow never felt to be possible while we were living in Britain.

Another kayaking trip in the winter of 1992 was to the Florida Everglades and into Florida Bay. This was also run by the Nantahala Outdoor Center, which had arranged all the permits required to camp

Brittany and Zach at Camachee Cove

overnight on the chickees—basically platforms above the swamp. We had guides, for which we were grateful, as it was easy to lose your sense of direction in the often narrow bayous. This event was probably held during the only known freeze in the Everglades. No one had sufficient clothing along.

We kept the Flair for a year, and having decided that we loved what a motorhome could do for us, visited a dealership that sold Safari Motorhomes. It was love at first sight. We purchased a Kalahari, 33 feet long with excellent décor, but with a very underpowered GM diesel.

During the year of Flair ownership, it had posed a problem as to where to park it when not in use. We had bought several lots on the street behind the Raintree, so we decided to build a rental house on one of the lots and build a motorhome garage into it. This worked out fine until we found that the Kalahari wouldn't fit into a garage designed for a 28-foot unit. That led to the first of four alterations to the house, as our coaches got bigger.

With our new Kalahari, it was our intention to go west in the summer of 1993, and explore the interior of the continent. Although we didn't know it then, there were to be excitements and disappointments with this trip, on which we had planned to go as far as Oregon and Washington states. We had our first breakdown in Alexandria, Louisiana, which was rectified, and we were able to continue to the north and west toward Utah. As we entered the more mountainous regions, and were pulling up a steep grade the engine threw a fan blade, cutting the coolant line. This stopped us dead, but we were able to obtain a new hose, refill the radiator, and, after checking with GM service, continued our journey. We drove to Idaho Falls, where another blade was lost, and further phone calls were made to GM and the Safari factory in Harrisburg, Oregon. GM, via their service representative, said it would be okay to continue to Harrisburg, where they would send parts as needed. We had picked up Charles and Smitty Willis, who were to travel with us for a few weeks, and were of great help in making the very tense journey into one of fun. We were far from confident when we left Idaho Falls, but all went well until it was time to cross the Cascade Mountains from Sisters, Oregon, to Eugene. Just as the Kalahari reached the top of the steep grade of Santiam Pass, doing less than 20 mph, there was a loud noise and we lost all power. I managed to drive it onto the shoulder and put on the hazard lights. On inspection at the back of the coach, it was discovered that another fan blade was missing and this one had cut the oil line. The back of the coach and the Saturn we were towing were covered in thick black oil. The engine was seized up completely, and this coach was not yet six months old. Cell phones at that time came in a shoulder bag, but surprisingly there was service. After a call to the Safari factory, which patched us into GM service and a towing company, it was decided to tow us to Bend, Oregon, where Safari owned a factory service facility for Beaver Coaches. In under two and a half hours from breakdown, we were all in the service department, with our car undergoing steam cleaning so we could use it.

Lorna

This was obviously going to be a long repair, and next morning we were told that we needed a new engine, that would arrive by air freight the next day. We booked into a rather plain but fun motel, which allowed us to grill food on our barbecue outside the door. Meanwhile, Charles and Smitty took off for a trip into Washington State and northern Oregon, leaving us to supervise repairs. The coach was completed in under two weeks, and Alex and I decided that a trial run up into northern Oregon would be in order. It checked out fine, but it still had the problem of lack of power. We decided to trade it for a new Safari Sahara 33 footer, so in a few days we continued our journey to the Pacific Northwest. It was at this time we started the habit, which we still use when traveling, that on arriving at the campground, we go to the nearest Forest Service Office. In this way we were able to assess the amount of walking and sightseeing we could do in each place. I must admit for the first few years of RVing we did race from place to place, as if we might not have time to see it all.

It was in Oregon at this time when we seriously took up hiking, and we would leave the campground early in the morning, returning late in the afternoon, every day that we were not traveling to the next place. At first the hikes were easy to moderate and often included a special falls or big trees, etc. As the summer progressed, we were doing over 10 miles on most days. We took our new Sahara back to the factory for a checkup and a few problems, and headed for home. The new unit was too tall for the garage door, so adjustments had to be made to the door height.

When Alex and I decided to go motorhoming, Alex stipulated clearly that this mode of travel would not replace our trips to other countries. I assured her that this was not my intention. Currently Alex prefers to spend her summers in the motorhome and begrudges time spent traveling elsewhere, but this is part of the evolution of our traveling, which has remained active to this day.

As if to prove that my intentions regarding travel other than in the motorhome were true, in 1992 we went bareboat sailing with our friends Ken and Bobby Budd from England to the islands of Greece. We repeated that trip to different islands in 1993. Also in the winter of 1992, we traveled to Palenque, Mexico, where we met up with Nantahala again to raft and paddle down the Usumacinta River between Guatamala and the Mexican Yucatan. This trip took us to a group of Mayan sites that can be visited no other way, including Bonampak with its still-intact murals, that are copied in the Mexico City Anthropological Museum. In 1993, on our way home from our trip to Oregon, we turned north to Minnesota, to go canoeing in the Boundary Waters. This was a habit that we continued more or less every year throughout the 1990s. We always tried to start the trips on Labor Day Monday, so we were paddling in as everyone else was coming out. Altogether we did nine trips and covered a large area of the Boundary Waters, entering through Ely and Grand Marais, Minnesota.

Occasionally by prearrangement we were joined by friends on these adventures. We carried our own Winona canoe on the roof of the Sahara, which was good for our Boundary Waters adventures, but did not prove useful in our travels out west, as it is not the best place for flat-water canoeing. The Winona at 34 pounds was a huge advantage over renting a large aluminum canoe at 73 pounds. The canoe increased the height of the motorhome, and on arriving at a low bridge in Montana, we had to hold up traffic while we removed the canoe from the roof, portaged it across the bridge, and put it back on the roof on the other side. The following and subsequent years we carried the canoe on the roof of the tow car.

40 CONTINUING ADVENTURES IN THE SAHARA

I have started a new chapter, as our motorhoming experiences really intensified in 1994. We were so anxious to leave on our next adventure that we pulled away from St. Augustine on April 6, in our Safari Sahara, bound for no particular destination. The direction was west, the mission to have fun and see as much of the U.S. as possible. I can't begin to mention every place we went to that summer, nor describe the experience of visiting some of America's finest scenery. We stopped in the town of Natchez on the Mississippi River, getting to walk sections of the Natchez Trace. Then on to Vicksburg and the chance to see the site of the siege, which had changed the direction of the Civil War. We went on into Texas and had our first exposure to Texas barbecue, at Squat N Gobble, billed as the best barbecue in Texas. It wasn't a meal time, so we had a tour of the pits, etc., and the owners insisted on giving us a sandwich each for later. It was a first and unique experience for us, and we began to realize how friendly Texans are.

On to Austin, and the capitol and governor's mansion. San Antonio and the Alamo came next, as we made our way to Big Bend National Park. At this point we started our summer hiking, but found it too hot for comfort. The decision to go north to gain some altitude was a wise one, and before long the now familiar cities of Albuquerque, Santa Fe and Taos were the antidote for the heat of Texas. We really started to hike in earnest, and were up in the mountains any day we were not traveling. From Taos and the surrounding area, we discovered some of the many Anasazi ruins dotting the country. These ruins then and now hold a fascination for both of us. Pecos, Aztec, Bandelier, Mesa Verde, and many others were toured and photographed.

From our first experience of New Mexico, we headed through Colorado, not knowing what we were missing, to Utah. Here we found the beauty of Bryce Canyon, the wonders of Canyonlands both upper and lower, Natural Bridges, Capitol Reef, Cedar Breaks, and, of course, Zion National Park. Being from such a small country as Britain, all of these incredible places were hard to believe, and we had the ability to walk in them, often with little company. I must mention our entrance to Zion Canyon from from the east. We knew that there was a 1.1 mile tunnel that we had to go through, and as we drew up to the entrance station, we paid our $10 and were told to drive straight on. I had never turned on the headlights of the Sahara, and there I was in total darkness. Foolishly I drove on and relied on the light from the air shafts to help me see the way, with Alex saying, "Right a bit, left a bit," etc. We were both relieved when we came out the other end unscathed.

From Zion we traveled up the Beaver Valley toward Salt Lake City, where we were to pick up Zach and Brittany, for the first of their many adventures in various motorhomes. We had to adjust our style of traveling to accommodate their tastes, so first stop was the dinosaur quarry in Vernal, Utah. Next was Arches National Park, where we were able to coax them all the way to the Delicate Arch, which was a good hike for eight and six year olds. We got there by saying we would stop at the next cairn, and then the next. In this way we taught them the idea it might be better to get out and walk to see things that are really worthwhile. The same applied to Canyonlands, where they were able to go into the rocks and play about in the holes made by the wind over the years. What they really wanted to do was see snow, so we headed for the high country in the Manti-La Sal. Sure enough after traveling a long way on dirt roads, we came to what we were looking for. We built two snowmen, complete with rocks for noses and eyes, and this was their very best day. We took them back to Salt Lake City, and sadly put them on the plane back to Florida. We had a really wonderful time with them, apart from their habit of sleeping when we were driving, as they were too young to pay attention to the scenery. This ignoring of their surroundings went on for a long time, but, of course, now they are interested in everything.

We went on to the Grand Tetons National Park with Charles and Smitty Willis, who we picked up in Salt Lake City. One of the loop hikes that Alex and I did around Cascade Canyon, apart from the beauty of the flowers and the scenery, was the longest day hike we had done at 12 and 1/2 miles.

On to Yellowstone National Park and more of the same. On the 7th of July, we had 6 inches of snow and thought about Zach and Brittany. We only gave Yellowstone two days, and we were off toward Oregon and all we had missed the previous year. Crater Lake followed the John Day Fossil Beds, and then into the wine country, to discover the wines of Oregon that we had hardly heard about. By chance, we drove up a road that would later become very familiar to us. John and Nancy McClintock founded their Vista Hills Vineyard at the top of the hill on this same road. At this time, the whole hill was covered with filbert trees. John and

Nancy have some 40 acres under cultivation in pinot noir and pinot gris grapes, which is not bad for people who were drinking Gallo Hearty Burgundy just a year or so before. They are now surrounded by some of the greatest names in Oregon wine.

After a trip up the Columbia Gorge—what scenery!—we said goodbye to Charles and Smitty in Portland, and went on with our trip through Oregon, visiting the coast and several state parks. By this time we were falling in love with Oregon, and all its byways. At Mount St. Helens National Park, a day hiking around the volcanic devastation was really worthwhile. We noted miles of trees sheered off by the blast, and only wildflowers coming back to replace them.

From there we traveled to Mount Rainier National Park, staying just outside in Ashford, Washington. This park and the mountain it contains was probably the high point of the trip. We hiked every day to some new high spot, enjoying the abundance of wild flowers that grow all over the mountain and meadows. Our favorite was Van Trump Park, a 2000 foot plus climb that was just breathtaking. We have been back several times since, but have never seen it like that day. Of course, we felt we had to leave and get on to the next adventure, as we had not realized the importance of giving up speed and distance to the reality that is today.

As we headed east through Idaho and Montana, all our notes show that it was too hot to do much of anything. The lasting memory for my driving through these wonderful arable lands was the extent of the grain fields and how as you looked through the fields, the stalks were in line—mile upon mile of them shortly to be harvested by the train of harvesters we met on the roads. After a trip into the Badlands National Park, where, if anything, it was hotter than ever, we arrived in Minnesota for some canoeing.

Our first paddle was down from the headwaters of the Mississippi through wild rice at the sides of the river. A demonstration of the harvesting technique was given by Harvey, a forest ranger, guide and generally well-informed individual. He was particularly vocal about the number of city folks who came and built their suburban-type homes in the forest. He was a memorable character, and so was the trip he led. One thing that we did learn that day was that as non-native Americans, we were not allowed to harvest any of the rice. From the headwaters we traveled on to Ely for our annual Boundary Waters fix. Alex was very nervous and did not sleep for three nights, as we were to do this alone. Everything was fine, of course, and we enjoyed the paddling, the solitude and the loons.

Back down through Duluth and on to Wisconsin and the Dor County peninsula, where I was able to enjoy apple pie and Alex was able to enjoy cycling, first in the Apostle Islands and then on a couple of Rails-to-Trails sites. Fall was approaching, and the leaves were changing as we headed toward the upper peninsula of Michigan, where it was cemeteries that we were looking for. The old mining communities throughout the peninsula were full of Cornish miners, with their distinctive names. We were able to enjoy quite genuine Cornish pasties for lunch. The Cornish Societies were very active, and if we'd had more time perhaps we would have attended a meeting. The reason we were staying north was to meet up with Wendy in Toronto, and do a trip with her. She had always spoken highly of the Bruce Peninsula in Ontario, where she and her daughters had spent several summers in Southhampton. It was a beautiful area, and we traveled up the peninsula to Tobermory, where we were able to picnic under the lighthouse. On our return to our campground, we canoed up the river and found two rangers catching huge Chinook salmon, 25 to 30 pounds, just below the dam. The fish that were marked were clubbed with a baseball bat, and those other lucky unmarked fish were tagged and helped over the dam, where they would spawn next spring.

As in all our traveling that year, we didn't allow nearly enough time for the Bruce Peninsula, or for Wendy for that matter. It was home now that became the consuming goal. With brief stops on the Blue Ridge Parkway and Atlanta's Stone Mountain, we arrived in St. Augustine on my birthday, October 3, 1994. So ended an adventure, which we had great difficulty describing to our friends. Unless you have seen the immensity of these western states, you wouldn't understand the meaning of Colorful Colorado, Montana's Big Sky country, or any other terms used by the tourist boards to describe their states. We had enjoyed nearly every minute of the trip, covered thousands of miles, and skimmed over places that we hoped to give more time to in the future.

41 THE START OF REAL HIKING AND BACKPACKING, 1995

We pulled out of our garage on the 6th of April 1995, heading for the West, which by now was a given. There was only one thing to do before we left Florida, which was to meet Lorna, Bryan, Zach, and Brittany in St. George Island State Park. We arrived in the morning, took a site, and asked if we could pay and reserve a site for the family, who were arriving later. We were told no, and of course when they arrived, all the sites were taken. We left the campground and our paid-for site, and went back to the mainland, where we got two sites in the Good Sam park. Bryan and I got up early the following morning and parked outside the state park office to await the departure of one unit. We immediately presented ourselves to the ranger, and said that we would take that site. We then returned to the mainland to get our RVs, as she told us that we could not rent the space until a camper was at the gate. We were back in a very short time, and camped for the remainder of the weekend in this beautiful state park. I wrote to the state park authority and had a kind letter of apology for the inconvenience we had suffered, which said that the rules had been altered to allow for families to be together. This was a small incident that would in no way dampen our enthusiasm for the summer to come.

We pushed on westward to places that we had heard or read about. Nothing was going to stop us from revisiting the Grand Canyon. On the 2nd of May, we arrived and took up residence in a campground for four nights. This was the first time we had been on the rim. We made the most of it, and hiked 6 miles down the Bright Angel Trail and 3 miles down the South Kaibab Trail. We resolved to get a permit for September and hike to the river, camping overnight. A permit was obtained, and the first of 22 descents into the canyon and its backcountry was made. On this first simple hike, we descended on the South Kaibab Trail, and came out on the Bright Angel Trail. We spent one night in the campground and had the first of many dinners at Phantom Ranch. I was in love with the canyon and its ever-changing scenery and was able later to transmit my enthusiasm for this awesome place to my hiking companions who were not on this particular hike. Two Grand Canyon hikes a year was the normal diet for several years thereafter.

On into Las Vegas for our first visit, and we certainly had never seen anything like that before. Death Valley and some real desert hiking, then we came out and headed for California, which was also a first. At the side of the road was an exhausted cyclist, who was riding from Death Valley, the lowest spot in the Continental U.S., to Mount Whitney Portal and beyond to the summit on foot. This was an organized race, but he had run out of steam after the first 5000-foot climb. We asked him if he wanted a lift, so his bicycle was put on board, and he followed it very willingly. We let him out at Lone Pine, California, where we stopped for a couple of days. We planned to climb from Whitney Portal to the peak, but the weather dictated otherwise, as it snowed all night.

On we went, through Sequoia, Kings Canyon and finally Yosemite. Each of these national parks has a significant number of hikes, so we were able to do a new one every day, by now somewhat comfortably, managing 15+ miles per hike. Never had we experienced anything like the beauty of Yosemite—the waterfalls were all at their spring flows. To get close to them at the top or the bottom literally took our breath away.

It was our plan to go into San Francisco to pick up Zach and Brittany for the second annual visit. We picked them up, whisked them around the city, and then back to Yosemite, where we stayed for a while. We promised that at the end we would return to San Francisco to see the sights. They love the falls, and we were able to encourage them to hike a little to see some of the places that were not accessible by road. After visiting Isleton and the Crawdad Festival, it was back as promised to San Francisco, where they rode the cable cars and other exciting attractions. They were to return to their parents the next day, and they were both looking forward to it.

After dropping Zach and Brittany at the airport, we picked up my sister Wendy, who had flown in from Toronto for a couple of weeks. We traveled north into British Columbia and then Alberta. In both places, we were completely awed by the scenery we saw in the mountains. After Wendy flew back, Alex and I checked out Vancouver Island, where we stayed for an unheard-of 17 days, not all in the same place, however. By now hiking was becoming a real obsession and very few days passed without a walk of some kind. We tried salmon fishing in the waters of Brown's Bay, but fishing failed us badly, and after many hours in the boat trolling up and down, we returned to shore some $200 poorer with no fish. We haven't tried fishing since.

On our return to the mainland, we began to make our way eastward through Idaho, Montana, South Dakota, and into Minnesota and Wisconsin. We took time out for our usual Boundary Waters canoe trip. After this it was south to arrive home in time to pick up Gaere and leave again on our first Grand Canyon hike, which was a success, and something Alex and I would repeat with variations over the next few years, until we were joined by our friends John Tesdorpf, John James, and Ricky Fitzgerald. They altered the dynamics of these tentative backpacking trips forever, but that comes a few years on.

In the late part of September after our return to St. Augustine, we flew to Turkey for the third bare-boat trip with Ken and Bobby Budd. This was the end of the season for these trips, so anchorages had few other boats in them. We picked up our boat after a horrendous flight and then a bus ride from the airport to Marmaris in southern Turkey. We arrived in the middle of the night instead of the evening, so it took us a while the next day to store up and get under way. Our instructions were open ended, but they gave us a date when they required us to be in Bodrum, which was to the west along the coast. As always with Ken and Bobby, the sailing, eating, and drinking were fun from the moment we woke up to finally giving in and going to bed. We were instructed before we left that under no circumstances were we to spend a night in the ancient harbor of Knidos. We didn't consider that this applied to us, and decided to stay after visiting this entirely ruined city of ancient times for the best

Sailing in Turkey

part of a day. It was too late in the afternoon to sail to a better harbor, and we thought as it was a calm evening with a blue sky, it would be okay. We had dinner in the cockpit and eventually went to bed. Not more than an hour later, a wind of near hurricane force got up. Seemingly the blasts were from straight above and down on to our boat, and we were the only vessel in the harbor. This kept up all night, making sleep impossible, so in the morning we thought we were going to have a terrible passage around the headland, which was clearly visible

Alex with Ken and Bobby Budd

from our anchorage. We set out with deeply reefed sails and had a hard sail for an hour or so. Then the wind completely disappeared as we rounded the headland, and we had to motor for the rest of the day. Knidos had been well worth the visit, for the remains of a lost civilization which was everywhere under our feet.

There were far too many experiences on this voyage to recount here, but I think our favorite after Knidos were the small fjord-like bays with perhaps one house in each bay. Often someone would row out, and ask if we wanted dinner that night. If the answer was yes, they would row out and get us. After a wonderful fish or lamb dinner cooked over an open fire, they would row us home to bed. There were seldom any other boats, so we had the Mediterranean to ourselves. In Bodrum, Alex and I bartered for a handmade carpet with a number on the fringe which denoted it was made by a prisoner. We paid $750 for it, rolled it up, and brought it home. It is one of our proudest possessions. At the end of the trip, we were offered a free week to sail the boat back to Marmaris, but neither of us had time, so we declined.

In 1997, we did a repeat performance of this trip, but on this occasion we rented a boat in the Virgin Islands. We both were looking forward to showing Ken and Bobby the islands which we had known so well. Unfortunately, the voyage did not go as well, because the boat's bottom was fouled with weed on collection, and one thing after another went wrong. It was hardly the same as our wonderful experiences on *Intsholo III* almost 20 years before. That was the last of the bareboat charters we enjoyed with Ken and Bobby. We do see them every time we go to England, as they live conveniently just two hours by road from London Heathrow. There is always a bed and glass of wine ready on our arrival.

In 1997 we started our trip out west with Alex's sister Pam and her husband John sleeping on our bed and traveling with us. The idea was to show them some of the route we travel with a destination of the Grand Canyon, which they had never seen. Along the way, we stopped in New Orleans and the French Quarter. This was the first time we had been there also, and we decided that we probably wouldn't go back, which we haven't. Then we drove on into Texas to show John the Alamo and San Antonio. He really enjoyed the visit, but the Mexican food was not to his liking.

From there we traveled west on Interstate 10 to Fort Stockton, the first of a series of visits to that plain town. It was so windy that it was difficult to open the door of the coach. We still keep going back—in fact, we spent our 52nd wedding anniversary there in 2011. On to Carlsbad Caverns, we had a rainstorm that flooded Main Street to a foot or more. John was by this time thinking what do these people see in this? Then we went on to Santa Fe and Taos, finally ending up in Sedona, Arizona, which was fast becoming one of our favorite places. From there, we took them back to Phoenix to catch their plane home. We were very sorry to lose them, as we had a really great visit. I think in retrospect John, in particular, found the road trip too long, and perhaps places of interest too far apart. They had seen and hiked considerable parts of the Grand Canyon rim, and we had picnicked on the very edge. I don't know what part of America has more to offer than this most spectacular area.

It was off to the north rim of the Grand Canyon for Alex and me, as we had planned an ambitious hike from there to the south rim, taking the shuttle back to the motorhome on completion. We had met up with Jarl and Marion Natwick, fellow Safari owners, who had just arrived at the Jacobs Lake Campground. They immediately volunteered to drive Alex and me the 60 miles to the trailhead on the following morning. We were up at 4:45 am and pulled out of the campsite by 5:30 am. Our trip down to the bottom went copybook, and after lunch, we relaxed in the creek, very cold and refreshing. Next morning we were up by 5 am and hiking down the North Kaibab Trail to Phantom Ranch, where we took the same site as we had the previous fall with Gaere. It was here that I lost all credence as a leader of hikes, etc.

We had agreed to get up at 3 am to pack up and start hiking out; i.e., up at first light. I was pretty wound up like the new watch on my wrist that John Davis had given me as a thank you present. I couldn't sleep very well, and in a stupor looked at my watch. I thought it said five to three. I woke Alex, and we prepared to leave, packing the tent and having breakfast, all very silently so as not to wake our fellow campers. We both put our packs on, had a last look around, and Alex asked, "What's the time, Tris?" I looked at my watch, and to my horror it said 1:30 am! The dialog that took place, all in a whisper, with a touch of vitriol in every sentence, I shan't recount. Suffice it to say, I suggested unpacking. "No." I suggested taking advantage of the nearly full moon, and hiking out. We began the hike out after much muttering, which continued until our arrival at Indian Garden some three hours later. The trouble was that shortly after hitting the trail, the moon on which I was counting was obscured by clouds, so we got out our Petzl headlamps and picked our way up the trail. At Indian Gardens, we rested. I made tea and a second breakfast was eaten. After three-quarters of an hour, we headed out for the remaining 5 or so miles to the rim, arriving at 8 am. There were a few early risers at the top, and they asked where we had come from. On hearing the reply, "Phantom Ranch," I'm sure no one believed us. I pointed out to Alex that we had missed the heat of the day, and ducked fast to avoid her hand as it descended on me. We had a third breakfast in the lodge dining room. I don't think eggs and bacon had ever tasted so good. Of course, Alex forgave me, and we caught the shuttle back to the north rim and our waiting coach. This was the greatest adventure yet and would lead to many other long hikes together and in company.

Before leaving the north rim, we took the car off the plateau and down the Wire Pass road, which leads north into Utah. We saw some activity on our right, and stopped to see what was going on. It was explained, and we were able to watch the first California condors released into the wild. I have since seen a number of these birds flying around the canyon on hikes. That sighting wasn't the purpose of our trip, so we continued to a spot that was unmarked, but looked as described. It is called Buckskin Gulch, one of the few entry points to Paria Canyon. This by no means unique but longest slot canyon stretches 39 miles to the Colorado River. I have always been more enthusiastic than Alex about the unique narrow slots carved through the rock by seasonal water and floods. The sheer scope of this one is so amazing and at that time very few knew about this entry point, so we walked between the walls sometimes a thousand feet above us for about 3 miles in and out without seeing another person. It was eerie then. It is now a victim of over-popularity, with a car park, entry permit required and lots of people. We have visited and hiked other slot canyons, but never one that made such an impression.

Zach and Brittany made a three-week visit that summer, and were treated to the volcanic wonders of southern Oregon and northern California. They particularly enjoyed the lava tubes and sliding down the slopes of a still snow-covered Crater Lake. Part of their trip was a visit to Harrisburg, Oregon, where in one hour I decided to change coaches for an X Edition 37-foot long Safari. Zach pointed out that his Mom and Dad had taken four hours to buy a truck. At 37 feet, the new coach was too long for our garage, so I called Lorna and suggested some ideas for lengthening it. By our return, this was accomplished. Lorna and Bryan joined us in a rented Cruise America from Portland, and we went into Washington State and over to Victoria, B.C., for the day. Unfortunately, their camper was a lemon and we spent a great deal of time seeking repairs or getting towed into service. They left with Zach and Brittany after a week or so. We went back to Harrisburg to pick up our new X Edition and continue our western trip through Washingston State and into the North Cascades National Park, where we did several long and strenuous hikes into mountains that are steep compared to anything we had done before. The average was over 1000 feet per mile. The views were spectacular from the top of every one we climbed. The best part was that there was almost no one in the park. All we saw were two bears, one picking apples at the base of the mountain.

We moved on to Glacier National Park where we were to meet Charles and Smitty Willis, who were renting a house on Whitefish Lake for a month. We spent several happy evenings in their company and even slept over one night. Time was passing and the Boundary Waters were calling, so we moved on into Minnesota for a couple of weeks before we headed for home and our extended garage. What a year we'd had!

In the late winter of 1998 as we were already thinking about preparing for our western travels, Alex and I were washing the car outside our garage in Camachee Cove. A car pulled up, and John Tesdorpf jumped out. We hadn't seen him for some time, and he was full of his plan to hike with some friends through the jungles of Guyana to the falls called Kaitur. I was, of course, interested, little knowing at the time that this would alter our hiking lives forever. I must first explain that John is a can-do sort of person, as this was a daunting enterprise of 85 miles in a trackless jungle. They, meaning a very mixed bag of inexperienced hikers, were planning to fly to Georgetown, Guyana, get a small airplane to fly them to a trailhead, if one existed, and hopefully follow the rudimentary map to their goal. John, Ricky, and John James were all strong and 20+ years my junior. This didn't apply to Brendan at 70, or Severin who was 25, who were both unfit. We had a meeting where I reluctantly told them that their planning was faulty, and they needed much more consideration for the terrain, temperature and time required for their endeavor. There was a distinct silence when I had finished, and I think I heard a few gulps of realization. We all got on with the planning and stocking of food and equipment for this hike, and it became a model for the hikes that were to follow, in many different locations.

We did fly into a small airstrip and what met our eyes was not what was expected. A major fire was filling the air with acrid smoke, and the scenery, instead of jungle, resembled a desert. We all looked at each other and if the airplane had still been on the ground, I think some of us would have climbed back on board. At this moment, and right on cue, two boys of perhaps 13 and 15 came out of the shack and offered themselves as guides. We all looked at each other in disbelief, as if to say, "How can these boys help us?" With no discussion of payment, they said they would lead us to Kukakabara, which was the first night we had marked on our map. It was almost midday, and the equatorial sun was beating down. We could seeing the cooling jungle off in the distance, so we loaded our packs and set out behind the boys, who were wearing only flip-flops on their feet. We came to a stream before long, and the weaker members of our group flopped down in it to cool off. One said, "I don't think I can go any further," and Moon Mountain was rearing ahead of us in the jungle. Severin's feet were already bleeding, as he insisted he only ever hiked with his laces undone and no socks. I suggested that we move on, and they follow as best they could, perhaps not the best way to win friends. The country had changed into jungle with intermittent savannas and downright grueling mountains to climb.

The savannas had been caused by the slash-and-burn agricultural techniques employed by the Indians. I must point out that through all of this vast land, there are no roads or tracks of any kind, just mazes of pathways going in most directions. The villages only contact with the outside world was the small planes, usually chartered by the Jesuit missionaries to supply necessities and bring in materials for the several cottage industries that had been started.

After awhile we finally arrived at Moon Mountain, which had been smiling down on us for a long time. We must have made a pitiful sight as

Ricky and John at Kaitur Falls, Guyana

we all struggled up in our own way. I must say that the two boys were way ahead, with only their cloth slings over their shoulders, holding very meager possessions and the only food they would eat, cassava bread. All trails go in a straight line, no matter how steep the mountain, and it didn't appear to be a problem for the Peters boys. I passed J.J., and he told me that he was going to die, and I don't think he was too far from the truth. Finally all but two, who were still far below, made it to the top. There was a spring-fed stream there, where all the village women were gathered doing their washing. With no modesty at all, we jumped in and cooled off. The village was only a short distance away, and somehow they all knew we were coming. They put us all in a hut with beds, and we slept the sleep of the dead. The hike progressed through jungle, across rivers, the occasional village where we were always made welcome, in and out of savannas which proved to be cooler than the humid jungle. Each day brought us nearer our goal. The two who were having so many problems stayed in Kukakabara, and said they would fly out on the next plane. We skirted the Orun River, a tributary of the Amazon, for some miles with us on one side and Brazil on the other. We of course had to wade across, actually the only time I have been to Brazil. This river is used extensively for alluvial diamonds, and we saw many spots where this illegal mining was taking place. On arrival at Orunduick, we had a couple of days of playing in a series of waterfalls in the village, and who should turn up but our two missing hikers. They had hiked with one overnight on the short route to Orunduick. I had lent Severin a book, a signed copy of an Ivan Doig, and he said he had left it behind. I was so mad that I said I would walk back to Kukakabara to get it, and they could pick me up on their return trip in the plane that would take us to Kaitur Falls. John volunteered to come with me, so we set off early on the following morning with a young guide, who was even faster than the Peters boys. We soon realized that if we didn't ask him to leave us alone to get lost, we would die of exhaustion. He left us, and we staggered into Kukakabara at about 5 pm. We were fed a chicken dinner and put to rest in a comfortable bed. The book was on the bed where Severin had left it.

The following morning, we got directions as to where the landing strip was, and after an interminable hike through some jungle, we arrived just before the plane. The short flight to Kaitur Falls was only spoiled by the realization that we had serious problems with B.O. brought on by lack of washing both of ourselves and our clothes for 11 days. The falls were perhaps one of the most sublime sights we had ever witnessed, dropping from the mountain plateau to the river below in an uninterrupted 825 foot fall, to a cauldron at the bottom. The river wound its way back into the jungle so far below us as we sat on the edge of the precipice and contemplated everything we had done to get here. Yes, it was worth it!

As I said earlier hiking would never be the same again, and although Alex wasn't with us on this one, she followed the hike from beginning to end, as if she had participated, and would do so in the near future on other trips. When I got back to St. Augustine and had my pictures processed, I sent the pictures of the schoolchildren to their villages. I had a wonderful letter from a Mr. Peters addressing me as Dr. Tristan, thanking us both for the photographs, and saving the life of one of the village wives who had been bitten by a fer de lance snake while washing clothes in the same stream that we had bathed in. In actuality, neither of us knew what we were doing, but by dumb luck we must have done something right.

42 1998, 1999 AND OUR 40th WEDDING ANNIVERSARY

The usual route was taken to Arizona, and two hiking trips were already planned for the early summer. The first was our descent into Havasu Falls, parking our rig in Seligman, Arizona, and driving the 98 miles to the trailhead by car. By 7:15 am, Alex and I were on the trail through the canyon to Supai Village and we arrived at the campground a couple of miles farther on by lunch time. The campground lies between the two main falls, and the creek flows through it. In every respect this should have been a wonderful experience, but it was dirty and unkempt. The Supai residents were belligerent and unhelpful. The falls, on the other hand, were very beautiful with turquoise pools at the bottom of each. You could swim in them if you were able to put up with the 70 degree F. water temperature. To visit the bottom falls, it is necessary to lower yourself down through a tunnel with the aid of chains, a little scary, but worth it. On this, our first visit to these falls, we were rewarded by the upper falls being divided into two equal parts and falling a hundred feet or so into the pools below. After a recent flood, this is no longer the case, and the large creek now flows over in a single stream.

Back to Sedona, and off to the Grand Canyon for a hike from the south rim to the north rim, this time on our own. We were able to take a shuttle bus back to our coach after our hike, and after dinner and a night in the North Rim Lodge.

Our next enterprise was from Flagstaff to the Navajo National Monument, where we had picked up a permit to hike into Keet Seel, a 10-mile trip to a very unspoiled Anasazi pueblo. After picking out the number one campsite, we were the only hikers that day. We were given a tour by a ranger guide, who lived there between Memorial Day and Labor Day. This was the only condition under which you could visit the site. It was annoying to find adequate fresh water in the campsites, as we had been told there was none, and consequently had carried a lot. We went back to Flagstaff, then drove down to Phoenix to fly home to move out of Camachee Cove, our home of 15 years. We had sold it to move into a home, which we were yet to find, in Marsh Creek. We packed up all our furniture and belongings, and moved them into the expanded motorhome garage. We went back to our motor coach to welcome Ian and

Elma Hunter from South Africa and did a few hikes from Priests Gulch and Telluride. Ian was unable to settle in the coach, so he rented a cabin. After their departure, we drove to Denver to pick up Zach and Brittany for their annual trip.

We had chosen Yellowstone National Park for this year and we were able to add the Grand Tetons National Park for more excitement. We finished up with Zach and Brittany, Pam and John Davis, Lorna and Bryan, who had driven out in the "Fountain of Youth" Mini-Winnie, plus Charles and Smitty Willis in their own coach. Quite a crowd, but we all had fun in the area around Buena Vista, horseback riding, 4-wheel driving, hiking, eating and drinking, as well as rafting down the Arkansas River, where we nearly froze to death in a freak hailstorm that half filled the raft.

We then traveled up into Montana and finally Alberta, where we did all the things that tourists do: the Banff Springs Hotel, and Lake Louise with its myriad tourists, mostly Japanese at that time. On the way to Jasper, John Davis treated us all to a ride on one of the Brewster buses that go on to the Athabasca Glacier. While camped in Jasper National Park, we witnessed the birth of an elk, immediately behind the coach. After a while, the mother put the baby into some juniper bushes, and went off to eat and drink. That baby was almost invisible in the bush, and didn't move even when approached. The mother and baby were gone the next morning. We took Pam and John back to Calgary, from where they flew home, leaving us free of any visitors or guests. It was pleasant to be on our own again.

We traveled south to Waterton National Park, where we had heard the hiking was really good. The Crypt Lake hike was perhaps the most exciting we ever did. After a boat ride across the lake with 60 other hikers, we disembarked and the race for the top began—we were the third and fourth hikers to get to the scary bit, a scree slope with a trail across with nothing but space below. Then into a 65-foot tunnel, and out of the other end to a ledge with a chain to hang onto with a drop of 2000 feet below. Alex was a little nervous, but made it across. On her return, she was perfectly alright. Two other hikes are worth mentioning: Cameron Lakes, which was a shuttle to the top and a walk back to the campground, was very long, and Avion ridge, even longer, with staggering views out over the Rockies. It was a given that Glacier National Park would be the next stop. We were able to do several overnights from there, in fact one of the hikes took us back across the border to Waterton Lakes. The scenery in both of these parks is literally world-class. I filled albums with my Hasselblad, which 15 years later still haven't been matched by any scenery anywhere that we have traveled.

The route home to Florida this time was more or less direct from Glacier. We stopped in Branson, Missouri, and I am unsure what I thought about this place, as it made me feel old. Our time in Florida that winter was without incident apart from trading the X Edition for an Ivory Edition Safari. This one was only 33 feet, so it would fit the garage easily. The interior décor in this coach was exceptional, in fact it was the vehicle with which we had the least trouble after purchase of all that we have owned. In fact, we collected it and transferred our belongings into it at the dealership and drove west from there in 1999.

Our route west in 1999 was not much different from others we had made. Santa Fe loomed large in the trip as it does to this day. A visit to El Morro Rock was a highlight, and after the visitors center, we walked around this huge monolith to observe thousands of names inscribed by travelers since the late 1500s. The reason for coming to the rock was obvious. There, under the shadow, lay a large pool of fresh water, the only water for miles around. Another trip was to Sedona, with a hike up Wilson Mountain where we encountered a very large bear, when we were

Morning In the Grand Canyon

With John on Tristan's 15th trip into the Grand Canyon

almost back down to the trailhead. We then met a group of realtors, who were having a beer after hiking the same trail. They made us very welcome with beer and conversation. We were actually making friends from the coach, one of the benefits we were learning from slowing down the pace a little.

On the 16th of May 1999, Alex and I celebrated our 40th wedding anniversary at Jacobs Lake, about 60 miles from the north rim of the Grand Canyon. After a bottle of Veuve Cliquot and a rack of lamb, we were prepared for the arrival of Gaere, John, Ricky, and Terry for a descent into the canyon. We set off, but unfortunately it was too aggressive for Terry, a new hiker to our group. John took him back up to the rim, then made the descent on his own, catching up with us at Cottonwood campground about halfway to Phantom Ranch. This was a long backpacking day of over 14 miles for us, and more for John. It was a good thing he took the trouble to take Terry back up; on his returned to Florida, Terry was admitted to the hospital for a triple bypass operation. We had a great time on this hike with humor running high, meals at the ranch, fishing in the Colorado River, and a trip to Ribbon Falls on the way back up. John left his brand new pack on the side of the trail, and upon his return he found a squirrel in it. It had chewed through the top. Words failed him—or did they, as all of our packs were okay. I tactfully pointed out we didn't leave them on the trail, but in a scrubby tree. We were truly sorry to see them drive off in their rental Lincoln Continental, which after miles of off-road driving and being impaled on a rock which got in John's way, was not fit to take back to Hertz or whomever.

Alex and I continued our adventures with a trip to Zion National Park. We hadn't been for five years and the hike to Observation Point seemed easy now. So, we set the scene for a backpacking trip that we might do the following year. After a shuttle ride to Lava Point, we headed down and up and then down again into the canyon via the east rim. Very steep, very hot, very hungry. In an effort to get to the shuttle on time, we had left our food in the fridge. Of course we made it, as there were no choices involved. The following day, with the car instead of a shuttle, we prepared to backpack in to the Kolob Arch, which was a further section of the long backpack trip I was planning for the future. This was a totally successful overnight, and left only one section to be explored.

Back to Flagstaff and Sedona, from where we would pick up Zach and Brittany in Phoenix for their annual walkabout. We took them to the south rim of the Grand Canyon and it was arranged that their parents would meet us a few days later. They were 12 and 13 by then, so we could expect a lot more from them, but their tendency to sleep through even the most amazing scenery while traveling persisted. Together with Lorna and Bryan, a trip was made around the canyon to the north rim and on to Bryce Canyon National Park, which was definitely their favorite. After dropping them both off for their flight home to Florida, we proceeded west into Oregon to visit with John and Nancy McClintock at their vineyard in Dayton for the Fourth of July holiday. After this, it was north into Washington State where we met Bill and Ann Robertson and Charles and Smitty Willis, both now in their own motorhomes. It was our plan to travel in convoy up into Canada and visit some of the sights of British Columbia. This was our first experience of traveling in company and proved to be a good one. We did a lot of hiking and sightseeing until it was time to break the convoy and go our separate ways. Alex and I stayed in the Rockies, and did some of the seminal hikes of the area, O'Hara Lakes, Cameron Lakes, and Avion Ridge being just a few, enabling us to see scenery that is without parallel anywhere in the world, with several overnight backpacks to more inaccessible spots.

By September, we dropped down south to Oregon to fly to Hawaii for two weeks with John and Nancy, on their coffee plantation in Kona. This was our first time in Hawaii, and we were impressed with everything. We really saw a great deal of the Big Island. John and Nancy were wonderful hosts, and their house and pool could not have been more idyllic. The daily event I remember most clearly were the early morning walks in the neighborhood around their home. The air was fresh, the views outstanding, and the luxuriant vegetation made a lasting impression. After our return to the motorhome from Hawaii in early October, we headed for Florida and home. The motorhome had given us great service, traveling and doubling all the while as our home. We had traveled 11,055 miles at an average price per gallon of $1.30 and a total cost of travel of $1839. Things were going to change, but we didn't know it then.

43 2000, A BUSY YEAR

Our travels in 2000 were, to say the least, intense and quite varied. In the winter of that year, John, J.J., Ricky, Alex and I started to plan the most ambitious hike yet. It was the complete Inca Trail from the Urumbamba River to Machu Picchu, a distance of 62 kilometers or just over 38 miles of some of the most rugged mountains anywhere. After a bone-shattering ride in a minibus with all our gear from Cuzco to the end of the road, we crossed the river on a swing bridge that was high above the raging waters of the Urumbamba. We all had rather heavy packs, but were confident that we could make the mileage required daily.

The first day brought us through a high mountain village, where I have to say I nearly lost it. The combination of dehydration (unnecessarily) and straight fatigue caused nausea and stomach cramps. I was grateful that not far past the village we found a camping spot. That evening we were visited by a man of perhaps 40 and his son of 16 or so. They offered to carry our packs and lead us over Deadwoman's Pass (14,000 feet) the following day. This would cost $25 per pack. I gave up my pack, and J.J. gave up his, in an effort toward economy. I took Alex's

John, Alex, Ricky and J.J. hiking to Machu Picchu

pack. The following morning at first light, the march began up into the cloud forest and on to the first part of the stone trail that would lead us to our goal.

We ascended the pass 60 steps at a time, with our two guides—no, packcarriers—laughing at our problems. They were wearing flip-flops and we were wearing boots. At the top and the payoff, they returned to their village, while we trudged on with our packs. Although we had spent several days acclimating in Cuzco, we all suffered with lack of breath. To John and Ricky's credit, they both carried their own packs for the duration. I, on the other hand, apart from the economy angle, didn't want to appear wimpy, so Alex's pack was a real face-saver. As we proceeded nearer Machu Picchu, we kept meeting more and more guided and porter-assisted adventure groups. The extraordinary thing was we were continually passing them, meaning we were not doing that badly. The next night we camped at the filthiest spot imaginable—it was a festering mess of human waste. This was

Ricky, Tristan, John and J.J. in the cloud forest

a problem everywhere on the trail, once we had joined the adventure groups, who were doing shorter routes from the train.

Arriving at Machu Picchu

On day three, we started early and by lunchtime had reached the gates of the national park about 10 miles from Machu Picchu. We tried to find a campsite that would accommodate the five of us, but were chased out of each one by very officious porters or their leaders, so, thinking that there would be something down the trail, we started out again, only to be met by a sign saying that camping beyond this point PROHIBIDO! There was no choice but to do the 10 miles to Machu Picchu, then go down to Aguas Calientes and hope we could find a hotel. We were all utterly exhausted, having covered 38 miles in three long days. The recommended time for that hike was four or five days.

We found rooms in the Hotel Machu Picchu, where a cleanup, dinner, and lots of Chilean wine deadened the pain. The following day, Ricky, Alex and I toured Machu Picchu, with no one there at all—just a few lonely llamas grazing between the buildings. The secret was to get there before the train or the hiking adventurers made it. John and J.J., having been there before, didn't make a second visit. After a second night at the hotel and a dinner of trout pizza across the road, we discussed our next move. We already had tickets for the train back to Cuzco, and would be met by our very friendly helper named Felix. John had other ideas, and insisted we should all go back in an enormous Russian military helicopter. The takeoff with zero visibility was one thing, but as we gained altitude, pinnacles appeared out of the clouds to left, right, and straight ahead. We made it back to Cuzco, of course, or this book would not have been written.

The Peruvian government changed the rules a few days after our hike was finished, and I hope it wasn't our example that made the new rule necessary. In the future, all hikes had to be with officially recognized and licensed guide or tour operators. This effectively froze out the enterpreneurial, self-sustaining small groups such as ours. In fairness, apart from the two $25 pack-carrying charges, we contributed nothing to the tourist industry other than a couple of hotel rooms for two nights in Aguas Calientes and a few mementos to take home. We had brought all our food with us for the hike itself.

We had a memorable night in Cuzco on our return, when John, J.J. and I chose the national dish for dinner; i.e., guinea pig. They were borne out by a waiter, who placed them proudly on the table in front of us, heads on and teeth showing in a snarl that showed their resentment at being cooked up for three gringos. Ricky's comment has remained with us to this day. He said, "Three smoking rats." None of us enjoyed it, and I wouldn't recommend it.

Just to round off a busy spring, we flew to England and went to Cornwall to see John and Pam, after which we went on a trip to France, visiting some of our old haunts. It was fun, but unremarkable, so I shan't elaborate. This gave us a late start on the trip west—it was mid May before we pulled out, and the weather was already hot. We traveled in a fairly straight line to Utah via Las Vegas to pick up Zach and Brittany, Gaere, and Ian Hicks, who came from Cornwall. We were planning to do the long hike of 40 miles from the top to the bottom of Zion National Park. We were 11 people on this hike, as we were later joined by Ann, Bill and their grandson Danny, plus J.J. and Rhonda. All were in place by the day before the start, and many hiked in the canyon in preparation. Packing gear was a large job for so big a group. Part of the preparation was to leave a car at the top of one of the trail sections, where the trail intersected a dirt road. The car was like a tanker, with many gallons of water stored for our arrival.

Everyone piled into the arranged shuttle the following morning, which took us to the North Entrance of Zion National Park. Packs on, and away we went, first down to the La Virkin creek, then on to seldom-visited Kolob Arch and an even more rarely visited waterfall. We made camp, and I deservedly suffered my first reprimand for inadequate tentage. In my infinite wisdom, I had only brought the flysheet of the tent, which allowed every bug in that part of Utah to chew on us all night. Ian and Gaere were perhaps as badly off, with no tent at all. They noisily rigged up a tarp during the night.

We continued across the Hop Valley floor, after gaining almost a thousand feet in the first mile. Ann was having a recurrence of her dizzy spells, and was soon out of water. This was more serious, and it took a long time to get Ann across the very hot shadeless valley to the car at the top. There is a connector trail there of another 4 miles, but under the circumstances, we ferried people past this trail and picked it up at the end, saving 4 miles and getting to our second camp by late afternoon. Alex and I, as purists, have since hiked this connector just to complete the hike.

Ian, who had arrived without a toothbrush, suggested that he use the car to go and get one, and Gaere offered to accompany him. They did return, complete with a cooler full of beer and a toothbrush. The beer was appreciated, but bad for discipline—nobody was watching!

Day three started after another mosquito-infested night. Everyone was in very good spirits as we set out for Lava Point, and Sawmill Springs somewhat below it. Here Alex and I filled everything that would hold water, and cached it just off trail for our passing in the morning of day four. This was probably the hardest day with a lot of elevation changes and very little water available—only one spot between Sawmill Springs and the top of the east rim. In the circumstances, as we reached a trail junction on the top of the east rim, it was decided that a group should go on an alternate trail to a spring that ran seasonally, then bring the water up using a circular route back to the east rim. Ian, Gaere, J.J. and I were selected for this duty. Bill and the others continued along the rim until they arrived at site #3, a designated campsite, with a fabulous view down into Zion Canyon. The water was running, and the four of us took a very cold shower under a little waterfall. All we had to do was complete the circuit with four heavy bladders of water. Only three of the bladders made it. That night as the sun was going down over the east rim, I took one of my best photos ever.

On day 5 we had a long way to go, and started soon after daybreak, but first I had to take a picture of the sun coming up and the full moon going down over the canyon. We hiked through beautiful rock and cliff scenery past Angel's Landing and down Wally's Wiggles to the lodge. Here, collectively, we emptied the smoothie machine, Ian having three. What a hike—so much laughter despite the health issues. I am sure no one involved will ever forget the details or the beauty that we passed each day.

East rim of Zion Canyon

44 A DISCOVERY THAT CHANGED OUR LIVES

After completing the Zion hike and taking the children back to Las Vegas for the flight home, Alex and I wanted to continue the summer on the high note with which it had begun. We headed east from Utah, and stopped first at Dolores, Colorado, and then Durango. Both were areas we liked and had great hiking. In order to plan the next group hike, we did some exploring along the Continental Divide Trail and the Colorado Trail out of both places. What we found, of course, was beautiful scenery and plenty of opportunities for long hikes, so we made notes and bought maps.

On Friday, July 21st, 2000, we set off from Durango for a town we had heard about in the mountains, which had a superb campground. We arrived at lunchtime, and were taken to site 46, next door to a very friendly couple named Bryan and Lorna, who were in a fifth-wheel trailer. Of course, we told them of the remarkable coincidence of their names being the same as our daughter and her husband, and we knew that we were in a friendly environment immediately. The front row of RVs in Mountain Views by River's Edge Campground (i.e., the north end) has totally splendid views, and here we were with one of them. We settled in, and knew that we were going to love this place, with its 360 degree views of the mountains. In the afternoon, we visited the small town of Creede, which seemed to have most of the things we would want, including a Forest Service Office on Main Street. On duty was Dennis, who over the years would become a friend and advisor on all things hiking in the surrounding countryside.

The following morning, Alex and I were off to the Wheeler Geological Area, a 16-mile hike to an area of remarkable rock formations. We have only repeated this hike twice, as it is very tiring. Charles and Smitty Willis joined us for a few days in their coach, and forays were made in all directions, mostly by car, as they were not hikers. We went over Stony Pass, and down into Silverton, which was accomplished in our Suzuki, with a canoe on the roof! We met up with Bob and Pat Schmidt, who have a furniture making shop in town. I had met Bob and Pat in St. Augustine while we were opening the Raintree. I had no idea they were in Silverton, and only a chance remark from a friend made it known. It was great

Evening in Creede

meeting with them again, and we have been friends ever since. He has since made us some remarkable furniture and a kitchen, of which we are very proud.

Creede was becoming the kind of hub that we didn't even know we were looking for. The idea of just sitting in one place and doing everything the area offered hadn't occurred to either of us. After two weeks of intensive hiking and 4-wheel driving, we decided to move on. I don't think that we met the owners of the campground on this visit, as we were very private people, and would go out each day on another adventure, never telling anyone where we were going or when we would be back. Not very smart, but it was the way we did things then. Before leaving, we decided to backpack up to the Continental Divide Trail via Ute Creek. A two-night, three-day hike, and no one knew where we were—we just disappeared. Leaving Creede, we were sure that we would return the next year, and so it turned out.

Traveling northward to Estes Park and Rocky Mountain National Park, we met up with Ann and Bill again, and planned an overnighter to Bluebird Lake. Unfortunately, Ann had a recurrence of her previous trouble with an irregular heartbeat. Alex and I hiked on and were surprised when they both turned up a couple of hours later. It was not a good feeling, so we returned to base the next morning.

After saying goodbye to Ann and Bill, we headed east to the Boundary Waters, where John and Ricky were waiting for us. There had been a significant storm the year before, and an estimated 20 million trees had either been blown down or broken off. Needless to say, numbers of them were across the portages, making progress very slow and arduous. We all had a great time and a story to tell when we came out ten days later. We had no fish stories, however, as neither John nor Ricky caught a single one.

From there we took a new route home via many interesting places never before visited. We traveled several bike trails in Wisconsin, including the Elroy to Sparta tunnel trail, with a campground right on the trail. I wished Alex liked cycling more. We collected Wendy in Pittsburg and went into Virginia to visit some battlefields and on to Harper's Ferry. The fall colors were at their best as we traveled south toward the Shenandoah Valley, Appalachia, and eventually home after meeting Lorna and Bryan plus kids, on the Suwannee River, where we had a wonderful weekend with them to finish a memorable summer.

Our motor coach on our lot at Mountain Views Resort

So, these wonderful years rolled on, each summer spending time in the motor coach visiting more extraordinary places, with Creede taking on an ever more important role in our travels. It seemed we would add two weeks to our stay there each year, until, in 2005, the owners, Roland and Helen Zimmerman, offered resort lots for lease. Late in 2005, we leased one, and made arrangements to have it customized for our new Beaver Patriot Thunder. In 2006, we could hardly wait to get out to Creede, and see for ourselves what had been done. That was not to be, as that summer was the year that we built a new home in Marsh Creek, next door to the previous one. We took our new Patriot out to Creede, parked it on our lot, and thought that we would be back periodically. In fact, apart from ten days in July with Gaere, it was late September before we could get out to pick it up and take it back to its new garage, adjoining the house we had built. Gaere was the contractor on the house, and he did a wonderful job.

We did return to our lot in the summer of 2007, and the pleasant job of making new friends in the resort area began. Now these are some of our best friends, home and away. People such as Dan and Carla Russell, who had bought the lot opposite just 20 minutes before we said we would like to buy it. Hal Murphree and Verdi Irwin moved in next door, and Les and Pat Jackson, who liked it so much they built a house, and Bill and Rena Bennett, who purchased at much the same time, and so on.

With friends in Creede

Brittany and Zach at Emerald Lake

I must say a few words about Creede, as it has become such an important part of our lives. In the 1880s and 1890s, there were reputedly some 20,000 people living in everything from tents to shacks. The boom was silver, and Creede became a silver city in a never-seen-before boom that hit the San Juan Mountains and the surrounding area. Creede's Main Street is witness to this, with many late 19th century facades of the businesses that thrived there. There is a still-operating theater, which stages events through the summer, to cater to the cultural side of the community. The town itself is geographically narrow, only three blocks wide between steep-sided cliffs on each side, leading to the canyon created by Willow Creek. The creek flows swiftly through the town, and enters the Rio Grande River about 2 miles away, at the Mountain Views Campground. The town has some, but not all, essential services—a good supermarket called the Kentucky Belle, a hardware store, many restaurants, hotels and motels, and gift stores. Altogether, it makes a quaint and pleasant impression on any visitor. The drive up through the canyon is an opportunity to see the remnants of Colorado mining first hand. Many buildings remain, and the magnitude of the cribbing and supports needed for all the mines and the railways are still plain to see.

These years when we were expanding our time in Creede were not without travel to foreign and domestic destinations. The Grand Canyon remained a magnet for exploration and one or two trips per year were a must. Now considering ourselves experienced Canyoneers, we spent most of our time hiking in the backcountry. We did a hike with Zach and Brittany, accompanied by their parents Bryan and Lorna, J.J. and Rhonda, his wife, along the Colorado Trail east of Durango, as planned and explored in 2000. Our foreign travel included England and Venice in 2001, Spain in 2002, Hawaii for Wendy's 70th birthday in 2004, and Prague in 2005. The standout trip, however, was to Corsica in 2004. Alex, John Tesdorpf, and I flew to this lovely island, with the intent to hike across it. In May of that year, we landed in Ajaccio, and after a night to collect our marbles, we caught a very old electric train for the all-day journey to the other side of the island. In Bastia, we caught a local bus. The driver said he would stop at our trailhead, and of course he did. The route was unclear in the beginning, but the mountains ahead pointed the way we needed to go. Soon we were entering the first of the villages in which we were to stay. This was luxury hiking, no tents or dried food—instead, a comfortable bed with dinner and wine each night in a gite. (Gite: a sim-

A group hike out of Creede

ple, usually inexpensive rural vacation retreat, especially in France.) Each day after breakfast, we would head out with a packed lunch, and a hike

San Luis Peak, 14,014 feet in elevation

ahead of us. Because it was early in the season, there was no one else in the gites or on the trail, and it was beautiful. On arrival at the other side of the island, we all took a ferry ride back to Ajaccio and the hotel. John went on to Sweden, and Alex and I took off for a week in a car touring the island and its beautiful old cities and towns. It was a great holiday, and a new experience, although we had been to Corsica on our boat years before.

In 2007, after moving onto our new site in the campground, we had been gathering hikers from around the campground to join us on some of our daily jaunts. We never realized how many people wanted to hike with us. At this point, Roland and Helen asked if we would lead a regular hike for all who wished to join in each Thursday. By the end of the season, we had a collection of hikers, all of whom were now friends and clamoring for more hikes. We have stuck to the Thursday hikes but have expanded to three or more hikes per week for the stronger and more capable hikers. This enabled us to meet John and Sue Romine, who in turn introduced us to the South Fork Hiking Group. Our cup literally was running over. I have to mention just a few of the people from the campground who have become such firm friends in this period. Lind Utz, Dan and Carla Russel, Hal and Verdi, Tom Owens, Cindy Crochet, and many more. In 2008, we were ready to take on the first 14,000-foot peak, and the chosen mountain was Handies Peak. Eleven hikers started, and eleven reached the top. In 2009, another 14'er fell—San Louis Peak, again eleven started and all got to the top. By 2010, we were becoming ambitious, and it was two 14'ers in a day: nine reached the top of Red Cloud and three reached the top of Sunshine. Who knows what will happen in 2012?

In 2008, Alex and I took an RVing tour of New Zealand's North and South Island. It was a great trip, but we were both unwell for much of the month we were there. Considering all that,we did a great deal, although we missed the bungee jumping.

Tristan and Alex at their 50th anniversary party

In 2009, Alex and I celebrated our 50th wedding anniversary at the Raintree, with almost exactly 50 people. It would have been 50, but Les and Pat decided to surprise us. Four other Creeders also traveled to join us—what an evening it was!

Since that night, we have been joined by an ever-expanding group of people who we love to spend time and energy with. Dan and Becky, David and Penny, Whit and Kathy, Angela and Jon, Bob and Marguerite, these and other friends all make our lives richer each year.

Finally, I have to mention one person who has come into my life in a special way, and not until the summer of 2011. I was planning Zach and Brittany's annual hike, which was to be on the Continental Divide Trail in July. I asked a couple of friends if

Lorna and Brittany

they were interested, and they declined. Then I asked Lindy Sisk if he would be up for the hike. The answer came back, even before he knew where we were going, a resounding "Yes!" On their arrival, we got Zach,

Brittany, and Lindy together, and they not only approved, but were enthusiastic at the choice. So, Lindy came into all of our lives, and whether out of gratitude or that he felt sorry for me, he has painstakingly transcribed this book from about Chapter 23 on. I must explain the whole book has been written in longhand on legal pads. Brittany shares the credit for the transcription, as she did all of the earlier chapters, and would have continued if she hadn't gone to law school in August 2011.

To finish this chapter, I must add the purchase of our latest motor coach. In November, 2007, just hours before the recession that is still gripping the country, we both agreed to buy a 43-foot American Eagle to replace the Beaver Patriot Thunder. The coach would fit in the garage of the new house. It has been and still is the best motor coach we have owned. It was unfortunate that the economy collapsed afterward, but we have had no regrets, and look forward to using it for years to come.

Brittany and Zach on the Continental Divide Trail in Colorado

45 THOUGHTS

I have not mentioned anywhere in the book what my feelings are about certain subjects. The first would have to be religion, which from my start in a non-religious environment has not matured into a belief in any specific dogma, or sense of belief in anything more than a confidence that I would lead a life that would be acceptable behavior in any society. I have never, and still do not, believe in anything past death, as I have been quite satisfied with this life.

The second issue would have to be politics and government in the three countries in which I have lived. Canada, which I left at age 16, had no input into my political thinking. As I came out of adolescence in England, and particularly when I joined the army, I was deeply distressed by the seemingly yawning gap between the various socio-economic groups that made up the country of which I was so proud. David Gollop and I read a great deal of political analysis, which made us feel that a more equitable solution could be reached in society. David went on to join the Communist Party and became a leader in the trade union movement. I went back to civilian life and started on the road to capitalism that I had previously so disagreed with.

It soon became obvious to me that all government was both wasteful and fraught with corruption and broken promises. My decision to become uninvolved with the electoral system, neither to vote nor take any real interest in the politics of the day, seemed to be a rational one at the time. As I matured and became more financially successful, my leanings were, and still are, toward conservative thinking. I still harbor a deep mistrust of government in all forms. I pay my taxes, and vote, not really believing that any contribution I make is, in any way, meaningful. I know this is a cynical way to be, but that is where I am at the moment.

46 THAT'S IT — SO FAR

The last chapter was dealing with my thoughts and our lives up to now, year 2011. I shouldn't leave out some of the highlights in our family story in the recent years. Perhaps the most important one is the long-deserved happiness that was to be the reward of Lorna's marrying Chris Cantabene, on October 1, 2007. Chris has worked at the Raintree for some years, and he brought a no-nonsense attitude to the kitchen. His love for Lorna is apparent always, and we had the opportu-

Chris, Lorna and Alex

nity to observe this at first hand on a trip to the French canals in September of 2011. It was Lorna's 50th birthday, and it was celebrated with lots of French wine and meals prepared mainly by Chris. It was an honor to be included in such an event. Lorna turning 50 was hard to comprehend—where have our lives gone?

By default, Gaere had celebrated his 50th birthday in March 2009. This was not marked by a trip, but was taken as a milestone in our long and happy marriage. Our two children have every reason to be proud of their achievements in life—both running successful businesses, Lorna with children and a new home with Chris, Gaere and Carolyn in their home, which they have so lovingly renovated. It is very normal for Alex and me to be greeted by people who say, "You must be Gaere's (or Lorna's) Mum and Dad." This is now our claim to fame. We are very proud to be the parents of both of them.

Chris has two children, Caitlin, 24, and Chelsea, 13, who we are integrating into our lives slowly but surely. Zach and Brittany, who are now 26 and 24, respectively, have played such a tremendous part in our lives, and we have both watched them as they have grown into really exceptional adults that any grandparent would be proud of. They hold their own if they are at a dining table or hiking at 13,000 feet.

The friends that we have made in our lifetime together have enriched our lives with shared experiences that are impossible to forget. Our only regret is that just a few of them have fallen through the cracks of time, and we are no longer in touch with them. This so much applies to my best man, David Gollop, John and Patience Bunnell—John was a confidante and partner—and Philip Grainey, our opening chef at the Raintree. These people have all left our lives, and we can only guess at the reasons why. Perhaps I fell short of their expectations of me? Or perhaps our lives went in different directions? I have been lucky not to lose many friends to premature death. Early in our married life, John Blewitt was lost with the complete crew of the Newlyn Lifeboat, while attempting to save the lives of the crew of a coaster. John and his wife Caroline were very good friends. There have been others, but none that has made such a deep impression as John.

Finally, I must write a few words about my current friends. At the top of any list would have to be John Tesdorpf, who, after coming back into our lives comparatively recently, has, in his sometimes frustrating way, been a rock-solid companion on many adventures, as well as in everyday life. I respect his considered advice on anything that I might give him to think about. I would miss him if he went absent from the list.

Six friends of 50 years or more, Ken Budd and his wife Bobby, who I met so long ago and have shared so much with, are high on my list of lifetime friends. Andy Ramsay and his wife Ann, became friends from the moment we met. Finally, Derek Charldwood, who, with his wife Pat, have always been "there" for both of us.

Last but not least, someone who would never appear on a list of any kind—Alex, who has been my constant companion and lover for more years than we would ever have thought possible. When I, as a very insecure 16-year-old, went into the Pixie Cabin Cafe in Newlyn and spotted her across the room with her friends, I knew I just had to get to know her, and so it proved. Through military service and beyond into marriage, and into times in our lives that seemed so difficult at the time, my love for her has endured, and I have come out the winner, as it would be impossible for me to imagine what life's alternatives would have been. It is still an adventure as we prepare for another year together, after almost 60 years of companionship and marriage, I just say to myself that I must be one of the luckiest men in the world!

That's it—so far.

ACKNOWLEDGMENTS

I first thought seriously about writing this book over a year ago, after reading an article in *Costco Connection* giving some tips in writing memoirs. It was as I was sitting idly waiting for a knee replacement to become functional that I picked up a pen and started on the journey that was my life in retrospect. The unburdening of the troubles of my early life has been a relief, and made it possible for me to forget most of it. However, the reminiscences of the past in general opened up thoughts about good fortune and the wonderful people I have met and am still meeting.

My thanks go to my granddaughter Brittany Fraser, who, without hesitation, agreed to the job of transcribing a lot of illegible handwriting. My thanks also go to my new friend Linden B. (Lindy) Sisk, who picked up the baton when Brittany entered law school, and ran with it, with, I'm sure, the same troubles she had endured.

Thanks also to my sister Wendy, for her untiring efforts to improve my grammar by editing and sending the finished product back to Lindy, who then inserted them into the copy. Finally this acknowledgment would not be complete without a thank you to Ruth Butler, who was able to use her expertise to assemble the book and photographs into a recognizable order.

Lastly, I owe Alex thanks for being patient, while I spent hours at a time scribbling away. She has been full of suggestions when I asked for them, but never forgot that it is my story.
Need I say more?

The first adventure in the Fourth Quarter—Lago Azul, Patagonia

Printed in Great Britain
by Amazon

47884368R00158